ADVANCE PRAISE FOR
The Long Game

"*The Long Game* is Derek Chollet's penetrating and wise examination of the foreign policy of a deeply unorthodox president. Rational, cool, and analytical (much like the man he is writing about), Chollet takes us deep inside the formerly opaque decision-making process of an administration that has up-ended longstanding assumptions about the way America should behave in the world. Chollet's conclusions are controversial, and will be debated fiercely in Washington and beyond, but no one could deny that he has brought intellectual rigor to his important task. Nor could anyone deny that he has had a front-row seat to some of the great international dramas of our time."

—JEFFREY GOLDBERG,
National Correspondent, *The Atlantic*

"Derek Chollet defines and explains the Obama foreign policy as grand strategy. *The Long Game* goes against the conventional wisdom of our moment. Though an insider's account, it views the present as history and puts down a marker that will shape how historians interpret the Obama years."

—GEORGE PACKER,
author of *The Assassins' Gate* and *The Unwinding*

"Foreign policy in the twenty-first century requires realism mixed with an element of idealism in order to navigate the intensifying anarchy of the world system. Derek Chollet shows this philosophy in action in this terrifically brisk, insider account of the Obama administration's travails in the Middle East, Asia, and Europe. Agree with it or not, I know of no more compelling defense of Obama's record."

—ROBERT D. KAPLAN,
senior fellow at the Center for a New American Security
and author of *In Europe's Shadow: Two Cold Wars and
a Thirty-Year Journey Through Romania and Beyond*

"Drawing on his front-row seats in the White House, State Department, and Pentagon, Derek Chollet provides a very insightful picture of President Obama's foreign policy. Memoirs are first drafts of history, and future historians will need to pay close attention to this one."

—JOSEPH S. NYE JR.,
Harvard University Distinguished Service Professor,
former dean of Harvard's Kennedy School of Government,
and author of *Is the American Century Over?*

"Obama's foreign policy has been misunderstood as much as it has been criticized, and a virtue of Derek Chollet's lucid account is that it explains even more than it defends. As both a participant and a keen observer of American foreign policy, Chollet is well-positioned to provide powerful insights into what guided the president through these confusing times."

—ROBERT JERVIS,
Adlai E. Stevenson Professor of International
Politics, Columbia University, and author of
American Foreign Policy in a New Era

"In *The Long Game*, Derek Chollet has given us a comprehensive, detailed inside account of the ideas and strategy underlying Barack Obama's foreign policies. Chollet, who worked in several positions in the Obama administration, describes what went into Obama's policies toward Egypt, Syria, Libya, Iran, Russia, and Ukraine. Even when he disagrees with a few of Obama's decisions, Chollet lucidly lays out the thinking behind them and responds to the most frequent criticisms. At least until Obama writes his own memoir, Chollet's insightful book will probably stand as the best single guide to his reasoning and his policies."

—JAMES MANN,
author of *The Obamians* and *Rise of the Vulcans*

THE LONG GAME

ALSO BY DEREK CHOLLET

The Road to the Dayton Accords: A Study of American Statecraft

America Between the Wars: From 11/9 to 9/11
(with James Goldgeier)

The Unquiet American: Richard Holbrooke in the World
(coeditor with Samantha Power)

Bridging the Foreign Policy Divide
(coeditor with Tod Lindberg and David Shorr)

THE
LONG
GAME

How Obama Defied

Washington and Redefined

America's Role in the World

DEREK CHOLLET

PUBLICAFFAIRS

New York

PublicAffairs books are available at special discounts for bulk purchases in the U.S. by corporations,
institutions, and other organizations. For more information, please contact the Special Markets
Department at the Perseus Books Group, 2300 Chestnut Street, Suite 200, Philadelphia, PA
19103, call (800) 810-4145, ext. 5000, or e-mail special.markets@perseusbooks.com.

Library of Congress Cataloging-in-Publication Data
Names: Chollet, Derek H., author.
Title: The long game : how Obama defied Washington and redefined America's
    role in the world / Derek Chollet.
Description: First edition. | New York : PublicAffairs, 2016. | Includes
    bibliographical references and index.
Identifiers: LCCN 2016010114 (print) | LCCN 2016010384 (ebook) | ISBN
    9781610396608 (hardcover) | ISBN 9781610396615 (ebook)
Subjects: LCSH: United States--Foreign relations--2009- | Obama, Barack.
Classification: LCC E907 .C459 2016 (print) | LCC E907 (ebook) | DDC
    327.73--dc23
LC record available at http://lccn.loc.gov/2016010114

10 9 8 7 6 5 4 3 2 1

For my own long game:

Lucas and Aerin, and most of all, Heather

CONTENTS

"Good policy depends on the patient accumulation of nuances; care has to be taken that individual moves are orchestrated into a coherent strategy. Only rarely do policy issues appear in terms of black or white. More usually they depend on shades of interpretation; significant policy deviations begin as minor departures whose effect only becomes apparent as they are projected into the future."

—HENRY KISSINGER

"Politics is not about objective reality, but virtual reality. What happens in the political world is divorced from the real world. It exists for only the fleeting historical moment, in a magical movie of sorts, a never-ending and infinitely revisable docudrama. Strangely, the faithful understand that the movie is not true—yet also maintain that it is the only truth that really matters."

—MICHAEL KELLY

"Games are won by players who focus on the playing field—not by those whose eyes are glued to the scoreboard."

—WARREN BUFFETT

INTRODUCTION

THE LONG GAME

"I am more concerned with what we haven't done than what we have," President Obama said in a July 2011 meeting in the White House Situation Room, where he met with a handful of his top advisers to plan his upcoming agenda. As his senior director for strategic planning on the National Security Council staff at the time, I had helped prepare the meeting. For several weeks, the president had been consumed by the domestic debt crisis and grinding talks with congressional leadership to avoid a budget default, but as he turned his attention to the world, he seemed energized, and was in an expansive mood. While we had dutifully come ready to discuss his upcoming schedule of meetings, speeches, and trips, he wanted to think bigger.

"Since 9/11, it has been a decade of war," the president said. "We have an opportunity to make the next decade one of peace." He went on to add, "We've established that we're tough enough." Just two months earlier, he had ordered the operation that killed Osama bin Laden, and American planes were then bombing Libya. But, he said, "What's been lost is the hope side of the equation."

He described the moment as a "pivot": having spent the previous three years "trying to clean things up" after the Bush presidency, "we need to start a generational opportunity and challenge the international community." Obama pushed his team to be more creative, and said that we needed to do more to knit together the narrative of economic strength and global authority. Obama wanted the US to be respected abroad not just for its military prowess, but also for its growing economy, domestic vitality, and moral example. "That's where I want to go," he said, "although we don't know if we can get there because history intrudes."

In the years that followed, history intruded in ways no one sitting around that table could have imagined. From the disintegration of Syria and rise of ISIS, to the chaos in post-Qaddafi Libya and turmoil in Egypt, to Russia's intervention in Ukraine and its resurgence as a military threat to Europe, the world order is under greater stress than at any other point since the end of the Cold War. In 2016, US leadership is in doubt at home and abroad, and many are again talking about America's inexorable decline.

For how much of this is President Obama to blame? Have his policies diminished or strengthened America's position in the world? When historians assess the Obama years, will they be seen as a period of recovery and repositioning America for the future, or one of abject failure that dragged the country down?

With such an astonishing diversity of threats unfolding simultaneously, it has certainly proven harder for the Obama administration to drive events than be driven by them. As the world seems to unwind, it is even harder to find the "hope side of the equation." But that does not mean the president has forgotten about it or doubted its desirability.

OBAMA BELIEVES AMERICA is an indispensable nation, but one that must be careful in its ambitions. His policies at home and abroad have been about renewing and sustaining American power, not squandering it. And he has worked to diversify the way that America exerts its influence.

Like most other presidents, Obama is wary of one-size-fits-all answers. During the 2011 US-led bombing campaign in Libya, for example, he rebuffed efforts to describe it as a widely applicable model, privately warning about the dangers of a "cookie-cutter" approach to the world's problems because things are so "case dependent." In this sense, his outlook is similar to that of one of America's greatest strategic apostles, George F. Kennan, who decried the "congenital aversion of Americans to taking specific decisions on specific problems" and "their persistent urge to seek universal formulae or doctrines in which to clothe or justify their actions."[1]

Despite this aversion to bumper stickers, Obama has structured America's statecraft around certain principles and priorities. Although he may never describe it this way, Obama has what academics call a "grand strategy," a concept the Duke University scholar Hal Brands describes as "a purposeful and coherent set of ideas about what a nation seeks to accomplish in the world, and how it should go about doing so."[2] A grand strategy, as Brands puts it, should be "firm and focused enough to keep American policy anchored amid the geopolitical squalls" so that it "can advance towards its highest objectives over time."[3]

The defining element of Obama's grand strategy is that it reflects the totality of American interests—foreign and domestic—to project global leadership in an era of seemingly infinite demands and finite resources. This is playing the "long game." And those who evaluate it should keep in mind Brands's explication of "the central dilemma of American grand strategy: the fact that it is an essential and potentially very rewarding undertaking, but one that is damned hard to get right."[4]

So why has Obama's foreign policy performance proven so controversial, dismissed as a failure not just by his political opponents, but also, more surprisingly, by much of the Democratic foreign policy elites and overseas commentariat that once swooned over him? This disaffection is especially curious because Obama has largely remained true to the policies he outlined before taking office.

In sharp contrast to his predecessor George W. Bush—who campaigned for the presidency promising a return to a more humble foreign policy but presided over an era characterized by overreach and arrogance—Obama has followed through on what he promised in 2008: restoring America's power at home by focusing on the economy; revitalizing alliances; pursuing tough engagement with adversaries; reducing the US role in Iraq and Afghanistan while not getting overwhelmed by massive new military engagements; modernizing the military while deemphasizing it as the primary tool of American power; rebalancing towards the Asia-Pacific; trying to involve Congress in decisions about the use of force; executing an even more lethal fight against terrorists while ending excesses like torture; and pursuing bold policy initiatives on such issues as climate change, trade, and nuclear disarmament.

Yet to listen to Washington's foreign policy establishment (of which I have been a card-carrying member for over two decades), Obama's record is one of fundamental failure: Under his leadership, America has been "in retreat," bereft of a strategy. Less partisan critics categorize Obama as a "retrencher," ambivalent about American leadership and only interested in keeping America out of trouble. [5] Reaching further, some question not just the president's policies, but also his view of America itself. They assert that Obama is an "apologist" who doubts whether the United States can be a force for global good (and among the loud voices on the fringe, there are those who question the president's very "Americanism"). It is because of this, they claim, that the Obama years have left America weaker and unwilling to shoulder the burdens of leadership. The consequence, they argue, is that the US is less confident, less feared, and less admired. If only America were "stronger" or "tougher" then it could solve the world's problems.

A completely contrasting critique comes from those who believe Obama has drifted too far from his ideals. They point to increasing the use of drone strikes and developing terrorist "kill lists" (including the targeting of American citizens), bombing more countries (seven) than George W. Bush, failing to close the prison at Guantanamo Bay, snooping in your phones and pursuing bold new free trade agreements that could harm American workers. The problem, they claim, is not Obama's reluctance to deploy power but his unbridled use of it, the result being another "imperial presidency" that is subverting the law.

Obama is thus a paradox: to some he exudes weakness and is afraid to act, but to others he flouts the rules and is too quick to pull the trigger. He is alternately characterized as a woolly-headed, liberal idealist or as a cold-hearted, unsentimental realist. He takes too few risks and too many. So where is the truth?

As the Obama presidency nears its end, a different picture is starting to emerge for those willing to take a broader and deeper look at his foreign policy record and America's position in the world.

Instead of Obama leaving a legacy future presidents will run from, I believe Obama's foreign policy legacy will be one future presidents will be measured by; indeed, he has done more to shape American foreign policy—and a new generation of foreign policy leaders—than any Democratic president since John F. Kennedy. Simply put, Obama has redefined the purpose and exercise of American power for a new era.

Of course, the president and his administration have made plenty of policy mistakes. Some missteps have been the result of wrong assumptions or lack of information; others of botched execution or unforced errors. But on the issues that matter most for the Long Game—how and where America uses military force, how the US approaches its enemies and works with its partners, and how America should conceive of its power and exert its leadership—Obama's mark will be enduring and largely positive.

Obama likes to use sports analogies, often referring to the latter part of his term in office as the "fourth quarter" when, he adds, big things happen and games are won or lost. So if his foreign policy legacy could be summarized in the newspaper's sports section, what would the final score be? I believe he would be ahead on points—say, in football terms, 28–21—but this score will look better and better with time. And however narrow, in history's own long game the Obama era will represent a definite win.

PRESIDENTS OFTEN BENEFIT from the warm glow of historical hindsight once they are safely out of office. Consider how Obama's immediate predecessors were judged when they left Washington and how they are remembered today.

Ronald Reagan departed the White House in 1989 wounded by the Iran-Contra scandal and with many wondering whether he had gone too far in trying to work with the Soviets; now he is remembered for playing a seminal role in ending the Cold War. In 1993, George H.W. Bush limped out of office criticized that he failed to define what he called the "new world order" and tarnished by the fact that he had not taken out Saddam Hussein when he had the chance after the first Gulf War; he is now lionized as one of America's most effective foreign policy presidents. Bill Clinton was seen as weak in 2001, ill-disciplined and crippled by scandal; today he is praised as the first president who understood globalization. Even George W. Bush, who left office in 2009 with a reputation in worse shape than any president since Richard Nixon, has seen history soften some of the edges of his failures. So, looking toward 2017, Obama has reason to be optimistic.

But Obama's faith in the Long Game is more than just a way to deflect the criticisms of the moment or soothe one's psyche. It defines his unique style of foreign policy—one that is best suited to leadership in the twenty-first century. He prizes deliberation, is comfortable with complexity and nuance, and is deeply skeptical of decisions driven by passion or the desire to seek maximalist solutions, especially over the short term. He resists knee-jerk responses and empty gestures. As one adviser aptly described it, Obama is a "consequentialist," far less interested in appearances than in what actually works.[6]

To HELP HIMSELF make decisions, Obama has closely adhered to a few core tenets—a kind of foreign policy "checklist," to borrow from an idea popularized by the author and surgeon Atul Gawande.[7] Like others who must navigate situations of extreme complexity, uncertainty, and risk (such as astronauts and surgeons), foreign policymakers can benefit by outlining and following a few basic principles.

Although foreign policymaking is a mix of art and science—Obama would say it is more of an imperfect art—a checklist can help leaders make objectives clearer, adjudicate among priorities, and avoid mistakes.[8] This is not a to-do list of things one wants to accomplish, nor is it a how-to list that tells what to do in specific circumstances. It is better thought of as a general guide to match means with ends, helping one remain mindful of pitfalls, avoid shortsighted choices, and identify what is most important.

Obama's Long Game checklist has eight criteria: balance, sustainability, restraint, precision, patience, fallibility, skepticism, and exceptionalism.

These eight tenets have never been formally promulgated. They weren't the topic of any White House meetings. You won't find them in any strategic plan or classified document. However, they serve as the framework that has shaped Obama's foreign policy and efforts to redefine American power.

Obama has aimed to achieve *balance* among America's many interests around the world, working to achieve manageable trade-offs among competing priorities.

He has tried to ensure that his foreign policy is *sustainable* in terms of resources, governmental bandwidth, and domestic support—both during his term in office as well as for his successors.

Because the US has a tendency to overreach, investing too much in one issue while underinvesting in others, he believes a strategy that is balanced and sustainable requires a large degree of *restraint*. For a power as dominant as the United States, the question is rarely whether it has the capability to do something, but if it makes sense to do so relative to its competing priorities, finite resources, and overall interests.

This is especially true when it comes to the use of military force, which is why Obama values *precision*, using particular tools for specific problems. He wants to ensure the means achieve the end. This is perhaps the key feature of his counter-terrorism strategy, which is not lacking in lethality but seeks greater precision to take out terrorist leaders.

Another Obama hallmark is *patience*. Famously deliberative, he is willing to take the time (and endure many meetings) to get it right. But more than that, he believes in strategic patience—giving intricate policies the time to unfold, blocking impulsive moves, and outwaiting the adversary (as well as the attention span of many observers).

Perhaps most controversially, Obama is not afraid of admitting America's *fallibility*. Critics deride this as apologizing for America, but he believes that to be aware of and open about imperfection is a way to avoid mistakes and earn respect.

Obama also has a great deal of *skepticism* of the political and foreign policy debate, which includes many of the ideas pushed by the bulk of the professional punditocracy. Whenever there is a wise man consensus in Washington, his first instinct is often to defy it.

Finally, Obama is a champion of American *exceptionalism*, a conviction he has said he upholds "with every fiber of my being." This captures the optimism that is fundamental to his outlook; with the right decisions and policies, America is best positioned to lead. And by having the confidence to admit flaws and working to overcome them, constantly seeking renewal and innovation, one generates strength, credibility, and legitimacy.

OBAMA BELIEVES THAT success at playing the Long Game requires a clear North Star to aim toward, with persistent and steady progress to get there. Obama is comfortable with incremental outcomes, believing that some problems can only be managed, while just a few can be immediately solved—and the trick is to distinguish between the two. Obama explained his approach in 2015: one tries "to steer the ocean liner two degrees north or south so that ten years from now, suddenly we're in a very different place than we were. But at the time… people may feel like we need a fifty-degree turn."

Yet often, the president continued, the temptation is to oversteer. "If I turn fifty degrees," he said, "the whole ship turns. And you can't turn fifty degrees." This is how Obama looks at policy issues like race, the environment, and ending discrimination in the United States. And it accurately describes how he looks upon many of the issues that challenge the United States in the world, whether it is confronting terrorist groups, curbing the proliferation of weapons of mass destruction, or defending and revitalizing the liberal international order.[9]

Obama swept into office riding a wave of hope and exuding a sense of possibility, but he has governed with humility, acknowledging that it is often difficult for meaningful change to come instantly. As he told the *New Yorker*'s David Remnick, one of the things he has come to understand as president is that "you are essentially a relay swimmer in a river full of rapids and that river is history…you don't start with a clean slate, and the things you start may not come to full fruition on your timetable, but you can move things forward. And sometimes the things that start small may turn out to be fairly significant."[10]

This outlook reveals Obama's fundamental challenge: to conduct a Long Game foreign policy in a political and policy ecosystem that is becoming synonymous with reality television or taking on the characteristics of professional wrestling, rewarding over-the-top rhetoric and concocted drama instead of results that can only be truly appreciated with time. His Long Game approach may seem unexciting, often shining only after considering the alternatives. As Robert D. Kaplan explains, realism "is respected only after the seeming lack of it has made a situation demonstrably worse."[11] In the moment, a policy that seeks a pragmatic middle course can seem less dazzling and satisfying than one of shimmering but unreal ideological purity.

This is a big part of what makes Obama's Long Game so frustrating for so many in the political and foreign policy establishment. Too many critics live in a self-contained world dominated by this play-acting, where the answer is almost always for the US to do *more* of something and to act "tough," though usually what that something is remains very vague. But doing more of everything is not a strategy.

As one of Obama's most influential advisers, Ben Rhodes, put it, "the discourse in Washington becomes like a self-licking ice cream cone," something that benefits only those directly involved, without regard to the larger picture or what would actually work.[12] Or, as the president once testily described what he gets when he asks his critics what they would do differently, "what you get is a bunch of mumbo-jumbo."

Think of it this way: Obama is like a foreign policy version of Warren Buffett, a proudly pragmatic value investor less concerned with appearances or the whims of the moment, focused instead on making solid investments with an eye to long-term success. The foreign policy debate, on the other hand, tends to be dominated by policy day traders, whose incentives are the opposite: achieving quick results, getting rewarded with instant judgments and what will make the biggest splash, and reacting to every blip in the market.

Of course, today's geopolitical turbulence feels like more than the usual market ups and downs. It is understandable that when looking out at the world, Americans are frustrated, pessimistic, and scared. The Middle East is in turmoil not seen since the fall of the Ottoman Empire a century ago; Europe is facing its greatest test since the end of the Cold War with millions of refugees, fears of terrorism, and questions about the future of the European Union; Putin's Russia is acting in ways reminiscent of the worst days of the Soviet Union; China's continuing rise is challenging the status quo in Asia and increasingly around the world; and common global threats like a warming climate and terrorist groups continue to loom large.

These are big, systemic challenges, and the United States cannot solve them alone, if at all. Yet there is nostalgia for an era when the US allegedly called all the shots and could fix problems easily if it just tried harder or asserted itself more. That moment never existed. In fact, our most costly mistakes in the past have come when we were seduced by the idea of our omnipotence. Washington's policy decisions may not be able to solve today's big problems, but they do make a big difference for better or worse. So the question is how the US can best invest its power and use its tools to bring countries together to shape outcomes, set agendas, and address these problems in a sustainable way. That is what Obama's Long Game grand strategy has been all about—and, despite all the world's challenges, it has left America stronger at home and abroad, in a better position to lead.

* * *

THIS BOOK IS a personal reflection on Obama's effort to redefine America's role in the world, drawing on my experience of over six years serving at the State Department, the White House, and the Pentagon. It is not intended to be a comprehensive narrative history of Obama's foreign policy—several important memoirs and excellent first drafts of that history have already been written, and many more will come. Instead, by exploring some of the toughest, most consequential, and controversial national security decisions of the Obama administration—focusing specifically on its handling of the "Arab Spring" crises in Syria, Libya, and Egypt; its approach to powers like China and Russia; its response to the war in Ukraine; and its effort to deal with Iran's nuclear threat—this book examines the intellectual foundations of Obama's foreign policy. It also aims to shed light on why policymakers navigated the course they did and how they struggled with the choices that confronted them.

In doing so, this book is also an exploration of the broader debate about America's role in the world and the politics that infuse these arguments. One must see the Obama presidency in the context of the policy debates that followed the end of the Cold War and shaped American foreign policy and politics in the post-9/11 years. This includes the George W. Bush administration's fateful choices, as well as the efforts of Democrats to forge a coherent foreign policy agenda in the 2000s—to be seen as "strong" and to overcome their perceived weakness on national security. This history has influenced the choices Obama has made, and helps explain how he has tried to redefine America's global role—and the resistance he has had to confront while doing so.

The late diplomat Richard Holbrooke observed that "a memoir sits at the dangerous intersection of policy, ambition, and history," warning of the temptation to see events as linear and outcomes as foreordained—especially the decisions that turned out well.[13] Depending on one's perspective, successes are credited either to sheer brilliance or dumb luck, while failures are seen as the result of either honest mistakes or gross incompetence. To learn from history, one must try hard to understand what actually happened, appreciating the full context in which decisions were made and all the uncertainties and risks involved. That is the approach taken by this book.

Policymaking is the collision of aspirations and limits, in which leaders are rewarded for aligning their goals with resources, and punished when they become out of balance. When approaching issues, leaders must constantly make difficult decisions and manage unpleasant trade-offs, often with little information and no time.

Henry Kissinger describes the making of foreign policy as "an endless battle in which the urgent constantly gains on the important," observing that the central struggle for policymakers is "to rescue an element of choice from the pressure of circumstance."[14] This struggle is particularly difficult in today's world, where the pressure of circumstance seems so overwhelming. And nowhere is that more evident than in the Middle East, the region that has been America's twenty-first century crucible, and therefore where this story of the Obama administration's foreign policy begins.

CHAPTER 1

THE RED LINE

On the last Saturday of August 2013, Labor Day weekend, the United States was once again about to go to war in the Middle East.

Less than two weeks earlier, in the middle of the night on August 21, the Syrian military had attacked rebel-controlled areas of the Damascus suburbs with chemical weapons, killing nearly 1,500 civilians, including over 400 children. Horrific video footage showing people with twisted bodies sprawled on hospital floors, some twitching and foaming at the mouth after being exposed to sarin gas, had ricocheted around the world. This atrocity opened an ugly new chapter in a brutal Syrian civil war that had already cost over 100,000 lives, and America needed to respond.

The day after the attacks, President Obama's national security advisor, Susan Rice, called an emergency meeting at the White House to discuss what to do. Because it was the end of summer, many cabinet officials were out of Washington, so they participated by secure video while those of us in town assumed our customary seats around the Situation Room table.

We first tried to establish exactly what had happened and who had done it. There was considerable discussion of the intelligence we had collected. We knew chemical weapons had been used, but we wanted to be sure we could conclusively establish the Assad regime's culpability. The evidence turned out to be overwhelming: it included eyewitness accounts from medical personnel and information about Syrian military officials giving specific instructions to mix the chemicals and use them. This brazen assault had clearly crossed the "red line" that President Obama had enunciated a year earlier.[1]

The discussion quickly turned to whether and how the US should respond militarily. There were a variety of targets that could be hit, from the chemical sites themselves to military headquarters, runways, and even Assad's palace or presidential helicopter fleet. But there were many concerns about the danger to American pilots (Syria had one of the most sophisticated air defense networks in the world), as well as the possibility of escalation.

Everyone understood the risks. There was no question the US had the capability to act decisively, but there was deep uncertainty about where military intervention would lead. The mood in the room was tense but resigned. A decade after the invasion of Iraq, there was a sense that America was about to go over another Middle Eastern waterfall.

As Rice went around the room (or asked those on the screen) for a recommendation, nearly everyone advocated for quick action. The most notable voice of caution came from Denis McDonough, the president's influential and highly effective chief of staff. McDonough questioned the effectiveness of airstrikes and warned of the risks of getting bogged down in yet another Middle East quagmire. A forceful advocate, he seemed to be putting extra emphasis on this point to ensure that he preserved for the president what he called "decision space." I sensed he felt the need to play a role similar to that of

George Ball, the great diplomat who, in that same room decades earlier, had intentionally assumed the part of "house dove" during Lyndon Johnson's fateful deliberations about the Vietnam War.

The meeting concluded with a unanimous decision to prepare for military strikes. To do this right, it would take some time to prepare. Tasks were handed out to scrub the intelligence further with an eye to what could be released publicly, construct the legal basis for action, build a campaign for diplomatic support, intensify outreach to the Congress and, most important, begin to make the case to the American public.

Military planners at the Pentagon started working around the clock to prepare for a series of air strikes, with the specific aims of deterring Syrian leader Bashar al-Assad from launching more chemical attacks and degrading his military's ability to do so. As the assistant secretary of defense whose portfolio included Europe and the Middle East, I had two roles: in addition to working with the secretary of defense, Chuck Hagel, and other senior defense officials on various aspects of planning the strikes, I stayed in daily contact with my counterparts from the two countries most likely to contribute to them, the United Kingdom and France, to coordinate our positions and ensure nothing was overlooked. We also were in close contact with the Israelis, who, while not involved in the military planning or potential operations, were keenly focused on Assad's chemical weapons and knew something about conducting airstrikes in Syria, having destroyed a North Korean-supplied nuclear reactor in the Syrian desert in September 2007.

By Labor Day weekend, all the pieces were in place. The Pentagon planners had narrowed the target list to around fifty sites, with the initial wave of strikes involving Tomahawk cruise missiles fired from five Arleigh Burke-class destroyers positioned in the Mediterranean Sea. The ships were in position—in Pentagonese, they were "in the basket"—poised to launch strikes within minutes of the president giving the order. The French were ready to go as well. The British, however, had bowed out after the UK House of Commons had refused to support the Prime Minister's request that the country join the US.[2]

Secretary of State John Kerry laid out the public case for intervention. In a speech encouraged (and partly crafted) by the White House and delivered in the State Department's ornate Treaty Room on Friday, August 30, he outlined what we knew about the chemical attack and Assad's role in it. Citing the "indiscriminate, inconceivable horror of chemical weapons," Kerry made a forceful call for action, arguing that the whole world would be watching what the US did or did not do.

For Kerry, this moment was rich with irony. In 2004, his campaign for the presidency had been defined by, and ultimately faltered over, his position on the Iraq War. A key event in the lead-up to that conflict had been when then-Secretary of State Colin Powell went to the UN Security Council to make the case for war, citing specific evidence of Saddam Hussein's possession of weapons of mass destruction. Now Kerry was speaking to the world from the State Department about another threat posed by such weapons, detailing intelligence and delivering a stark warning about the costs of inaction. While he was careful to note that no decision had been made, the speech was an unmistakable signal that intervention was coming.

HEADING INTO THE weekend, the Pentagon had made plans for round-the-clock staffing coverage over the holiday, when we thought the operation would start. And on Friday night, we received word that the president wanted to see his top advisors at the White House at 10 a.m. on Saturday. We assumed this would be the final signals check before the Tomahawks flew.

Early Saturday morning, as I was walking with my wife and young son to grab a quick breakfast before heading into the Pentagon for what I expected to be a long and dramatic weekend, my Blackberry buzzed with a call from "Cables," the office of the secretary of defense's switchboard. It was Mark Lippert, an old friend who was then Hagel's chief of staff, with surprising news: the president had called Hagel late the night before and told him he "wanted to explore another option." Instead of ordering strikes immediately, the president wanted to pump the brakes and first go to Congress to ask for its authorization.

I was shocked. I had been in most of the White House meetings up to that point, and while the issue of legal authorities and Congress had come up, it was clear the president had all the domestic legal authority and international justification he needed to act. The question of asking for a congressional vote had never been discussed at length; some had suggested we should ask for a vote, but there was skepticism it would pass, and therefore a feeling the question should not be asked. For an administration that prized careful and inclusive deliberation, it was unusual that a decision this big would arise so suddenly without first being thoroughly pored over in the interagency process.

Once the surprise wore off, I found myself thinking that, while abrupt, unexpected, and unorthodox, this was the right move. Not because of any legal reason or question of constitutional powers, but because Congress and the American people needed to be fully invested in what we were about to do and prepared to accept the consequences.

It turned out that the president had decided to do this on his own the night before. After a now-famous walk around the White House South Lawn early Friday evening with McDonough, he told his advisors huddled in the Oval Office that he had decided to take the question to Congress. Subsequent accounts of the meeting described his closest aides being as surprised as the rest of us, with some arguing that it was a bad move.

There were many reasons for the president's hesitation. As he later explained to the journalist Jeffrey Goldberg, he worried Assad would use the UN inspectors on the ground as human shields (as had happened in Bosnia and Iraq in the 1990s) and that the strikes would merely dent Syria's massive chemical weapons arsenal, creating an even more dangerous situation. Most fundamentally, Obama believed that intervening in Syria could prove to be such a consequential decision—one that could evolve in an unpredictable and dangerous way, consuming the remainder of his presidency—that he was convinced it would be a grave mistake to act in haste and without the country fully engaged in what we were getting into.

As he would later explain in an address to the nation: "I believe our democracy is stronger when the president acts with the support of Congress. And I believe that America acts more effectively abroad when we stand together. This is especially true after a decade that put more and more war-making power in the hands of the president, and more and more burdens on the shoulders of our troops, while sidelining the people's representatives from the critical decisions about when we use force."[3]

For years we had been struggling over what to do about Syria. We had stepped up to the brink of conducting air strikes before, only to pull back. Recent experience had taught us to expect the worst. After a decade that had been dominated by the war in Iraq—a conflict that had begun with promises of easy victory and limited American sacrifices, only to bring terrible costs—the country needed to be in this together. Our eyes were wide open about what might come, and we had concluded the risks were worth it, but we wanted the American people to understand and support our case as well.

Moreover, Obama wanted to make a larger point about the exercise of presidential power and the use of force—something, he later said, he had been "brooding on for some time."[4] Having taught constitutional law before entering politics, he often thought in terms of precedents. He knew that his successors would be measured by his actions.

Since his first presidential campaign, Obama had argued that presidents had the constitutional authority to use force on their own, especially in an instance of a direct threat to America's security or an immediate emergency like genocide. But in instances in which there was no immediate threat and therefore more time to consider the full spectrum of potential responses (like in Syria), it was always preferable to act with the support of the Congress and with as many allies as possible.[5] As Obama said to his aides gathered in the Oval Office debating his decision, he wanted to "break the cycle" of presidents not going to Congress before using force. His recent experience in Libya—in which the US acted without congressional authorization, something I think in retrospect he saw as a mistake—only reinforced this conviction.

So when the president stepped into the sunny Rose Garden that Saturday morning, he announced that he had made two decisions: first, that the US would act against Syria, and second, that he would seek explicit authorization from Congress to do so. "I've long believed that our power is rooted not just in our military might," he said, "but in our example as a government of the people, by the people, and for the people." With that, the administration set out on a different campaign than the military one we had been preparing for: to convince the American people that intervening in Syria was in the country's interest.

Now THAT ALL of Washington had a stake in the decision, the next three weeks were a frenzy of political drama, raucous debate, and second-guessing. Despite Syria having dominated the news for so long, few politicians had thought deeply about it, relieved that it was not their problem. None were happy to share the responsibility of being accountable for what America would or would not do about it. And the foreign policy punditocracy was pirouetting between the wisdom of getting involved in Syria and Obama's decision to have this debate at all.

What transpired was one of the most revealing episodes in eight years of Obama's foreign policy. Despite the administration's strong advocacy and the support from a small minority of hawkish politicians, Congress and the American people proved strongly opposed to the use of force. They did not want to risk getting involved in another conflict like Iraq. In the end, however, the threat of military action ended up achieving something no one had imagined possible: the peaceful removal of most of Syria's chemical weapons.

Yet, while the outcome unquestionably made America safer, the episode is almost universally seen—by the national security establishment, foreign officials, including those from our closest allies, the media, and even current and former members of the administration—as one of Obama's most consequential mistakes, an enduring symbol of his foreign policy failures. That the outcome and the interpretation should be so at odds reveals how poorly understood foreign policy is once it is reduced to politicized sound bites and ninety-second news items. They simply eliminate the complexities of the problem and the knotted history that has created it.

THE TOUGHEST PROBLEM

Since the Syria crisis erupted in 2011, what to do about its massive chemical weapons stockpile was one of the most perplexing—and scariest—issues the Obama administration faced. At over 1,300 metric tons spread out over as many as forty-five sites in a country about twice the size of Virginia, Syria's arsenal of chemical weapons was the world's third-largest. It was ten times greater than the (erroneous) CIA estimate in October 2002 of Iraq's chemical weapons, and fifty times more than Libya declared in late 2011. Since the Syrian regime denied it even possessed these weapons, what we knew about them came from intelligence gathered by the US and others. But often these were just informed guesses, so we could never be sure of the stockpile's scale (which we thought could even be larger) or level of security.

Among the many concerns emanating from the Syrian catastrophe, chemical weapons dominated our attention. We worried whether Assad would use those weapons against his own people. We thought he might lash out and use them to attack an ally like Israel. And we were perhaps most focused on the possibility that the weapons would get in the hands of extremists who were gaining strength and taking hold of territory inside Syria.

At the White House and Pentagon, we constantly puzzled over how practically to take out the chemical weapons. The scope of the problem made it overwhelming, hanging like a dark shadow over every aspect of our deliberations. On numerous occasions intelligence indicated that such weapons were about to be used or the security of a storage depot was under threat, and the administration would scramble to prevent something from happening. Sometimes that meant talking directly to the Syrian regime to warn it off, or getting the Russians to pressure Assad, or preparing military options. Some of these scares found their way into press reports; many did not.[6]

This was the context for President Obama's first utterance about the use of chemical weapons as a "red line" in an August 2012 White House press briefing. The president had been very focused about the disposition of chemical weapons, and had sat through hours of tense briefings on the subject. While he believed the Syrian conflict touched many American interests—humanitarian, regional stability, and the rise of extremists—chemical weapons security was most urgent and directly threatened US national security. So when the president was asked by NBC journalist Chuck Todd about what might happen if there were indications the chemical weapons were insecure or about to be used, Obama spoke openly about his determination not to allow the weapons to be used or end up in the wrong hands.

"That's an issue that doesn't just concern Syria," he warned. "It concerns our close allies in the region, including Israel. It concerns us." The president said he had made very clear to Assad and others that "a red line for us is [when] we start seeing a whole bunch of chemical weapons moving around or being utilized." He further described it as something that would "change my calculus" regarding the use of force.[7]

Obama considered this a statement of fact rather than a new policy declaration—this wasn't the conclusion of a policy process or formal decision. In diplomacy, there is always a danger in thinking out loud. Some of his aides were surprised that he went as far as he did—I was one. The president's statement was undeniably true—if chemical weapons were used it would be a game-changer, regardless of whether he had publicly called it a red line or not—but we had not yet fleshed out a plan to enforce such a threat. In the months that followed, we scrambled to develop our military plans and establish the legal rationale for action.

As the August 2012 statement became widely interpreted as a sacrosanct commitment to act militarily rather than a self-evident analytical comment—therefore turning every stray report of Syria crossing the red line into a dramatic test of US resolve—Obama surely came to regret that he had taken the bait and uttered it in the first place. It serves as another reminder why it is never wise for a president to answer a hypothetical question.[8]

BY THE SPRING of 2013, concerns about Syria's chemical weapons had reached a fever pitch. There had been a steady stream of reports about chemical weapons use on a small scale, and importantly, solid intelligence with corroborating soil and blood samples. Mindful of the lessons of Iraq, the administration pressed the intelligence community for greater specificity. But we were careful to give intelligence analysts the space to make their conclusions—we all remembered that the Bush team had been accused of pressuring the intelligence community into concluding that Saddam had chemical weapons to justify intervention in 2003, and no one wanted to repeat that mistake.

The Israelis were especially worried. Syria's massive arsenal had been designed for use against them. So while they stayed quiet over most aspects of the Syria conflict (as long as the unrest did not turn on them) they had become very agitated about the security of the chemical weapons. The essence of Israel's military doctrine is to possess the capability to eliminate any threat by itself, yet Israeli defense officials had no answer to the threat of Syria's chemical arsenal. Of their many security concerns, this was their highest priority.

During a visit to the Israeli Defense Ministry at that time, I met with their senior official in charge of defending against weapons of mass destruction, who explained how they were distributing gas masks and antidotes to every Israeli citizen.[9] To address these concerns, the US had increased information sharing with Israel about the whereabouts and security of Syria's chemical stockpiles, and we started joint contingency planning about what we might do if such weapons got on the loose.

Israeli Prime Minister Benjamin Netanyahu was seized with the issue. He used his first meeting with the new secretary of defense, Chuck Hagel, in April 2013, to make a strong case for action. Meeting in his Jerusalem office, I recall Netanyahu raised his usual concerns about Iran and Hamas, yet at that moment he was most animated about Syria.

Nearly leaping out of his chair, the prime minister said we needed "to think outside the box," even suggesting that together the British, Americans, and Israelis should divide responsibility for securing each of Syria's estimated forty-five chemical weapons sites. I remember he urged us to discuss what we could do specifically—such as mining the sites to make them too dangerous to enter, seizing them with special operations forces, or destroying them with airstrikes. Although most of this seemed a bit too creative and we did not pursue any of these ideas with the Israelis, Netanyahu's stern message to us was clear. We knew we'd have to do something. The question was when and how.

THE NETANYAHU MEETING coincided with an ominous milestone in the Syria conflict. On April 25, the White House announced for the first time that the intelligence community assessed the Syrian regime had used chemical weapons on a small scale. With the red line crossed, the question of what we would do about it surged front and center.[10]

None of the options were appealing. This was a stark example of the fact that for many foreign policy problems, the choice is not between bad and good, but bad and worse. The challenge seemed so massive and complex that it was hard to know where to begin. At a White House meeting to discuss military actions, one senior Pentagon colleague remarked that "Iran is a tough problem, but it pales in comparison with Syria." The storage facilities were dispersed throughout the country, and there didn't seem to be any way to secure them without putting boots on the ground. Military planners estimated that this could take as many as 75,000 troops. The sites would be hard to blow up safely from the air, and we worried about the toxic chemical plumes airstrikes could create.

To the president's critics, the decision was a no-brainer. With the red line crossed, they wanted America to act immediately, and to them Obama's caution was more inept than prudent. In March 2013, the top two senators on the Armed Services Committee, Arizona Republican John McCain and Michigan Democrat Carl

Levin, urged the president to use precision strikes to destroy Assad's aircraft and SCUD missile batteries.[11] The conservative commentator Charles Krauthammer urged Obama to establish a no-fly zone by destroying Assad's air defenses.[12] And Hillary Clinton's former director of policy planning (and my former boss) Anne-Marie Slaughter took to the pages of the *Washington Post* to argue that "standing by while Assad gasses his people will guarantee that, whatever else Obama may achieve, he will be remembered as a president who proclaimed a new beginning with the Muslim world but presided over a deadly chapter in the same old story."[13]

The media joined the bandwagon as well, constantly peppering administration officials with questions about why they weren't intervening, almost taunting them to do so. But this seemed all part of another same old story: once we did act, and things would not improve and in fact might get worse, the mood in favor of action would likely shift. As one White House official described at the time, "The pressures on us to intervene now are enormous. But the day after you do something, the pressures go in the other direction."[14]

THIS CONTRADICTORY AND thankless dynamic—clamoring for military action, then expressing outrage that you are actually (or even considering) doing so—characterized the intense congressional debate about using force in Syria in September 2013, following the large-scale chemical attack.

Always mindful to protect their constitutional powers, congressional leaders initially praised the president's decision to ask for their support. But as public opinion polls showed most Americans skeptical of using force, the mood on the Hill quickly soured. Phone calls were pouring into congressional offices to urge a vote against action. A survey by the Pew Research Center at that time found that 48 percent of the public opposed air strikes against Syria; just 29 percent supported them.[15]

Immediately after the president's Rose Garden announcement, teams of administration officials flooded Capitol Hill to brief members and their staffs on all aspects of the issue—from the specifics of the attack and everything we knew about Syria's chemical weapons program to the types of targets we would hit and the kinds of weapons we would use. Members of Congress were suddenly very worried about the risks. They wanted to know for sure that using military force would work, that once we destroyed the sites the chemical weapons would be kept secure, and that Assad would not retaliate against our troops or allies like Israel.

They demanded answers to questions to which there were no certainties. Although we were confident the planned strikes would affect Assad's thinking, we could not guarantee it—nor could we say for certain what might happen next. The best we could offer was that we believed the strikes would degrade some of Assad's capabilities and deter him from acting again. We could not promise that a military response would solve the problem. In fact we had to prepare for the possibility that it may backfire.

As one of those dispatched to make the case, I spent the better part of two weeks with my colleagues on Capitol Hill meeting with all variety of members and their staffs. Sometimes we briefed a single member in his or her office or in a classified meeting room in the bowels of the Capitol; other times it was with a party caucus, a congressional committee, or a state delegation; in one instance, it was the entire House of Representatives. Since it was the congressional summer recess and many members were away from Washington (many of them flew in for briefings and then returned home), we arranged for large briefings with staff, all of them trying to get up to speed on the issue. In one such meeting, US Ambassador to Syria Robert Ford and I briefed nearly 400 House staffers in a packed congressional auditorium—it was reminiscent of a Vietnam-era teach-in, except we were advocating for the use of force, not agitating against it.

The case for action was swallowed with a healthy dose of skepticism. It wasn't easy for members of Congress: In a matter of weeks, the administration was asking them to travel the same treacherous journey it had been struggling with for two years in Syria. Now they too had to accept all the dangers and own all the consequences. Once members started to consider the risks of acting—especially now that they were part of the decision—most became unsure. Some even complained that the administration, in asking for their approval and obliging them to share responsibility, had put them in this position.

Although the vast majority of Congress worried that we would do too much, some complained that we would do too little—this latter group wanted to make the crossing of the red line a pretext to expand the mission and overthrow Assad. If one had followed the press up to that point, it was easy to believe that hawkish voices like Republican Senators John McCain and Lindsay Graham, who had been most prominent in advocating the use of force, represented a powerful base of support. But they were exposed to be very lonely. Long the administration's sharpest critics, they were now its strongest supporters; but on this occasion, they had little influence in persuading their colleagues.

Trying to navigate between these two extremes proved difficult. We had planned a discrete use of military power, at once devastating and tightly scoped. Yet this was tough to explain, and led to some mixed messages. To reassure those who worried about escalation, we stressed the limits of the campaign, with Secretary Kerry promising the strikes would be "incredibly small." But at the same time, the strikes would pack a punch—as Secretary Hagel said, they would be "more than pinpricks."

Despite our efforts, the president's case was losing momentum. The prospect for getting congressional approval looked dim. Republican Senator Marco Rubio said he was "unconvinced that the use of force proposed here will work" (a position he proudly defended on the 2016 presidential campaign trail).[16] Senator Ted Cruz explained he did "not believe a limited airstrike, as proposed by the president, will lead to success or improve conditions in Syria." He warned that if the "proposed military strike against Assad succeeds, al-Qaeda could be strengthened and terrorists could seize control of Syria's vast cache of chemical weapons."[17] Senator Rand Paul declared: "War should occur only when America is attacked, when it is threatened or when American interests are attacked or threatened. I don't think the situation in Syria passes that test."[18]

The rest of the world was no more enthusiastic about the prospect of American military intervention. Once the British bowed out, France was the only ally willing to join the US (the days of "freedom fries" seemed like ancient history); Turkey and Saudi Arabia voiced support but did not commit to participating in eventual strikes. Most Arab countries stayed silent, worried that lending support would expose them to retaliation, and some wouldn't back the strikes because they would not go far enough and leave Assad in power. The UN Security Council was tied up in knots because of Russia's opposition. Even the Israelis were skittish, worrying that instead of eliminating the threat of Syria's chemical weapons, military strikes could set them loose.

Then, just as the US seemed headed toward intervening in Syria on its own—without the support of most of the world, Congress and, by extension, the American people—a stunning twist occurred that led to an outcome none of us had expected, planned for, or even dreamed was possible.

AN OPENING FOR DIPLOMACY

It started with another ad-lib. During a September 9 press conference in London, Secretary Kerry was asked if there was anything Assad could do to avoid an attack. Sure, Kerry said in exasperation, the Syrian leader could admit that he had chemical weapons (something he still refused to do) and give them all up peacefully, but "he isn't about to do it and it can't be done." Like Obama's original red line a year earlier, this offhand remark wasn't intended to be a policy pronouncement. But soon after Kerry walked off the stage he received a call from his Russian counterpart, Sergei Lavrov, who was then meeting with a delegation of Syrian diplomats in Moscow and wanted to talk with the secretary of state about his "initiative."[19]

The idea of working with the Russians to deal with Syria's chemical weapons had been batted around for several months and had come up in several conversations between President Obama and Russian President Vladimir Putin. Kerry later said he had discussed it with the Russian foreign minister, and some Israeli leaders later claimed that they had had the idea first.

Washington and Moscow had deep disagreements over Syria. Russia continued to be one of Assad's only friends and the Syrian military's chief supplier. But even Moscow worried about chemical weapons. When we had been concerned in the past about the possible use or security of Syria's chemical stockpile, the Russians had reliably passed messages to Damascus. While they remained stalwart defenders of Assad, we tested how we could build on our mutual interest in preventing the spread of chemical weapons, but the overtures had never led anywhere.

The credible threat of military force changed that. Now Moscow was ready to pressure Assad to comply. Maybe this reflected their own concerns about chemical weapons; or perhaps this was driven by their desire to keep an ally in power; or possibly they were simply trying to stay relevant geopolitically. Whatever the reason, after meeting with the Russians in Moscow, the Syrians publicly admitted for the first time that they had chemical arms and committed to signing the Chemical Weapons Convention, the international treaty that bans such weapons. The Syrians were pledging to come clean—not just revealing what they had, but getting rid of their chemical weapons altogether.

Initially the administration approached the Russian offer skeptically. Putin had every reason to want to delay military action. Moreover, the idea of dismantling Syria's stockpile was daunting—there seemed to be thousands of steps before we could be sure something like this had any hope of working. But Obama wanted to test the proposition. After all, if *not* using force enabled the US to achieve something that was unquestionably in its security interests and had once seemed impossible, while also avoiding the risks entailed by military action, how could it not take such a deal?[20]

WITH US NAVY ships still ready to launch strikes, American and Russian diplomats spent several days hammering out the details of an agreement for the specific steps Syria would take to allow international inspectors to find, remove, and destroy its chemical arms. The Syrians signed on and the UN Security Council endorsed the deal, which for the first time authorized international action if Assad failed to comply. In just a matter of weeks, we had gone from plotting over how to deal with one of the world's largest arsenals of chemical weapons to implementing a plan to eliminate all of them.

The scope and ambition of the agreement—everything was scheduled to be complete in less than a year, in the middle of a civil war—were stunning. The *New York Times* aptly described it as "one of the most challenging undertakings in the history of arms control."[21] A mountain of complicated details had to be sorted out, such as how the inspectors would be kept safe, how the weapons would be transferred out of Syria, and who would assume the responsibility for destroying them.

Eventually the task would be performed through an elaborate multinational effort: international inspectors would locate and verify Syria's chemical materials and then supervise their transport to Danish and Norwegian ships, with Russia and China providing security. Then, because no country wanted to have Syrian chemical weapons on its territory, they would be placed on a US Navy ship, the *Cape Ray*, which was specially outfitted to convert the weapons material into hazardous waste so they could be safely disposed.

By June 2014, the Organization for the Prohibition of Chemical Weapons (OPCW), the international group responsible for overseeing this effort, announced that the over 1,300 tons of Syria's declared chemical weapons were now safely out of the country and on their way to being destroyed. For its efforts the OPCW was awarded the Nobel Peace Prize. As the *Washington Post* observed in June 2014, "the international effort to find, verify, pack, transport, and ultimately destroy the Syrian weapons has been unprecedented in countless ways. Never before have such lethal substances been packaged in bullet-proof containers and carried on flatbed trucks through the front lines of a war zone. Never before have such weapons been destroyed at sea."[22]

A FAILURE OR SUCCESS?

Without a bomb being dropped, Syria had admitted to having a massive chemical weapons program it had never before acknowledged, agreed to give it up, and submitted to a multinational coalition that removed the weapons and destroyed them in a way that had never been tried before. From my perspective at the Pentagon, this seemed like an incontrovertible if inelegant example of what academics call "coercive diplomacy," using the threat of force to achieve an outcome military power itself could not accomplish.[23]

Yet the near unanimous verdict among observers is that this episode revealed Obama's core weakness. Even the president's sympathizers call the handling of the red line a "debacle," an "amateurish improvisation," or the administration's "worst blunder." They contend that Obama whiffed at a chance to show resolve, that for the sake of maintaining credibility, the US would have been better off had the administration not pursued the diplomatic opening and used force instead. In this sense, a mythology has evolved from the red line episode—that if only the US had used force, then it could have not only have addressed the chemical weapons threat, but solved the Syria conflict altogether. This conventional wisdom warrants unpacking.

Some of this can be explained by politics, with partisans unwilling to give Obama credit for any success. More serious are those who argue less about the outcome than the way it came about. Presidents get rewarded for linear results, especially when things happen the way the policy sages say they are supposed to. Moreover, because one of the core attributes of being a Washington insider is being "in the know," one of the special few privy to what's really happening, surprises are frowned upon.

So Obama's sudden pivots—first by abruptly pausing to go to Congress, then by seizing an unexpected opening for diplomacy—struck many as unseemly. It did not help that unscripted comments both got the US into this situation (Obama's original red line) as well as out of it (Kerry's musing that Syria could avoid strikes by giving up its chemical weapons). Where the president saw nimble improvisations adjusting to new opportunities, the critics saw lurching indecision. Richard Haass, the president of the Council on Foreign Relations, spoke for many in the establishment when he described Obama's moves as "the most undisciplined stretch of foreign policy of his presidency."[24]

Many foreign leaders asserted that failing to respond militarily had damaged the administration's credibility. Although no Arab countries were willing to contribute their own forces and most Arab leaders even refused to support Obama publicly when he asked for it, nearly all blamed him for not intervening. Even though the chemical weapons threat was removed, they questioned whether they could trust the US to follow through on its commitments to them (as

Defense Secretary Hagel later asserted, they believed the president had "debased his currency"). Even some Europeans were disappointed—especially the French, who felt politically exposed as the only country that was willing to strike with the United States. When asked about the red line two years later, the French defense minister said, "We are sorry that it happened, and we keep being sorry for that."

GIVEN SUCH PERCEPTIONS, it is worth reflecting on what might have happened had the US barreled forward and attacked Syria. Would we have been better off? It is highly unlikely that the tons of Syrian chemical weapons would have been safely removed from the country. Even if an initial salvo deterred Assad from using more chemical weapons, he would still have had hundreds of tons remaining since the strikes would have only eliminated a small fraction of his arsenal.

Therefore it is safe to assume that there would be, with good reason, absolute hysteria about such weapons on the loose (consider the attention paid to the credible reports that some unaccounted-for weapons might be, or that extremists are cooking up their own crude weapons using industrial chemicals like chlorine). The rise of ISIS has been terrifying enough; it would be exponentially more dangerous if it had had the chance to get its hands on hundreds of tons of Syrian chemical weapons.

In fact, had President Obama acted as he was ready to do in the fall of 2013, it is likely that substantial numbers of American troops would have had to be deployed to Syria to secure those remaining chemical weapons depots over which Assad had lost control. If President Obama had passed up the opportunity for diplomacy and used force, and if that had in turn led to a loose chemical weapon being used to strike Israel or conduct a terrorist attack in the US or Europe, he deservedly would have been blamed and held accountable.

Perversely, critics at home and abroad treat the removal of Syria's chemical arsenal as an afterthought—as minor and insufficient—and instead choose to assert that Obama soiled America's reputation. It is as though they place higher value on being "tough," especially if it involves military force, than on lasting accomplishment. In the name of maintaining "credibility," they criticize Obama for not acting, even if doing so would have delivered a less advantageous outcome.

This is especially odd given our recent past. In Iraq, the US went to war in 2003 to address a WMD threat that did not exist, and the devastating result cost resources, took thousands of American lives and wounded many others, tarnished US leadership, and unleashed a regional firestorm we are still dealing with today. In Syria in 2013, the US addressed a WMD threat that *did* exist—and was of far greater scale, with as much as ten times the amount of chemical weapons materials the intelligence community wrongly estimated in Iraq—by *avoiding* the use of force. Yet this is widely perceived as a blow to American prestige.

How CAN THIS be? The first part of the problem is the definition of—and fixation with—credibility. Perceptions do matter, but I think Obama would agree with the point made by the political scientist Richard Betts, who observes that "credibility is the modern antiseptic buzzword now often used to cloak the ancient enthusiasm for honor. But honor's importance is always more real and demanding to national elites and people on home fronts than it is to [those] put into the point of the spear to die for it." Obama is deeply skeptical of the Washington establishment's obsession with credibility, believing that the logic sets a trap leading to bad decisions. As he once argued, "dropping bombs on someone just to prove you're willing to drop bombs on someone is just about the worst reason to use force."[25]

A second issue is process. Procedure and presentation are important, and Obama concedes that this was not a textbook execution of foreign policy. "We won't get style points for the way we made this decision," he has said.[26] By exposing the public to the sausage-making of policy—by thinking out loud, making clear all the uncertainties and risks, and shifting directions abruptly—the administration created an impression that it lacked confidence.

This perception was exacerbated by the sudden, and clumsy, move to go to Congress for approval. It was the right decision, but it should not have been made on the fly (and not *after* Kerry had been sent out to make such a Churchillian call for action) and with no consultation with our allies, especially the French, who were the only ones willing to act with us. To this day, many believe that going to Congress was just a cynical move by the president to pass the buck and avoid strikes. I never believed this to be true, and remain unaware of any evidence to prove such an assertion. Although Obama asked for congressional support, he always made clear he would act without it.

A third problem is dashed expectations. By drawing the red line, Obama unintentionally fueled the hope that he would respond with overwhelming force. Or, as many now assert, he should have used the crossing as justification to achieve a *different* goal, something that the military strikes were never intended to do: take out Assad.

There was always some ambiguity about how the US would enforce the red line. To some extent this was necessary: to establish deterrence, the US needed to keep Assad guessing about how it might respond, staying ambiguous enough to encourage him to think the worst, wondering if his life was in danger. Still, the overall effect was that by threatening force and then not using it, Obama seemed to make a promise he did not keep. This despite the many occasions—from the bin Laden raid to the Libya war to numerous counter-terrorism operations—Obama had shown a willingness to use force decisively and at considerable risk.

To be sure, it was harder for the administration to claim this as a strategic success because of the improvised way it arrived. In retrospect, the US could have tried earlier to use the specter of intervention to get Russia on board to pressure Assad. But it hadn't. Once the red line had been crossed, one can imagine a circumstance where the US went to Assad with a clear demand: "we'll strike unless you give up all of your chemical weapons." The substantive outcome would not have been any better, but perhaps it would have generated a greater sense of American leadership.

OBAMA IS WILLING to live with this perception as long as the result serves the country's—and in his view, the world's—long-term interests. Because he was defying Washington's expectations—what he mockingly calls the "Washington playbook"—he knew he would face a barrage of criticism. But he has stayed confident enough in the result to suffer some reputational costs. In retrospect, Obama remains immensely proud of his decision. As Jeffrey Goldberg describes, this moment was Obama's "liberation," and the more scorn critics heaped on him, the more convinced he became that he had done the right thing.[27]

"I'm less concerned about style points," Obama told an interviewer after he pulled back from using force. "I'm much more concerned about getting the policy right." If given the choice between removing Syria's chemical weapons or not, the preference should be clear. When asked about the criticisms, Obama said that "folks here in Washington like to grade on style...and so had we rolled out something that was very smooth and disciplined and linear, they would have graded it well, even if it was a disastrous policy. We know that, because that's exactly how they graded the Iraq war."[28]

What's instructive—and for many of Obama's critics, inconvenient—is to listen to the foreign leaders who are most complimentary of the way things turned out: the Israelis. Syria's vast chemical weapons arsenal was an acute threat to Israel—a threat for which it had no viable military answer. Israeli military officials later told me that they had done their own planning for airstrikes to take out the chemical weapons, yet all the scenarios had "horrific" civilian casualties.

While some Israelis were initially very worried that by pulling back from military action Obama had undermined his credibility, they were relieved by the outcome. The removal of Syria's chemical weapons is an accomplishment that Prime Minister Netanyahu, a leader who has had his share of disagreements with Obama, described as "the one ray of light in a very dark region." Such sentiments were echoed repeatedly by senior Israeli defense officials, who by 2015 considered the Syrian chemical weapons threat so insignificant they did not include gas attacks as a scenario in their annual emergency home front drills.[29]

THE RED LINE is remembered quite differently than what the phrase was really about—the massive threat from Syria's chemical weapons. Instead, it has morphed into a short-hand critique of Obama's handling not just of Syria, but of his exercise of American power entirely. Even inside the administration the phrase became loaded, as though it were a slur, politically incorrect to utter.

There is no question that the Syrian war is the greatest catastrophe of the post-Cold War world, with hundreds of thousands killed, millions of refugees, states disintegrating, and extremists filling the vacuum. But there *is* a question about what America can and should do about it, and whether Obama's approach reflects a sensible balance of competing interests and a healthy recognition of limits, or whether it simply derives from timidity and defeatism.

When and how America should use its military power has been one of the most vexing questions President Obama has faced. And it has been one of the most contentious issues within the administration. In Syria, Obama was ready to use force to deal with one major threat to US interests—chemical weapons—but ended up achieving an even better outcome through diplomacy. Since 2014, the US has been using force to address another direct threat to US interests: ISIS.

Numerous critics (including some former administration officials) have made the case that the US should be willing to use additional military power to achieve its other stated policy goals—to accelerate Assad's departure, build a lasting political settlement, combat extremists, or simply to reclaim leadership. The challenge is how one reconciles this understandable impulse to act with the desire to prevent a problem like Syria from overwhelming American foreign policy.

The debate is often defined as "doing something" or "doing nothing," but those are false choices. The policy disputes exist between these extremes—deciding the way to address a problem like Syria somewhere between being all-in (like the Iraq invasion in 2003) or standing aside entirely. How the United States navigated these competing interests and managed the trade-offs is one of the central stories of the Obama presidency. And it is a defining characteristic of his Long Game.

CHAPTER 2

THE FOREIGN POLICY BREAKDOWN

B arack Obama arrived in 2008 with some entrenched criticisms of his own about how Washington handled America's role in the world. His skepticism of the foreign policy establishment was rooted in more than the political expediency of needing to take on Hillary Clinton in the Democratic primaries. It reflected the core of his view of politics. He decried the "smallness" of Washington, its obsessions with the fleeting, petty, and trivial, and its penchant for division over consensus.

Obama had conducted his 2008 presidential campaign in a way that defied prevailing views of how it should be done—eschewing the cable news, political talking-head wisdom, while using innovative methods to attract new voters and compete in places most pundits ignored. The core message of his candidacy—"change"—was to him about more than simply replacing who sat in the White House. Obama wanted to transform the culture of politics, which he believed had become deeply misguided and corrosive. This was especially the case when it came to foreign policy. For Obama, the mentality and incentives of Washington's professional political and policy class were the main obstacles to pursuing a Long Game strategy.

Obama believed that conventional thinking had generated a huge strategic mistake, the biggest since Vietnam: the 2003 invasion of Iraq. Instead of laying the blame solely on the Bush administration and a government hijacked by a neo-conservative cabal (as many Democrats wanted to do, so as to absolve themselves of responsibility), Obama saw the Iraq War as a systemic failure in which the entire Washington establishment—Democratic and Republican politicians, foreign policy experts of all stripes, and the press—was responsible. And, importantly, it was an issue he had gotten right from the beginning.

ALTHOUGH OBAMA WAS more than an antiwar candidate, his early opposition to the invasion of Iraq fueled his political rise. His decision to speak out against the war in 2002 crystalized in one moment everything that he believed was flawed about the foreign policy debate—and how he wanted to change it.

"The American people weren't just failed by a president," he said in an October 2007 speech at DePaul University in Illinois, when few in the foreign policy world were watching. "They were failed by much of Washington. By a media that too often reported spin instead of facts. By a foreign policy elite that largely boarded the bandwagon for war. And most of all by the majority of a Congress... that voted to give the president the open-ended authority to wage war that he uses to this day."[1]

The DePaul speech, delivered before a crowd of nearly five hundred students on the fifth anniversary of Obama's famous statement against the Iraq invasion at a Chicago antiwar rally, was a broadside against what he called Washington "groupthink." To drive this point home, that same day he delivered this speech twice more, in Iowa. Throughout the campaign Obama had sparred with his more experienced opponents (including his future vice president and secretary of state) over such issues as how to engage adversaries like Iran and whether to get tough with countries like Pakistan. He turned their criticisms back on them, once saying during a Democratic primary debate that he found it "amusing that those who helped to authorize and engineer the biggest foreign policy disaster in our generation are now criticizing me" for such stands.[2] In the DePaul speech, Obama went further, observing that "you might think that Washington would learn from Iraq. But we've seen…just how bent out of shape Washington gets when you challenge its assumptions."

Such themes carried through his 2008 campaign, and he would return to them often as president. During his early years in the White House, establishment critiques would gnaw at him. But in the latter part of his presidency he wanted to take on such critics more openly—trying to engender a sense of accountability.

For example, Obama characterized opponents of the Iran nuclear deal in 2015 in similar terms to those who had criticized his policies in 2007—explicitly drawing a direct line of argument between the two. In a fiesty speech at American University in August 2015, he laid out his critique of this "mindset," intentionally calling out his critics:

> When I ran for president eight years ago as a candidate who had opposed the decision to go to war in Iraq, I said that America didn't just have to end that war—we had to end the mindset that got us there in the first place. It was a mindset characterized by a preference for military action over diplomacy; a mindset that put a premium on unilateral US action over the painstaking work of building international consensus; a mindset that exaggerated threats beyond what the intelligence supported. Leaders did not level with the American people about the costs of war, insisting that we could easily impose our will on a part of the world with a

profoundly different culture and history. And, of course, those calling for war labeled themselves strong and decisive, while dismissing those who disagreed as weak—even appeasers of a malevolent adversary.

In public and private, Obama would frequently express frustration with what passed for smart thinking from Washington's unceasing chorus of commentary. While Obama was open to ideas and liked to engage his critics—and at times, quietly hosted them at the White House for informal discussions to hear them out—he was usually left underwhelmed by what they recommended he do differently (he engaged both sides; for example, two of the more notable critics he met with privately were conservative Robert Kagan and liberal Andrew Bacevich). Obama would decry that the foreign policy debate was not, as he often put it, "on the level," meaning it sought to elide complexity and deny trade-offs just to score points or win the news cycle, with little consequence for being wrong. Sober reflection hardly attracts attention. Proving the point, the DePaul speech was barely noticed at the time, garnering scant coverage in the national press (this despite Obama having delivered it three times that day).

Obama's views as president are aptly summed up by an observation he made in 2007 as a candidate at DePaul: "Conventional thinking in Washington has a way of buying into stories that make political sense even if they don't make practical sense."

ALTHOUGH OBAMA FRAMED his candidacy against the establishment, he was hardly a fringe candidate or some reincarnation of George McGovern. He still drew upon the ideas of leading foreign policy thinkers, and benefitted from the tough lessons Democrats had learned during the Bush years. While the 2008 primary debate between Obama and Clinton became quite bitter (especially among their rival camps), their actual policy differences were exaggerated.

In fact, Democrats found themselves more unified and ready to debate foreign policy in 2008 than in any other election since the end of the Cold War. To be sure, some of this confidence was a result of Bush's foreign policy failures, and the fact that Obama's 2008 opponent, John McCain, could be tied to so many of those policies, especially the war in Iraq. But just as important, Democrats had coalesced around a set of ideas to bring bold changes to American foreign policy.

To understand the foreign policy debates of the Obama years—and to appreciate better Obama's perspective on American foreign policy and how he set out to change it—one must consider the broader historical context.

A SECOND CHANCE

Obama's Long Game approach was far more than a knee-jerk response to the Bush years and America's post-9/11 policy decisions. It was another chapter in the quarter-century-long struggle to define American leadership after the Cold War.

For the quarter century since the fall of the Berlin Wall in 1989, conservatives and liberals have grappled with the very nature of the world order and America's place in it. The core questions included: How much should the United States care about the legitimacy of its actions—such as adhering to international law or working through international institutions? How much should it care about what happens inside other countries? When should the US use military force to solve problems?

Fundamentally, the debate has revolved around how the United States should pursue its interests; how the exercise of American power can be reconciled with limits; what, if anything, is necessary to justify US actions; and how one should define "strength" and "leadership" in today's world.

The end of the Cold War presented a paradox. Even though the Soviet Union had been defeated, America's initial triumphalism soon gave way to pessimism. The US may have been victorious, but after the Cold War many American leaders and analysts believed the country was in decline ("the Cold War ended, and Germany and Japan won" was a popular quip). Some politicians argued that traditional national security policy would take a back seat to domestic issues, or "softer" challenges like international economics and globalization.

The collapse of the Soviet Union also scrambled US domestic politics. For decades, the core of conservative foreign policy had been to be tough on Communism, and their assertions of strength were used to cudgel liberals as feckless and weak. In many ways, the Soviet threat had been at once the grip holding modern conservatism together and the wedge driving liberals apart. With the Cold War over, both sides were compelled to remake themselves.

During the 1990s, conservatives and liberals found agreement on certain foreign policy questions, such as the interventions in the Balkans or the enlargement of NATO. But common ground on some issues did not create a new foreign policy consensus. However vigorous these debates sometimes proved to be, they remained in the confines of elite circles. The broader public never really engaged in them.

That changed only after 9/11. For many Americans, the September 11, 2001 terrorist attacks marked a stark turning point for the United States' role in the world. After years in which American leaders seemed to careen from crisis to crisis, none of which quite rose to the level of grave threats to national security, the US now faced a determined enemy and a generational struggle. Foreign policy in the "post-Cold War era" finally had an overriding purpose: to defeat al-Qaeda and its ilk. America, it seemed, needed to fight "the long war"—which became the organizing framework for US foreign policy.

During the 2000s, analysts such as former national security adviser Zbigniew Brzezinski offered sobering assessments of the mistakes the US made under the "long war" banner. In his 2007 book *Second Chance*, Brzezinski argued that during the Clinton and Bush years, the US had led "badly," and that "after its coronation as global leader [in 1989], America is becoming a fearful and lonely democracy in a politically antagonistic world." American leadership was headed in the wrong direction, too often defining itself as a matter of military strength alone, and succumbing to fears that led us into misadventures like Iraq. So the US needed to seize a second chance. Obama and his team had read this book and shared its assessment—in fact, Brzezinski was one of Obama's informal advisers during the 2008 campaign.[3]

IN HIS OWN book that helped launch his 2008 White House bid, *The Audacity of Hope*, Obama expresses the view that, in many ways, the post-Cold War era was one of lost opportunity (most campaign books are dismissed as ghost-written policy pablum, but Obama's is worth reading carefully, and once in office he would often remind people that it provides a clear description of his views). Although there were accomplishments—such as ending some long-festering conflicts and promoting democracy and free trade—Obama concluded that "in the eyes of the public, at least, foreign policy in the nineties lacked any overarching theme or grand imperatives."[4]

The stage for the immediate post-Cold War period had been set by President George H.W. Bush and his principal national security advisers, Brent Scowcroft and James Baker, who had earned plaudits for their skilled handling of complex events that came at a dizzying pace. In less than four years, the Berlin Wall fell, the Warsaw Pact disappeared, Germany reunified, Saddam was kicked out of Kuwait, and the Soviet Union crumbled.

The Bush team handled all of this with prudent and steady management. But they failed to translate these huge successes into a lasting strategy that the American people could understand and rally around. George H. W. Bush's attempt to begin sketching a doctrine—his much-maligned "new world order"—was never much more than a slogan. If anything, the idea quickly became shorthand for an unimaginative, traditional conception of stability, not a bold way forward. Bush admitted his discomfort with the "vision thing." (And Bush's successes abroad sowed the seeds for his demise at home, as Americans found his domestic agenda less compelling.) Obama is an admirer of the elder Bush, yet he, too, saw that "his skill in building international coalitions or judiciously projecting American power did nothing to salvage his presidency."[5]

Bill Clinton had a different problem. He was brimming full of ideas and had a lofty if somewhat abstract vision for America as the "indispensable nation." In the 1990s, Clinton helped put American foreign policy on a steady course, accumulating so much military and economic might that some foreign leaders described the US as a "hyperpower." Yet Clinton was frustrated that he had not brought enough Americans along: "I still don't think I've persuaded the American people by big majorities that you really ought to care about foreign policy, about our relationship to the rest of the world, about what we're doing," he said in one of his last foreign policy speeches as president.[6]

George W. Bush and his team agreed. In the year 2000 they swept into office asserting that Clinton had failed because he had not defined a lasting doctrine for America in this new era. They, too, were seduced by simplicity—if the United States looked strong and acted forcefully, the world would follow and problems would come to a heel.

IN THE IMMEDIATE aftermath of the 9/11 terrorist attacks, it seemed that conservative foreign policy was ascendant. Despite the Clinton administration leaving the White House with an impressive record of foreign policy accomplishments—boosting free trade, enlarging NATO, making progress in the Middle East peace process, bringing peace to the Balkans—Democrats still found themselves saddled in the 2000s with the reputation of weakness. George W. Bush had run for office belittling Clinton's leadership for being both arrogant and feeble, and he had surrounded himself with widely-recognized foreign policy heavyweights such as Dick Cheney and Colin Powell.

The Bush team exuded confidence and certainty, and while it may seem hard to remember now, at the time most Americans thought that they had good reason to do so. Because of their association with the Cold War's end, these Republicans had a mystique that even Democrats admired. They conceived of themselves as the professionals who had defeated the Soviet Union and believed they needed to bring back decorum in Washington after the tumultuous Clinton years. Their sense of purpose—and self-regard for their own hype, which was widely shared in Washington's power corridors—was summed up by the slogan Cheney used on the 2000 campaign trail: "Help is on the way." They wanted to restore America's role in the world to the grand imperative that had defined the Cold War.[7] Yet by the time George W. Bush left office, America faced a deep crisis at home and around the world—the worst it had faced since the 1940s, when crippled by the Great Depression and World War II. After eight years in power, conservatives were in disarray on foreign and economic policy.

Some of this was due to the Bush team's mismanagement of crises both at home (the response to Hurricane Katrina and the American economy's near collapse) and overseas (the Iraq War), which tarnished their brand as clear-eyed, competent guardians of national security. In Bush's wake, the Iraq-era conservative generation—like the Vietnam-era liberal "best and the brightest" generation of the 1960s—was widely discredited. Their image of competence was shattered and their ideas challenged.[8]

The implosion of the Bush foreign policy had also exposed the divisions among conservatives that had been masked in the immediate post-9/11 years, when a new sense of threat from Islamic extremism had unified the right. But by the 2008 election that consensus had broken.

A symbol of this collapse was Colin Powell's endorsement of Obama for president in 2008. When explaining his reasons for doing so, Powell offered a rationale that would become a hallmark of Obama's foreign policy decision-making: Obama, he said, demonstrated "the kind of calm, patient, intellectual, steady approach to problem-solving that I think we need in this country."[9]

Powell's support for Obama was important politically, but it highlighted a larger divide that still riddles Republicans. Powell represents a strain of foreign policy thinking that was once dominant, but is now far out of fashion. This school is represented by the elder Bush, who, while believing deeply in American leadership, hoped the US could exercise its influence through global institutions like the UN that had been hobbled by the Cold War's divisions. "Bush 41" and his core team cared about legitimacy and believed it had to be earned, and they reasoned that working through institutions was a key way of doing so. And while they kept faith in the strong use of American power—and when necessary, the unilateral use of force—they also valued restraint.

One of history's ironies is how the instincts of the first George Bush were rejected by the second—and, significantly, it is Bush 43's worldview and conception of American power that became the center of gravity for conservative foreign policy (judging from the 2016 Republican presidential campaign, more accurately it is the Cheney worldview, which was the most hawkish, nationalist, and extreme version of Bush 43's approach). George W. Bush and his team were less worried about generating legitimacy. Their understanding of American exceptionalism was a little like papal infallibility or Richard Nixon's understanding of presidential power: if we do it, it must be right.

THE ASCENDANCE OF the Bush/Cheney foreign policy was a key impetus behind Obama's rise. Like many Americans, Obama recalls how in the wake of 9/11 he expected the Bush administration to lead by forging a new kind of approach to use America's special strengths and attractive power to build a new international consensus against global threats. Instead, Obama observed, "What we got was an assortment of outdated policies from eras gone by, dusted off, slapped together, and with new labels affixed." But most concerning to Obama, "the Bush administration resuscitated a brand of politics not seen since the end of the Cold War."[10]

For a time, this kind of politics worked as liberals floundered. The 2004 presidential campaign illustrated the dilemmas that Democrats faced. Even though the Iraq War was not going well, national security ultimately proved Democrats' political undoing. The proximate reason was the support most Democrats had given to Bush's decision to launch the Iraq War, which effectively neutralized the issue politically by making it harder to criticize (John Kerry's unfortunate argument that "I voted for it before I voted against it" exemplified the contortions the issue generated). Moreover, there was still a sense within progressive circles that national security could not be a "winning" issue politically. Inside the Kerry campaign, there were constant discussions about how soon they could drop the topic of foreign policy and switch to domestic issues that they believed would win the election.

One lesson Democrats drew was that to be politically successful in a time of war, they needed to look "strong" and "tough," and so Kerry made his military service in Vietnam a central part of his candidacy. Yet that experience proved his undoing, as the successful efforts by the Bush campaign to undermine the credibility of Kerry's war record became a large part of his failure as a candidate. Instead, the one person who emerged from the 2004 campaign as a star was then a little known Senate candidate from Illinois, who famously delivered the keynote address at the Democratic Convention in Boston, arguing that "war must be an option sometimes, but it should never be the first option."

The painful 2004 loss established the foundation for Democrats' rebirth on national security, as progressives were determined to regain their footing on these issues. Most of this happened behind the scenes, under the helpful camouflage of the Bush administration's foreign policy which was self-destructing by the day. Democrats had studied the efforts of conservatives in the 1970s and 80s to build an infrastructure of expertise and policy advocacy that could help build consensus around their efforts, and in the four years after the 2004, progressive national security experts and leaders met and plotted their way out of the wilderness.

They formed study groups and established new organizations to help carry this message forward and create a new generation of leaders, such as the Truman National Security Project, which was established in the days after the 2004 presidential campaign to help build a young generation of Democratic national security leaders, purposely harkening back to the strong Democratic foreign policy hands like those who had served under Presidents Truman and Kennedy, and think tanks like the Center for American Progress and the Center for a New American Security.[11]

A key part of these efforts was to strengthen the ties of Democrats with the military. Despite the eight years of a Clinton presidency and a largely successful civil-military relationship that had developed over those years, Democrats were still tarnished with the sense that there was an inherent divide between them and the military. Part of this was cultural—with roots in the Vietnam era—but it also stemmed from the ambivalence many Democrats still had about the use of force, and that view was newly visible.

OUTSIDE WASHINGTON'S FOREIGN policy elite, there was a larger struggle going on within the Democratic Party, a ferment created by a new class of activists and donors. There were many who discerned from the 2004 election the opposite of what Washington national security experts and politicians had concluded. They believed that the problem for Democrats was that they were too much like Republicans, and that rather than try to remake themselves, Democrats needed to return to a purer form of liberalism. They asserted that by supporting the Iraq War—and by not advocating for defunding the effort and for the immediate withdrawal of American troops—Democrats themselves were culpable in the failures of the Bush years.

This battle was principally about Iraq, but it had actually started years before. The convulsions within liberalism began in the late 1990s, illustrated by the rise of the anti-globalization movement and division over the military interventions in Bosnia and Kosovo and the 1998 air strikes against Iraq. They only became more severe and divisive in the post 9/11 years.

Such tumult reflected the pain of the contested 2000 and 2004 election losses and deep anger with George W. Bush. But it was more than that. When it came to national security issues, liberals had become divided in a way not seen since the 1970s, when Vietnam had split the Democratic Party and sparked a reaction, pitting the "new Left" against the liberal establishment. A similar dynamic unfolded in the 2000s, as a new generation of internet-fueled liberal activists (call it the "new-new-Left") raged not just against Bush, but against the Democratic establishment in Washington.[12] At the forefront of this were groups like MoveOn.org, which pressed relentlessly for the

Democratic Party to take a stronger stance against the Iraq War. When combined with a conservative movement that was itself splintering and a media culture that was becoming more partisan, instant, and atomized, the result was a more embittered and chaotic policymaking environment.

These internecine battles got ugly. Nothing demonstrated that more vividly than the fate of Connecticut Senator Joseph Lieberman. A respected Democratic senator for eighteen years, and Al Gore's vice-presidential running mate in 2000, Lieberman was a foreign policy hawk, who had advocated for intervention in the Balkans and getting tough on Iraq. Lieberman was just a few Florida votes away from being vice president of the United States, and ran for the Democratic presidential nomination in 2004. Yet by 2007, Lieberman had become a pariah among the "new-new-Left." He lost a primary election to an antiwar candidate who was bolstered by outside money, and returned to the Senate as an Independent. In 2008, he endorsed and actively campaigned for John McCain for president against Obama.[13]

This political fratricide sent shockwaves among Democratic foreign policy elites. To the extent that Clinton's presidency had exorcised the ghosts of McGovern—allowing progressives to be comfortable with American leadership, power, and intervention—the new debate seemed to reopen old wounds.

BARACK OBAMA'S VOCAL stance against the Iraq War gave him legitimacy among this new cadre of liberal activists and donors. But he was not some bleeding heart. Obama made clear he was not against all wars, only "dumb ones." He argued that while the top concerns of many of these liberals (like withdrawing from Iraq or fighting AIDS) had merit, "they hardly constitute a coherent national security policy...like it or not, if we want to make America more secure, we are going to have to help make the world more secure."[14]

Moreover, Obama relied a great deal on those Democratic thinkers and ideas that were the product of the efforts to get stronger on national security after the 2004 election. So, in a way, Obama embodied the hopes and ambitions of both sides. He also embodied their contradictions.

WHAT DOES "STRENGTH" MEAN?

While Obama campaigned for the presidency by positioning himself against the professional foreign policy elite, his approach to foreign policy reflected the views of mainstream progressives, especially as they contrasted with conservatives. Obama might have vigorously campaigned against Hillary Clinton, but in fundamental ways, he embraced the consensus that mainstream Democrats had rallied around after her husband left office.

Many of the policies that progressive foreign policy thinkers had championed and developed in the 2000s—responsibly managing the transitions out of Iraq and Afghanistan; bringing new focus to the war against al-Qaeda; maintaining military strength and willingness to use force while achieving greater balance between defense, diplomacy, and development; revitalizing core alliances, especially in Europe; addressing issues like energy security, climate change, and nuclear non-proliferation; putting greater emphasis on the US role in the Asia-Pacific—became the core of Obama's foreign policy.

In a broader sense, these policies reflect fundamentally different worldviews between liberals and conservatives. For example, the liberal consensus sees the world as "us and them," where nations' fates are linked and therefore they have to work together to address common problems, while conservatives see things in more antagonistic terms, as "us versus them," in which the US stands apart. Conservatives believe that what is good for the US is good for the world, while liberals believe that what is good for the world is good for the US.[15]

Conservatives prioritize freedom of action, which helps explain their obsessive focus on issues like missile defense and suspicions of international institutions and law. They prize the idea that an America protected cannot be blackmailed. This also fits within a larger strategy: to ensure invulnerability, the US needs to shed any artificial constraints on protecting the country's interests, whether treaties or agreements or institutions, that could hinder its ability to act unilaterally.

Liberals see America as the "indispensable nation" and consider US leadership vital to solving problems. But they believe in the power generated by legitimacy, and maintain that treaties, alliances, and agreements are vital ingredients of influence. Such tools can also help create a shared set of norms to shape state behavior, widening the circle of the global order led by the United States.

Liberals are also more comfortable contemplating the limits of American power. Although critics belittle such talk as defeatism or underappreciating America's greatness, it is a reflection of reality in the changing global order. Bill Clinton said after his presidency that the "most important thing is to create a world we would like to live in when we are no longer the world's only superpower," and to prepare "for a time when we would have to share the stage."[16] Every nation is limited by finite resources and competing demands. Even though the US has fewer limits than any other, it, too, can overextend. So the challenge is how to calibrate its approach.

THIS IS ALSO an argument about how a country defines its strength. What does it mean to be strong? As he campaigned for president, Obama answered this in two ways.

First, Obama believed that being strong abroad started with being strong at home. To say that you could only concentrate on one or the other was a false choice. When Obama came into office, he saw an America that few believed was strong at home—in the middle of a financial crisis, with education and health care systems that were in shambles, and a deeply polarized political system. With this trajectory, it was hard to argue that America was in a position to continue to lead in the twenty-first century. At that time, the country was far from the model that both liberals and conservatives claim it to be.

So what was needed was what Obama called "nation building at home." This phrase provoked a torrent of criticism by many foreign policy thinkers who tend to think of domestic issues as detached from what makes America great in the world. But in fact, Obama thought they had it exactly wrong. If not strong at home, America would not be able to project its power abroad. It would not be respected abroad. It would not be the inspirational leader to so many around the world. America's inner strength is an indispensable part of its outer strength. As Peter Beinart observed, "if American power swells overseas but the quality of life for Americans deteriorates at home, then American foreign policy has failed."[17]

Second, Obama believed that the way you measure strength is by actually being strong, not just boasting that you are strong. He had little tolerance for posturing. It was something that his closest aides said most frustrated him about the Washington scene. And as his presidency evolved, he was determined to expose those elements of the foreign policy debate he considered the most preening, where politicians and pundits proclaimed the need to be "strong" and "decisive" seemingly just for the sake of doing so, with little regard for what that actually meant in practice. Obama later observed that it was unwise "to indulge in either impetuous or, in some cases, manufactured responses that make good sound bites but don't produce results. The stakes are too high to play those games."[18]

Therefore, the question is not whether America should lead, but how, and Obama favored Theodore Roosevelt's adage to speak softly but carry a large stick. In *The Audacity of Hope*, Obama quotes Roosevelt with admiration, observing that the US "has not the option as to whether it will or will not play a great part in the world. It must play a great part. All that it can decide is whether it will play that part well or badly."[19]

OBAMA OFTEN RETURNED to this critique about leadership and strength, and toward the end of his presidency he sought more opportunities to articulate it. One of his most forceful presentations was his September 2015 speech to the United Nations, where he made the provocative comparison about the similarities between the notion of strength championed by leaders like Vladimir Putin and that espoused by many of his Republican critics.

Conceding that the US is not "immune" from such thinking (he was referring to the GOP candidates for president, who were taking macho boasting about strength to new heights), Obama explained to the world's leaders that "we see in our debates about America's role in the world a notion of strength that is defined by opposition to old enemies, perceived adversaries, a rising China, or a resurgent Russia; a revolutionary Iran, or an Islam that is incompatible with peace. We see an argument made that the only strength that matters for the United States is bellicose words and shows of military force; that cooperation and diplomacy will not work."

As Obama made clear, such thinking was a recipe for failure—not just for the United States, but for the global order. "A politics and solidarity that depend on demonizing others, that draws on religious sectarianism or narrow tribalism or jingoism may at times look like strength in the moment, but over time its weakness will be exposed," Obama said. Speaking to his critics directly, Obama warned that "history tells us that the dark forces unleashed by this type of politics surely makes all of us less secure. Our world has been there before."

Obama also took issue with how the Washington wisdom defined "strength." He believed that too often, strength is explained as bold action with military might, and acting in the name of being "tough." While he fully believed that military power was essential to the nation's defense, it could neither be the only instrument of influence nor the only pillar of "strength."

Obama believed the foreign policy establishment prized the illusion more than the reality; it was too focused on demonstrating credibility for its own sake, regardless of the consequences. As the writer Jonathan Schell observed more than forty years ago—during the Nixon era, when the craze to show "strength" and "resolve" created Watergate and Vietnam—"what counted was not the substance of America's strength or the actual state of its willingness but the image of strength and willingness."[20] This kind of thinking led to grave mistakes. After all, when the United States had prevailed, it was because it had been patient and persistent in defense of its values at home and abroad, because it had maintained strong alliances, because it had sustained a vibrant domestic economy and an innovative, open society, and because it had wielded smart and principled leadership.

That's why Obama believed the country needed to embrace a different narrative of what it means to be "strong," shifting its foreign policy paradigm from the "long war" to the Long Game.

BY LEADING "BADLY," the America of the first decade of the twenty-first century had failed Teddy Roosevelt's test. The country emerged from the post-9/11 years wildly out of balance, both at home and abroad. Policies justified in the name of being strong had in fact left America weak.

US foreign policy had become defined by war, yet the American people had not been enlisted to do much of anything. Americans were asked to live normally, to act as though nothing had happened, to shop. It was an era in which it seemed perfectly fine to conduct a war without sacrifice, funding a global military campaign on "supple-mental" budgets—the federal government's equivalent of a credit card without a limit—without any attempt to pay for it with new revenue. As the journalist George Packer explained, this "revealed the unreality that lay beneath [Bush's] call to arms…never was the mis-match between the idea of war and the war itself more apparent."[21] Domestically, there was a similar disconnect between scale and sac-rifice—where, for example, it seemed reasonable for an individual to earn a modest income but still be able to purchase a million-dollar home with no money down.

To borrow from the author Michael Lewis, this was the era of the "big short," in which the country was swept up by the fantasy of eco-nomic strength defined by easy money and no sacrifice. Just as a handful of traders benefitted by betting against the deep flaws in America's fi-nancial system due to the housing mortgage crisis, countries like China benefitted by shorting America's global power due to its economic mis-management at home and overreach in Iraq. "Troubled asset" became the euphemism that defined America's 2008 financial crisis; the same phrase describes the instruments of US influence abroad when Obama assumed office. And importantly, two of America's most influential establishments—financial and foreign policy—were culpable.

By nearly every measure, the US in 2008 was a declining power, dangerously close to strategic insolvency. It was engaged in two wars with unsustainable budgets and a military force stretched to the breaking point. Its standing in the world was greatly diminished, with its core allies in Europe feeling more distant and its partners in Asia feeling ignored. In the fever of fear after 9/11, the US had pur-sued policies—like torturing enemy captives and opening the prison at Guantanamo Bay—that had undermined its ideals. The global chessboard was changing—with the rise of powers like China and India—and the US always seemed a step behind. On too many issues where common action was required—such as climate change or nuclear weapons proliferation—the US had taken positions that only served to isolate itself.

At home, the very core of American power was decaying. The US was in a deep financial hole, driven there by a similar mindset of instant gratification and little accountability, and the very survival of entire sectors of the US economy—like banking and the automobile industry—was in question. Millions of Americans had been thrown out of work or lost their homes (or both), US education was faltering, and health care costs were skyrocketing. In 2008, the stock market lost one-third of its value; by Obama's inauguration, the US economy was shedding 800,000 jobs a month.

During the Clinton and Bush 43 years, the question had been not whether American power was dominant but what it would do with its might. For Obama, the future of American power was very much in question, and the priority was to save the country from itself. To do so required bold moves in both domestic and foreign policy—forging a grand strategy that would be a wholesale makeover of American power.

YET THE FOREIGN policy debate Obama inherited only made this task harder. The black-and-white, "with-us-or-against-us" mentality that came to define conservatism during the Bush administration, combined with an angry and insular political Left, provided very little space for common ground or common sense. The incentives driving the debate had become increasingly partisan, rewarding those who pushed hardest toward the extremes or provided the most enticing click bait.

This represented a "foreign policy breakdown." In a book written over thirty years ago, *Our Own Worst Enemy*, three respected analyst-practitioners—Leslie Gelb, Anthony Lake, and I.M. Destler—warned of such a moment, in which a politicized foreign policy debate, amplified by an increasingly ravenous media, would combine to make it nearly impossible to fashion an approach to the world that is coherent, consistent, and necessary to meet the challenges of the future. Their argument is worth dusting off, because the hallmarks of this breakdown are glaringly apparent today. By the end of the Obama presidency, the situation is worse.

Consider the attributes of the breakdown they described: "Political play acting is better rewarded than hard work; political speech-making passes as serious policy making." At the same time, foreign policy debates "give more weight to ideological 'certainties' rather than to the ambiguities of reality." Foreign policy elites "help drive policy into domestic politics and push debates toward the extremes." And perhaps most harmful, "tolerance and trust, the essential ingredients of a healthy democratic system, are always sought for oneself but rarely given to others."

This sounds very similar to Obama's own perspective on what has coarsened our politics and made the debate simplistic: "The spin, the amplification of conflict, the indiscriminate search for scandal and miscues—the cumulative impact of all this is to erode any agreed-upon standards for judging the truth," he wrote in *The Audacity of Hope*. This is even more challenging as the public discourse becomes hypercharged, with nuanced commentary becoming like white noise.[22]

The result is a debate that undermines strategy, making it harder for leaders to design and sustain their policies, sabotaging American power and influence just when it is most required. Again, the words of Gelb, Lake, and Destler ring true. "At precisely the moment when we need to husband our strength and use it more efficiently; at a time when there is no choice but involvement in world affairs; in an era when others look to us for maturity and sophistication in dealing with international problems of growing complexity...at that moment we are taken less seriously."[23]

It is for this reason Obama believes in the imperative of defying this breakdown. "[F]or me to satisfy the cable news hype-fest would lead to us making worse and worse decisions over time," Obama recently observed.[24] When considering America's role in the world, he has sought to bring back a sense of proportion between ends and means; to uphold principle, but to usher a return to pragmatism. He believes that while the US cannot solve every problem on its own, it is uniquely able to bring countries together and set the agenda. Most importantly, Obama has wanted to correct what he saw as the collective irresponsibility of the political system—elites, media, politicians, activists, and donors—that he articulated in his 2007 DePaul speech.

Obama maintains deep optimism about America's global role as a force for good, and in the strength and wisdom of the American people. But he believes that too often, the political debate stands in the way. Such an atomized policy and media environment makes it more difficult to think strategically, let alone maintain the focus and discipline necessary to implement a strategy.

In other words, the "foreign policy breakdown" makes playing the Long Game even harder. This dynamic would be the defining struggle of Obama's presidency.

CHAPTER 3

REBALANCE, RESET, RESURGE

Every new president enters office surfing a wave of expectations and opportunity, but must grapple with the undertow of peril. That was especially true for Barack Obama. Few presidents have been elected who carried such a mix of high hopes and excitement combined with domestic crisis and global danger. Robert Gates, Obama's first secretary of defense who was one of Washington's most experienced policy hands, recalled, "It is hard to think of a president who entered office facing more challenges of historic magnitude."[1]

Obama and his team had to wrestle with the worst global financial crisis since the 1930s; a US economy in freefall, with millions thrown out of their homes and losing their jobs; draining wars in Afghanistan and Iraq, with over 150,000 troops in harm's way; a massive new global counter-terrorism effort; rising powers like China and surging regional players like Iran; and urgent global issues like a warming climate. It was a double-sided problem: the international agenda was unforgiving, while the reservoir of

American capacity and credibility to project power was in danger of being depleted.

This was a daunting inbox, and there was a profound sense of urgency. Yet Obama was determined to play the Long Game. He wanted to take a hard look at America's existing foreign policy priorities and see how they squared with the country's long-term interests. He wanted to know where we were "underweighted" or "overweighted" in the world—and how we could regain and sustain America's leadership position. His initial approach to handling this difficult inheritance, and his attempt to devise a strategy for the future, had three components: rebalance, reset, and resurge.

REBALANCE

The imperative to *rebalance* was based on a set of assumptions that there was a fundamental imbalance in US foreign policy in 2009.

One assumption was that there had been not enough attention given to the foundation of American leadership at home, including the US economy, jobs, education and health care. Another was that there had been an over-emphasis on the military instrument of power at the expense of other tools in the national security toolbox, such as diplomacy, international economics, and development assistance. There was the sense that while counter-terrorism certainly remained a priority, the United States needed to reestablish its credibility by trying to close the Guantanamo Bay prison and renouncing torture. It also needed to do more to address pressing global challenges such as climate change—an issue many of Obama's political opponents denied was even a problem—and the spread of weapons of mass destruction.

In this sense, Obama set out to go beyond just dealing with the issues that other forces had set upon him (as important as that would be); he wanted to drive a new affirmative agenda. That is why he acted not just to save the economy, but to change it fundamentally by enacting financial reform, implementing a nearly $800 billion economic stimulus package, and overhauling the health care system. It is why Secretary of State Clinton, with the crucial help of Defense Secretary Gates, stressed the importance of elevating diplomacy and development to work alongside defense as the "three D's" of American power. And it's why Obama used his first year in office to set out a bold agenda to tackle challenges such as climate change and nuclear proliferation.

Most prominently, the "rebalance" reflected the imperative to shift regional priorities from the preoccupation with the problems of the Middle East—which remained vitally important but had, in Obama's view, consumed far too much of America's time, attention, and resources—toward expending more leadership bandwidth in the Asia-Pacific.

AMERICA HAS ALWAYS been a Pacific power. For decades it has underwritten the regional order through its network of alliances, deep economic ties, and robust military presence. Asia's transformation has been defining the global order—the region's rise is the most important strategic development since the end of the Cold War. Asia is the center of gravity of twenty-first-century geopolitics: nearly half of the world's population is there; it has many of the world's most dynamic economies, which generate more than one-third of global GDP; it has some of the world's largest and most capable militaries (whose defense spending is increasing); and it is home to the world's two most consequential rising powers, China and India.

The US interest in Asia is compelling. Asia's markets are vital to the American economy, providing important opportunities for investment and trade. American firms need access to Asia's growing markets and cutting-edge technology. The United States also has a stake in helping maintain the region's security, whether that means confronting North Korea's nuclear threat, supporting allies such as South Korea and Japan, or defending freedom of navigation in the

South China Sea (where the Chinese are asserting dubious claims to territorial rights). In these ways, America's future is inextricably entwined with Asia. The idea that the dynamics in Asia will matter most to the United States in the long run is the closest there is to a consensus among foreign policy experts. It is one example of foreign policy conventional wisdom that Obama shares.

Yet when Obama took office, there was a widely held view that that United States had been absent from the strategic transformation in Asia, spending years focused mainly on terrorism and the Middle East. America's regional allies felt that they had been neglected and that China was filling the vacuum. The outgoing Bush team bristled at this assertion—arguing that they in fact deserved more credit for their efforts in the region—but could never shake the perception that they were preoccupied elsewhere.

Intellectually, Obama was sympathetic to the argument that Asia needed more attention. And he was personally predisposed to prioritizing the region, having grown up in Hawaii and Indonesia. His most influential foreign policy advisors who helped shape the policy during the first term—especially Hillary Clinton, Robert Gates, and National Security Advisor Tom Donilon—believed that the United States needed to engage more in the region, so much so that many of them wanted to share credit for being the architect of his Asia strategy.

In a speech to the Australian parliament in November 2011, Obama summarized his core goal in Asia: to sustain a stable security environment and a regional order rooted in economic openness, peaceful resolution of disputes, and respect for universal rights and freedoms. To accomplish this, Obama pledged, the United States would be "all-in," and he directed his team to elevate engagement with Asia in three ways: by raising America's diplomatic game; reshaping its military presence; and advancing the region's economic prosperity, which was also vital to the health of the US economy.

THE KEY MOVES of the diplomatic rebalance were to bolster ties to US treaty allies such as Japan, South Korea, and the Philippines; deepen relations with emerging partners such as Vietnam; and open new ties to countries such as Burma. It also meant investing a great deal of capital in developing the relationship with India (here, Obama was building on the work of Presidents Clinton and Bush 43). Obama described the US-India relationship as one of the "defining partnerships" of the twenty-first century. A main objective of his policy was to encourage India—the world's largest democracy with an increasingly vibrant economy and strong military—to "look east" and become a greater player in Asia.

Another vital component of this diplomatic rebalance was for the United States to engage more and seek to reshape the region's diplomatic architecture—the alphabet soup of multilateral institutions such as APEC (Asia-Pacific Cooperation Forum), ASEAN (Association of Southeast Asian Nations) and the EAS (East Asian Summit), which the United States joined for the first time in 2011. The US also sought to develop more informal, smaller groupings to take on specific challenges. Two examples of such "minilateral" efforts were the Lower Mekong Initiative to encourage cooperation in Southeast Asia, and the Pacific Islands Forum to help Island states address common threats such as climate change.

Taken together, such activity added up to one of the most intense periods ever of American diplomatic activity in Asia. With a steady pace of trips, meetings, and events—what Clinton described as "forward deployed diplomacy"—the Obama administration enhanced the US position in Asia. It is often said that the most valuable commodity in Washington is the president's time, and Obama made the priority clear by making nine trips to Asia by the spring of 2016 and by hosting many Asian officials at the White House and at the Sunnylands Estate in California (his first Oval Office visitor was from Japan, and he hosted his first official State visit for the prime minister of India). This investment of time stood in stark contrast to Bush's intensive interactions with the leaders of Iraq and Afghanistan. The result was a renewed sense of confidence in US leadership in Asia. As Clinton reflected, "We had climbed out of the hole we found ourselves in at the beginning of the administration and reasserted America's presence in the region."[2]

The US military is the backbone of this presence. Under Obama, the Pentagon has deepened military engagement in Asia across the board. In 2012, the Defense Department released a strategy that made clear it would prioritize maintaining a robust military presence in Asia even while considering cuts in the defense budget. By the end of the Obama administration, the United States will have more peacetime military training and partnerships in the region than ever before. And the Pentagon is planning to station a higher proportion of American military assets in the Pacific—by 2020, 60 percent of America's naval and air capabilities will be stationed there.

However, Obama and his team always stressed that the rebalance to Asia was not just about ships and planes. The economic dimension was critical. In fact, the economic approach to Asia was directly tied to the health of the US economy, which needed to tap into new markets and customers.

So under Obama, the United States promoted new trade pacts like the US-Korea Free Trade agreement (which could increase American exports by as much as $10 billion), and used institutions like APEC to reduce economic barriers and bolster investment. The centerpiece of this effort has been the Trans-Pacific Partnership, or TPP, which is the most far-reaching free trade agreement in decades, bringing together twelve countries (including the United States) into a single trading community that represents well over $1 trillion in global trade. This achievement is important economically, but it also represents a strategic commitment to Asia for the long haul, tying the region's economies closer to the United States. In 2016, the question is whether Obama can muster the domestic support to get this trade agreement approved by Congress.

ENHANCING AMERICA'S REGIONAL leadership through such diplomatic, military, and economic moves is a vital part of managing China. Perhaps no country gained more from America's post-9/11 focus on terrorism and the Middle East or its economic woes. The Chinese hard-liners saw the 2008 financial crisis as the opportunity to bet against American power, and to challenge more forcefully for regional position.[3] For Obama, a key reason for the rebalance was to improve America's ability to deal with China's rise—a relationship he believes is the most important for the twenty-first century. This involved a mix of cooperation and confrontation, working on issues of mutual interest and standing up to China where interests collide.

Working with China is rooted in practical necessity. There are few global problems that can be solved without the United States and China acting together. Therefore the Obama team set out to develop a structure of cooperation between the two countries, centered on regular leader visits (Obama met with his Chinese counterpart more often than any previous president), and formal bureaucratic mechanisms such as the Strategic and Economic Dialogue, an annual gathering co-led by the secretaries of state and treasury which brought together nearly a dozen Cabinet and agency heads to meet with their Chinese counterparts. Such discussions sought to build trust and led to progress in many areas of practical cooperation such as global health, non-proliferation, and climate change.

These efforts unintentionally stirred suspicions among many US friends and allies. As the power gap between the United States and China, on the one hand, and the rest of the world, on the other, increased, some wondered whether this would lead to a new kind of global order led by a "G-2." This arrangement was never the goal. Nor was it ever possible because the US–China relationship, while increasingly cooperative on select issues, remained rooted in competition and distrust. As Kurt Campbell, one of the key shapers of the administration's approach to Asia, often observed, the US–China relationship is like water polo. On the surface, it is a rough game with rules where the goal is to achieve a "positive, cooperative, and comprehensive relationship," a mantra recited often by American and Chinese officials. But underwater, the relationship is one of pulling, scratching, and cheap shots, and the objective is to win outright.

Many aspects of China's rise take place in this darker place beneath the surface. It bullies its neighbors. It asserts its sovereign rights in the South China Sea and is effectively militarizing that region. It engages in aggressive mercantilist behavior in Africa and Latin America. It invests significantly in its military modernization, prioritizing capabilities to undermine America's military advantage. Despite all the talk of "win-win" outcomes, the relationship is fundamentally one of competition.

China has its own version of the long game, and plays it quite well, especially when America is distracted and its resources over-leveraged. China seeks a diminished US role in Asia, at the very least forcing Washington to share regional influence. While China does not desire to lead the world—it does not want to shoulder the burden of responsibility—it wants to prevent any other country from standing in its way.

For Obama, the trickiest questions have been when and how to confront China. The results have been mixed. The United States has used its military presence to reassure partners and to challenge Beijing's unilateral claims in the South China Sea (in an attempt to control access of vital sea lanes), yet China has built new military bases on reef islands. The Obama administration tried to convince its partners not to join a new financial institution to rival the IMF, known as the Asia Infrastructure Investment Bank (AIIB), but largely failed (with Britain leading the way to join) and subsequently found itself on the outside looking in. The administration could have handled this issue with more dexterity, trying to channel Beijing's ambitions constructively and without the premature opposition that only served to isolate Washington.

DESPITE SUCH SETBACKS, the rebalance to Asia has been a significant strategic shift, positioning the US for the future. The analyst David Milne concluded that Obama's strategy "toward Asia may be viewed as the Obama administration's principal foreign policy legacy thirty years hence."[4] Administration officials often remark how much better America's standing in Asia is today, saying that when they attend Asia summits, they don't hear much about US "retreat" or "credibility" or "red lines"—terms that dominate the conversation in other regions, especially the Middle East. But in at least three ways, the story of the rebalance also reveals some of the challenges to the strategy in both concept and execution.

First, although nearly every foreign policy expert believes the rebalance makes strategic sense, it is very hard to get credit for such moves in the moment. Secretary Clinton described the rebalance as a "quiet effort," one in which "a lot of our work has not been on the front pages, both because of its nature—long-term investment is less exciting than immediate crises—and because of competing headlines in other parts of the world."[5] The key payoffs of the rebalance—closer relationships and more effective regional institutions; a robust military presence; improved economic ties—are not blockbuster developments that attract fanfare. They can only be fully appreciated in time. The rebalance is what Obama had in mind when he spoke of turning a ship's direction just a few degrees at a time—what appears incremental can ultimately be profound.

Rebalancing requires patience and stamina, which can be tough to sustain when other events place demands on finite resources and time. Leaders can be distracted by other parts of the world and competing priorities, especially when prodded by the Washington debate, which tends to magnify disproportionally issues of the moment. During many of Obama's trips to Asia, events elsewhere crowded out the news, making it hard to get much attention. And some Asian officials and experts perceived that with the departure of such officials as Hillary Clinton and Tom Donilon, who were critical to designing the rebalance strategy and were deeply invested in it, implementation lost focus. That is unfair—especially because the most important driver of the rebalance wasn't any single advisor, but the president—yet such perceptions matter.

Domestic politics can also throw a strategy off course. Sometimes this is indirect—in October 2013 Obama had to cancel a four-country trip to Asia because of budget battles with Republicans in Congress that threatened a government shutdown. But other times politics has a direct impact—on the 2016 presidential campaign trail, Hillary Clinton has come out against the TPP agreement that she had championed as secretary of state.

Second, even if the Obama administration gets credit for having the right approach, it has been dogged by worries that the strategy's implementation falls short of its ambition. There is constant concern that, because the rebalance is one of those "important" issues that the "urgent" pushes aside, it is under-resourced. There is only so much military, economic and political bandwidth to go around. This is true today, but would even be more apparent should future presidents make different decisions. For example, if the US gets involved in another major ground war in the Middle East, it will be harder if not impossible to sustain the rebalance to Asia.

Maintaining American staying power has been a constant theme, especially in an era of tighter budgets and governing gridlock in Washington. In the administration's two most important strategic statements about the rebalance—Obama's November 2011 speech to the Australian Parliament and Clinton's October 2011 essay in

Foreign Policy—both went to great lengths to reassure regional partners who wondered about America's ability to deliver on its future
commitments. Obama pledged that while the US defense budget
would have to be cut, he would prioritize the American mission and
presence in Asia, while Clinton wrote that the US would resist the
temptation to "come home" and not be "distracted again by events
elsewhere."[6]

This created a third challenge. The parts of the world where
"events elsewhere" took place wondered how this strategic shift would
affect them. Those concerns help explain the somewhat esoteric debate about the strategy's terminology, and whether the approach to
Asia was a "pivot" or "rebalance." The terms were used interchange-
ably, but the use of the former fed suspicions in other regions that,
because one has to pivot away from something, they were going
down the priority list. This was true among Europeans, who fretted
that more American time and attention in Asia meant less for them
(my former Pentagon colleagues who worked on Europe joked that
they were the "ass end of the rebalance"). And it was also true for US
allies in the Middle East, who had been the subjects of America's
post-9/11 "distractions." To them, all the talk of the "pivot" caused
unnecessary stress.

Yet these key relationships—with Europe, with Russia, and with
the Muslim world—were the focus of another component of Obama's
effort to build a strategy for the long term—a *reset* to repair America's image and reestablish its leadership position.

RESET

In Europe, the reset began before Obama even got elected. There is
no better symbol of this than his July 2008 address in Berlin, which
he visited as a presidential candidate. It will likely be remembered for
a long time—if not necessarily for its message, then for the imagery

of over 200,000 wildly enthusiastic, mostly young Germans packed into Berlin's Tiergarten, creating an atmosphere more like a rock festival than a policy conference. As Obama's top campaign adviser, David Plouffe, later reflected, the Berlin event was an opportunity to "visually demonstrate an important premise: the world was still hungry for American leadership, but of a different, more cooperative kind that only Barack Obama could deliver."[7]

During the Bush years, the US-European relationship had been especially choppy. The policy debate had been dominated by influential analysts such as Robert Kagan, who argued that the United States and Europe lived on entirely different planets and were therefore drifting apart. The Europeans, Kagan observed, lived in a world of Kantian "perpetual peace," whereas Americans lived in a Hobbesian world of grave threats. Among leaders, insults flew across the Atlantic, with the Bush team belittling "old Europe" (traditional partners like France and Germany) and European officials openly deriding Bush's "cowboy" approach.

Such bitterness was especially evident in Europe's most pivotal country, Germany, which is a key example of the damage the post-9/11 years had done to America's image in the world (this impact is still being felt today, when Germans complain about an issue like torture long after Obama ended it). The year before Obama's visit to Berlin, opinion polls showed 86 percent of Germans disapproved of President Bush's handling of foreign policy, and 59 percent did not want the United States to play a leading role in world affairs. The US-German relationship was defined by mutual recriminations and suspicions, and even to express solidarity with the United States was a risky proposition politically. In 2003, Angela Merkel, then still virtually unknown in the United States, nearly undermined her political career by writing an article for the *Washington Post* to make the unpopular point that then-German Chancellor Gerhard Schröder didn't speak for all Germans when he criticized the Iraq War.

By 2008, Europe was clamoring for new American leadership, and Obama represented the ideal. To the thousands packed in the Tiergarten who hung on his every word, Obama embodied all of their dreams about the United States; to them he truly was, as Obama described himself in the speech, a "citizen of the world." Obama used the Berlin address to outline the idea that "partnership and cooperation among nations is not a choice; it is the one way, the only way, to protect our common security and advance our common humanity." But he also reminded his audience that this would be a two-way street, and that just as the United States would seek to reach out, the Europeans would need to step up.

In many ways, Bush's foreign policy had let European leaders off the hook. Because the United States had expected less of Europe—and because it had become politically easy, if not advantageous, to oppose the United States due to Bush's unpopularity—many European leaders had been able to shirk hard choices. That's why Obama stressed the common burden that the United States and Europe must share, one that, he said, "a change of leadership in Washington will not lift." In fact, Obama promised things would only get tougher, because "in this new century, Americans and Europeans alike will be required to do more—not less."

The Berlin speech laid the basis for Obama's approach to the transatlantic relationship: for all the talk of pivots and rebalancing, when it came to solving problems, Europe remained America's partner of first resort. Obama promised a new kind of leadership, but had high expectations in return. In this way, the speech also set the stage for the mutual disappointment that riddled the relationship during Obama's presidency. Just as Obama could not meet the unrealistic hopes that Europeans had placed on him to change the world with the snap of his fingers, as Europeans' frenzy of enthusiasm waned, many still proved unprepared to make tough choices to meet the challenges ahead.

THE SECOND RELATIONSHIP in need of a reset was with Russia. Obama's approach to Moscow, which was also first outlined during his 2008 campaign, combined both wariness and a sense of opportunity.

As a candidate, Obama was clear about the dangers Russia posed, especially after its invasion of Georgia in August 2008. During the first presidential debate with John McCain, Obama had warned of "a resurgent and very aggressive Russia" as a threat to global stability. Obama also expressed concerns about Russia's drift away from democracy and its bullying behavior toward neighbors such as Ukraine and NATO allies in the Baltics, saying that the Russian leadership needed to understand that "you can't be a twenty-first-century power and act like a twentieth-century dictatorship." However, Obama also believed that because Russia was simply too important to ignore, one had to find a way to work with it. For Obama, the key was to approach Russia with clear-eyed pragmatism.[8]

Since the end of the Cold War, the disputes over how the United States should approach Russia have never really been about what we wanted to achieve. Democrats and Republicans largely agreed that the fundamental goal should be to help promote a democratic Russia at peace with itself and its neighbors, working where possible to cooperate with the rest of the world in solving problems.

Therefore, the debate has always been over how most effectively to influence Russian behavior, especially when it turns negative. The policy struggle is about whether the United States should seek to engage or isolate Russia; whether our policies should do more to accommodate the Kremlin or confront it; and how one weighs the value of Russia's cooperation abroad with its progress toward democracy at home.

When Obama entered office, he found the relationship with Moscow adrift, believing that the accumulated differences of the previous decade had made it harder to work together on common endeavors—such as nuclear security, trade and economics, or dealing with Iran and North Korea. There were still deep concerns about Russia's political direction—in 2008 Putin had switched jobs with his prime minister, Dmitri Medvedev, but was still seen as the power behind the throne—as well as over the way Moscow dealt with its neighbors. Yet the administration believed it needed to find a way to work together on the issues where cooperation was possible. As Secretary Clinton put it: "Straight up transactional diplomacy isn't always pretty, but often it's necessary."[9]

That was the core logic of the Russia "reset." It was not, as the critics later insisted, some naïve attempt to work with Russia at all costs, to brush aside differences, or to establish a new era of harmony. The US-Russian relationship has always combined a mix of cooperation, competition, and disagreement, and the reset era was no exception. It was a policy driven by pragmatism, not ideology; to work with Russia where our interests converged, stand firm where they did not, and engage directly with the Russian people as they continued to press for political freedom and economic reforms.

This approach paid dividends for a time. But it did not solve all our problems with Russia—and some would come roaring back as Obama's tenure in office neared its end.

THE THIRD ASPECT of the reset was broader: to present a new face of the United States overseas.

This was more than just an attempt to generate good feelings. It was an effort to reestablish the credibility and sense of legitimacy that had been lost during the post-9/11 era. This was a significant reason Obama chose Hillary Clinton to be his first secretary of state—both because of her widely respected skills but also the message it sent by placing a former political rival in such an important role. Some of this restoration was also achieved by early policy changes such as renouncing torture and pledging to close the Guantanamo Bay prison. But Obama aspired to something even grander—to outline a new narrative for America's global leadership.

In a series of speeches in 2009, Obama set out to repair relationships and reintroduce America in order to, as he put it, "turn the page" on the George W. Bush era. The result was as ambitious a collection of foreign policy rhetoric as any president has delivered in a single year. Nearly all of the speeches were overseas, where Obama aimed to speak to great global challenges from the same perspective he had conveyed in Berlin—as a "citizen of the world." Obama wanted to reach ordinary people, believing that his background, his identity, and his message could project a new way forward for America abroad. He also used these speeches to outline the ambitious policy agenda that he believed would be fundamental to winning the Long Game.

In Prague, Obama detailed his plan to deal with the issue that still concerned him most, the spread of weapons of mass destruction, and outlined his aspiration to achieve a nuclear weapons-free world. In Ankara, Obama went to the Turkish parliament and pledged that the United States was not at war with Islam. In Accra, Obama stood before the Ghanian parliament and explained his hopes for democracy and development, urging Africans to embrace not "strong men" but "strong institutions." In Moscow, Obama spoke of his hopes for greater global cooperation, observing that "the pursuit of power is no longer a zero-sum game" and that "progress must be shared." And in Oslo, where Obama accepted the Nobel Peace Prize—an award he admitted was given prematurely, reflecting more hope than accomplishment—he delivered a message that the use of military force was at times necessary.

THE MOST HIGH-PROFILE of these speeches was delivered on June 4, 2009 in Egypt, where Obama took the stage in front of an audience of 3,000 people at Cairo University to speak about America's relationship with the Muslim world. This was, as the writer James

Traub observed, "the most ambitious, the most eagerly anticipated, and the most excruciatingly crafted foreign policy address of [Obama's] first term and perhaps of his presidency."[10]

Obama spoke candidly about the tension between the United States and many of the world's Muslims, blaming "small but potent" extreme minorities on both sides who "sow hatred rather than peace," fueling a "cycle of suspicion and discord." He said the United States needed to accept its share of the blame, citing the legacy of colonialism and Cold War policies where Arab states were treated more as pawns than partners. By acknowledging such fallibility, Obama exposed himself to critics back home who decried his "apologizing" for America. But this concession was instrumental to the president's argument—by acknowledging America's own imperfections, Obama forced his listeners to consider their own.

Obama outlined his desire to launch a "new beginning" with the Muslim world. He did not promise any large policy shifts or announce any major policy "deliverables"—he continued to support Egyptian president Hosni Mubarak, reiterated his commitment to fight terrorists, and pledged to work hard to achieve peace between Israel and the Palestinians. Instead, Obama offered something less tangible: a promise to engage Muslims with "mutual interest and mutual respect."

These words were well received, and for a time the Cairo message seemed to improve things. But it was soon undermined by the expectations it had created. Obama hoped, as Traub observed, a "change at the level of thought and feeling would in turn help bring about a change in policy." Obama later said that he had intended to show that "the US would help, in whatever way possible, to advance the goals of a practical, successful Arab agenda that provided a better life for ordinary people."[11] That sounded good, but left the Muslim world wanting more. If there is a lasting lesson from the Cairo speech, it is that while the use of words to create new narratives is necessary to reset the image of American leadership, words alone are not sufficient. Actions are needed, too.

Yet from the perspective of 2016, when the question of America's relationship with the Muslim world has again become politically explosive—exposing a strain of intolerant demagoguery in US politics—the core of Obama's message seven years ago in Cairo remains essential. As Obama said, "Islam is a part of America."

RESURGE

These efforts to rebalance US foreign policy and reset the image of America in the world unfolded against the backdrop of armed conflict. Although Obama championed a message of peace, he remained a president at war. His decisions on fighting and ending the wars in Afghanistan and Iraq would be among the most consequential that he would make. Which brings us to the third component of Obama's initial strategic shift: *resurge*.

Of all the tough decisions Obama confronted during his first year, perhaps the most difficult concerned the war in Afghanistan. During the 2008 campaign, Obama had made the flagging war effort in Afghanistan a central part of his foreign policy critique: instead of starting a "dumb war" by invading Iraq, we should have kept our eyes on the ball and finished the job where the 9/11 terrorist attacks had been conceived. Obama entered office calling for the need to resurge in Afghanistan—for more troops, more civilians, more assistance, more intelligence assets, and more international support.

During the 2008 transition, the outgoing Bush team conceded to those of us coming in that Afghanistan was "not where they wanted it to be," and had begun their own policy review to take stock of what they would do if they had more time. Perhaps the most revealing—and concerning—thing the Bush team told us was that, a decade after the initial invasion of Afghanistan, the United States did not have a clearly defined goal for what it was trying to do. You would get a different answer depending on whom you asked—to some, it was about fighting al-Qaeda; to others, we were there to help build a new society. Obama wanted his own assessment, so he ordered a process to be led by Bruce Riedel, a longtime CIA analyst and former Clinton White House official. Riedel's charge was to come up with a set of specific goals and a strategy to achieve them. (Having been on the NSC transition team and taken a position as deputy director of the State Department's Policy Planning Staff, I was assigned to Riedel's small team to help craft the document.)

For Obama, the most difficult questions were about military force. All of the campaign commentary that he was "antiwar" and therefore ideologically a dove grossly missed the point. He believed the military component was essential, and had pledged to do more. The challenge, however, was how much force to add and for what purpose. In Afghanistan, as elsewhere during his time in office, Obama was determined not to overextend the United States on projects it couldn't deliver on and, he believed, would only bleed the country further after it had bled for over a decade.

This is why Obama approached the question of how to resurge in Afghanistan so carefully. As a result of the "Riedel review," the administration settled on a clearly defined goal: to disrupt, dismantle, and defeat al-Qaeda in Afghanistan and Pakistan, and prevent their return to either country. This was reinforced by another strategic review the president initiated in the fall of 2009. Taking several months, this latter review—which was started after the military had asked for additional troops—was a far more systematic process in which the president was more directly involved (he had been distant from the Riedel-led review, focusing instead on the urgent priority of saving the US economy).

THE STRATEGY'S PREMISE was straightforward: instability in Afghanistan contributed to terrorism and insurgency in Pakistan, and safe havens in Pakistan were driving the insurgency in Afghanistan.

Therefore, both issues needed to be addressed together. The innovation was to frame this as one interlinked challenge, and as one theater of operations—"Af-Pak."

Militarily, this called for an initial surge of 20,000 troops into Afghanistan to add to the more than 30,000 already there, and replacing the American commander on the ground with a leader more focused on counter-insurgency, General Stanley McChrystal. Later in 2009, in response to McChrystal's request for more forces, Obama ordered more troops into combat. As of February 2010, just a little over one year after he took office, around 77,000 American troops were at war in Afghanistan, along with approximately 39,000 forces from forty other countries (while Americans were the bulk of the fighting force, Afghanistan was technically a NATO-led mission). By August 2010, the number of US troops in Afghanistan reached nearly 100,000.

Alongside these military deployments was a civilian surge. The administration sent hundreds of civilian experts to Afghanistan to administer rule of law, good governance, and agriculture programs, more than tripling the American government's civilian presence there.

The administration also restructured US civilian assistance to Afghanistan to reward good performance and ensure careful oversight and transparency (coming into office it found that too much of American aid was unaccounted for, and only 10 percent of US assistance flowed through the Afghan government—meaning our aid was actually undermining the government we were trying to build). In Pakistan, the administration initiated a massive influx of financial and development assistance to strengthen Pakistan's ability to partner with the United States and reassure them that we would be there for them for the long haul (in order to reduce their incentives to cut deals with extremist groups).

OBAMA'S AF-PAK STRATEGY followed several essential elements of the Long Game. It tried to achieve *balance* between the military, political, and economic components of the strategy—although the question of troop numbers took the most time and got the most attention, everyone agreed that the political and economic aspects of the strategy were more important for long-term success. It also sought to balance the approach itself—it was not simply an Afghanistan problem, but one of "Af-Pak."

Most broadly, Obama sought to design a policy aimed toward narrower goals, properly weighted relative to America's other global interests. The additional troops, civilians, and resources were never designed to be permanent—the idea was to escalate in order to exit, enabling and empowering the governments of Afghanistan and Pakistan to take control over time. No one ever believed that this approach would lead to perfection, but the administration sought to achieve an end state that, as we said at the time, was "good enough."

What this meant—and I believe what in hindsight the strategy achieved—is a decimated al-Qaeda in Afghanistan and an Afghan government and security apparatus that is more capable of standing on its own (although that is relative—the Afghan government does remain weak and vulnerable). To be sure, Afghanistan in 2016 still faces endemic political turmoil and significant security challenges—and will require outside military support for some time, as Obama is prepared to do by leaving a small enduring presence of troops there beyond 2016.

The strategy was also *precise*, most importantly in military terms. The "disrupt, dismantle, defeat" formulation as the aim for military power was focused specifically on al-Qaeda and its affiliates, and denying the Taliban the ability to overthrow the Afghan government. This narrowed the goal militarily, but also left open the prospect of a diplomatic negotiation with the Taliban, which the administration would quietly pursue later. By emphasizing the core goal against al-Qaeda, such precision allowed us to assess progress better and hold ourselves accountable (something that Obama was very focused on), and to prevent this from morphing into a massive, military-led nation-building effort like Iraq. The problem, however, was that the rhetoric of Obama's strategy sometimes veered beyond this more modest goal, embracing the logic of counter-insurgency (which at that time was the prevailing fad in the military) but without the kinds of resources necessary to achieve such ambition.

Finally, Obama's choices were driven by his assessment of what was *sustainable*. Throughout his deliberations Obama remained focused on the costs of the strategy, especially as his top priority overall was to deal with the financial disaster at home. This would be expensive—estimates were the US would spend $30 billion on Afghanistan in 2009 alone. One of the key lessons Obama had taken from the over $1 trillion war in Iraq was how it had helped drive the US economy off a cliff, and he did not want his strategy in Afghanistan to do the same. Beyond costs, he was determined not to allow the war in Afghanistan to consume US policy for another decade.

THIS LED TO the most contested part of Obama's Afghan strategy in 2009—the announcement of a timeline to start withdrawing American troops in less than two years and to transition responsibility to the Afghan government. Announcing such a timeline divided his advisors: Hillary Clinton recalled the timeline was "starker" than she wanted and "there was benefit playing our cards closer to our chests."[12] Unsurprisingly, some critics were harsher, asserting that this undermined the perception of US resolve, signaling to our friends that they couldn't count on us and to our enemies that they could wait us out.

The escalate-to-exit approach did make the strategy more difficult to communicate (I was in Brussels to brief NATO allies with Richard Holbrooke the day after the strategy was announced, and we labored to help them understand how these seemingly contradictory tasks would work). Obama understood these criticisms, yet believed that such clarity was needed to sustain public support for the mission. As he said in one meeting, "The American people need to know that the war is ending." Importantly, his secretary of defense agreed. "After eight years of war in Afghanistan," Robert Gates reflected, "Congress, the American people, and the troops could not abide by the idea of a conflict there stretching into the indefinite future." What after 9/11 had been a war of necessity to root out terrorists—the conflict Obama had believed was the one America needed to fight—had become, in Gates' words, "an albatross around the nation's neck, just as the war in Iraq had."[13]

When describing his strategy, Obama explicitly stressed the attributes of balance, precision, and sustainability. In his December 2009 speech at West Point where he outlined the new policy—the same venue where Bush had announced his "preemption doctrine" seven years earlier—Obama made clear that his Af-Pak decisions were taken in the context of addressing other priorities at home and abroad, especially the financial crisis. Quoting Eisenhower's adage about national security decisions, Obama said that "each proposal must be weighed in the light of a broader consideration: the need to maintain balance in and among national programs."

This weighing of ends and means, calibrating an approach within the context of the totality of American interests, is the essence of grand strategy. The military aspects could not be open-ended or considered in isolation. Since America's prosperity was the foundation of its power, the president explained, and because this new strategy would be so costly, it needed to be limited. Obama was blunt. "The country I am most interested in nation-building is my own," he said.

* * *

IN TERMS OF US commitment, effort, and resources, this new strategy aimed to put Af-Pak on the same escalate-to-exit trajectory as the other war that had, in Obama's view, consumed too many American assets up to that point. What Obama set out to achieve with

Iraq, of course, was a different kind of "resurge"—one whereby American military forces left the country, positioning the US to deal more effectively with its other interests.

For six years, Iraq had been the most defining, and divisive, issue in American politics. Questions about the war had consumed a generation of politicians and, in 2004 and 2008, dominated the presidential campaigns. Obama's decisive electoral victory effectively defused the debate. The question therefore was not whether the United States should get out of Iraq, but how—and what we would leave behind.

Although Iraq had been one of the central issues of Obama's campaign, the template for the withdrawal of the roughly 130,000 US troops had been established by George W. Bush. In November 2008, after the election but before Obama took office, the Bush administration concluded an agreement with Iraqis that set a deadline for the withdrawal of US troops. According to its terms, American military forces were to be out of Iraq's cities by July 2009 and out of Iraq by the end of 2011.

This kind of agreement—known as a "Status of Forces Agreement," or SOFA—is what the United States uses with partners around the world to establish the rules that govern its military presence, defining everything from what American forces are allowed to do to what happens when something goes wrong. Bush was determined to complete such a deal before he left the White House (unfortunately, the December 2008 ceremony in Baghdad to sign the SOFA will forever be remembered less for the accomplishment than for the fact that an Iraqi had stood up and hurled a shoe at Bush, nearly hitting him).

During the campaign, Obama had pledged to implement a "responsible" departure from Iraq by drawing down troops at a steady clip of one to two combat brigades per month (approximately 5,000–10,000 troops), for a complete withdrawal in sixteen months. Having all troops out a year and a half before the Bush timeline was a much faster pace than military leaders had advised, and they feared that doing so would threaten the hard-fought security gains of the surge and undercut US leverage to influence Iraqi politics.

Obama accepted this counsel, settling on a compromise that allowed him to stay true to his campaign commitments. Instead of having all troops out by the end of August 2010, he would use that date as the milestone to end the American "combat mission" in Iraq, which would mean fewer troops and a smaller footprint. But importantly, until the end of 2011 the US would maintain a "transitional presence" of as many as 50,000 troops to help advise and assist the Iraqis, especially on counter-terrorism. Then, by January 1, 2012, the American military mission would be over.

The president unveiled this decision in a February 2009 speech at Camp Lejeune, North Carolina (throughout his presidency, almost all these kinds of decisions were unveiled before military audiences). The announcement was well-received. And with it, the Iraq issue almost instantly evaporated from American politics. Democrats were satisfied that the United States was on its way out, despite grumbling from some that the pace was still too slow. Republicans were happy not to relitigate the Bush administration's decisions and handling of the war. Congress lost interest, and so did the press. And the American people were more than ready to move on to other things.

But the administration did not wash its hands of Iraq. Believing that pluralistic, inclusive politics were key to Iraq's long-term stability, the Obama team maintained a steady focus on events there. Although the president scaled back his involvement in the day-to-day policymaking on Iraq, he made Vice President Biden the chief troubleshooter. As one of the most experienced and well-known American leaders on Iraq and a relentless advocate, Biden dove into the work, making numerous trips to Iraq, chairing countless meetings and videoconferences, and working the phones constantly.

Alongside these efforts to shape Iraqi politics were the preparations to establish an enduring relationship with Baghdad. While the US military withdrew, the relationship had to evolve into one between two sovereign states. As a practical matter, this meant preparing for a difficult transition from military-led to civilian-led efforts in Iraq.

For years, the State Department had survived in Iraq thanks to the logistical and security support of the US military. Now it had to be ready to stand on its own. This would be among the most complicated and ambitious US diplomatic undertakings ever, including building the largest and most expensive embassy in the world, securing nearly 17,000 civilian personnel, many of whom would be private contractors, and allocating a massive influx of resources. Getting this transition right was a central focus for Secretary Clinton, who charged her key deputy Jack Lew (who would later become Obama's chief of staff and treasury secretary) with overseeing the effort.

The withdrawal of the US military raised another practical issue: Washington had less leverage and capacity to influence Iraqi decision-making. Even the best American diplomats would never have the same tools and resources the generals had to wield influence. Simply put, with the military gone, the Iraqis would rely on us less. Our relationship with Iraq would have to become more "normal"—relying on the same tools we use with other countries, such as political persuasion, economic and development assistance, and security cooperation. The implications of this became clear when the administration had to confront the issue of what kind of military relationship it would have with Baghdad—and whether any US forces should stay in Iraq—after the Bush SOFA expired in December 2011.

IN AUGUST 2010, the administration welcomed the completion of the combat mission in Iraq and pledged to continue the steady withdrawal of troops. But as the end of 2011 approached, Obama indicated he was willing to leave a small number of forces (around 5,000) behind to continue to assist the Iraqis with their security needs. While the administration had always envisioned having a robust defense assistance relationship with Iraq through such mechanisms as arms sales, it was ready to invest more. The question was whether the Iraqis wanted American forces to stay in their country, and if so, under what kind of legal framework.

It was the Iraqi leadership's choice, and they were conflicted. They frequently said they wanted the Americans to stay. Yet then they would turn around and say the opposite, celebrating each stage of US withdrawal as the departure of the infidels. It often seemed that the Iraqis told Washington officials (especially visiting congressional delegations) only what they thought the officials wanted to hear. As Chris Hill, one of Obama's ambassadors to Baghdad, recalled, "I'm not sure the Iraqis were entirely committed or entirely honest about saying whether they wanted troops or not."[14]

Whether they were driven by ambivalence, indecision, or duplicity, such uncertainty made it very hard to negotiate a new agreement to allow an enduring American military presence. This was especially important when it came to the thorny issue of legal protections for US personnel.

No one wanted to see an American soldier accused of wrongdoing and dragged into an Iraqi jail. For this reason, the Obama team insisted on having a legally-binding document with the political approval of Iraq's parliament. While the Iraqis had insisted on putting the Bush SOFA before their parliament, in 2011 they were wary of exposing the issue of an enduring American presence to Iraqi politics. Instead, they wanted the United States to agree to something that would not go through parliament and therefore not have the same legal guarantees—in other words, they wanted us to trust them. At best, it seemed they wanted the benefits of an American presence without paying the political costs.

The administration understood the strategic value of keeping some troops in Iraq. Even a small presence could help keep tabs on the nascent Iraqi Security Forces and assist with counter-terrorism efforts. But Obama did not want to force the issue and try to convince the Iraqis that the US military needed to stay. After all, Iraq was a sovereign country. In the end, Washington and Baghdad were unable to agree to a new deal. US troops left as planned in December 2011. From that point, less than 200 Defense Department personnel remained in Baghdad as part of the US embassy to administer the military relationship.

Was this a mistake? At the time, some administration officials argued that Obama needed to try harder; that he should have engaged in the negotiations directly; or that the administration should have used greater leverage against Baghdad by threatening support if they did not let the US stay. Yet what mattered most to the president was that he had a partner in the country he could trust and work with, and who truly wanted US help.

In Iraq in 2011, there was little evidence to convince him that was the case. As Michael Gordon of the *New York Times* and Marine Lt. General Bernard Trainor, two of the most sober chroniclers of the US tangle with Iraq since the first Gulf War, observed, "given the vicissitudes of Iraqi politics...a continuing if minimal American troop presence might have proven impossible under the best of circumstances."[15] And these weren't the best of circumstances. Both sides may have preferred for some troops to stay, but neither wanted to try very hard or sacrifice much to make it happen. So even if this was a "mistake," it was one made by both sides.

Given America's exhaustion with Iraq at the time, these decisions were hardly noted. After all, the vast majority of Americans wanted us out. However, we found ourselves rethinking these decisions less than three years later, when the Islamic State captured vast swaths of Iraq and threatened the country's future, and American troops headed back in.

FROM THE LONG WAR TO THE LONG GAME

Bookshelves are already bulging with detailed accounts of the Obama team's decision-making behind the "resurge" into Af-Pak and withdrawal from Iraq. Reflecting back on the consequences of these debates, their implications extend beyond the specific policy challenges they posed at time. The deliberations during Obama's first two years taught lessons that colored his approach to future problems. They also shaped enduring perceptions many have about the making of his foreign policy, as Obama tried to shift the organizing principle from the "long war" to the Long Game.

Three implications stand out. The first concerns Obama and the military, both in terms of his perspective on the place of military power in US foreign policy and his relationship with senior American military leaders.

Despite Obama's decisions to surge troops in Afghanistan and not leave precipitately from Iraq, his repeated admonition that there is "no military solution" to the problems of Iraq and Afghanistan or that he wanted to "end wars" was often heard as a sign that he wanted to withdraw completely and was unwilling to use force. Of course, the president's decisions to use American military power in Afghanistan—and later in Libya, Syria, Iraq and elsewhere—showed he was hardly averse to, as the military would say, "going kinetic."

Obama saw war for what it is: often necessary, but always tragic. In his 2009 Nobel Peace Prize speech, which was Obama's most important statement on the use of force, he made clear that the "instruments of war" are indispensable to the preservation of peace. But at the same time, he often said that he did not want "killing people" to be his only lasting legacy. And he did not believe the military should always be the primary instrument of American power.

Once more, this is about how one defines strength. As Obama explained in late 2015: "American strength and American exceptionalism is not just a matter of us bombing somebody." He was often frustrated that military might was seen as the only metric of strength and leadership. For Obama, more often being "strong" is a "matter of us convening, setting the agenda, pointing other nations in a direction that's good for everybody and good for US interests, engaging in painstaking diplomacy, leading by example."[16]

The application of force is tangible and easy to measure: troops and equipment are deployed, resources are spent, and things get blown up. But that's not the only tool of American power, and it's often not the most important one. To see and appreciate the power of the other tools of influence is often difficult, so it can be hard to get credit for using them. As Obama admitted, "sometimes the results don't come overnight, they don't come the following day, but they come."

THIS EFFORT TO recalibrate the instruments of US power did lead to tensions with military leaders. The intense debates over the surge in Afghanistan and the pace of withdrawal in Iraq (and later, what to do about Libya and Syria) stressed these relationships. But while they could be scratchy, they were hardly broken.

In fact, Obama's relationships with his military leaders were for the most part quite strong, and with many of them, personally warm. He and his closest advisers took great care to tend to civil-military relations, applying the lessons Democrats had learned during the early 2000s about how they approached the military. And during the course of his presidency Obama forged especially close bonds with his top military commanders, especially those like Army General Martin Dempsey, Chairman of the Joint Chiefs from 2011 through 2015, who was perceived by the White House as an astute, solid straight shooter who did not play games.

But as the Afghanistan and Iraq cases show, they did not agree on everything. Obama did embrace the basic strategy offered to him by military advisers—the surge in Afghanistan and gradual withdrawal from Iraq—but in both cases put restrictions on how force would be used, and set deadlines for withdrawal that he was determined to stick with.

There is a natural tension between what the military demands in resources and what political leaders are ready to provide. There is also a fine line between civilians asking questions for greater specificity about military planning or fine-tuning options (to ensure they do not extend beyond the stated goals), and meddling in military decision-making. Obama appreciated the fundamental difference of perspectives, often saying that he understood why military commanders asked for the resources they did, but that his job was to consider such requests in the overall context of other interests, competing priorities, and the trade-offs between them.

While the military leadership bristled at troop caps and withdrawal timelines, they were necessary to disciplining the process to fit the strategy. As Gates recalled, "Without these controls, the number of deployed troops would steadily inch upward, not because of some military ruse but because of the inexorable pressure from commanders as other assets are required... I believe the [troop] cap was the only way to avoid having the president wake up one morning and discover there were 130,000 troops in Afghanistan rather than the 101,000 he had approved."[17] Again, fighting the "long war" is different than—and must be subservient to—playing the Long Game.

Sometimes, the heat of debate would cause these differences to boil over. The second Afghanistan policy review in 2009 is an example. Numerous press leaks about the troop numbers Pentagon leaders were requesting caused frustrations in the White House that the military was "jamming" the president by raising the costs for him of "rejecting" their advice and, in effect, reducing his options (Obama certainly believed this to be the case). Intentional or not, such leaks accentuated these inherent tensions, leading to the impression that civil-military relations were more troubled than they actually were. Yet this was hardly the same kind of ugly struggle that plagued the Bush administration, when the "generals' revolt" over the direction of the Iraq war exploded in public, a factor that ultimately led to the firing of Defense Secretary Donald Rumsfeld.

THE DELIBERATIONS OVER the use of military power illustrated a second attribute of Obama's foreign policymaking that took shape during these early years: the dominance of the White House.

One constant theme of the critiques from many former officials and Washington pundits is that the Obama White House was overbearing and too prone to micromanaging. The result, these critics claim, is a policy process that stifled innovation and left the United States dithering while events passed it by. The easiest path for a pundit (or a disgruntled official) is to blame the process if you don't like the policy. To be sure, the Obama NSC process created its share of problems. As someone who was part of its decision-making for six years from the perspective of the State Department, Pentagon, and White House, I both experienced and am partly responsible for what's behind many of the complaints.

But one must consider these frustrations in a broader context and with more than a short-term memory. Every recent administration has been criticized for a flawed process, and by comparison, the dysfunction attributed to Obama's is fairly tame. There has been nothing like the kinds of breakdowns of the past. Just to cite a few examples, recall Henry Kissinger's paranoid machinations from the Nixon White House (e.g., wiretapping subordinates); the bitter disputes between Zbigniew Brzezinski and Cyrus Vance during the Carter years; the rogue Reagan NSC that made Oliver North a national figure and flushed through six national security advisers (two of whom were convicted of crimes conducted while in office); or the epic battles of George W. Bush's NSC, with Vice President Cheney's staff operating a kind of parallel operation. This history is a reminder that while slinging criticisms comes easy, it should be done with some perspective.

In many ways, such frustrations are inherent, as every White House struggles with managing the rest of the government. White House officials tend to approach the bureaucracy in one of two ways: believing it is doing too much and going beyond what the president has decided, or that it is doing too little and not fulfilling what the president wants done. During my time in the White House, I found myself toggling back and forth between these concerns. The answer to both is more oversight, which can often evolve into bureaucratic overreach.

Most White House colleagues were conscious of not wanting to centralize power too much, and at times they would try to pare back responsibility to allow the bureaucracy to do its job—such as by trying to call fewer meetings and delegating more decisions. But too often this only worked in theory, especially on questions that concerned the use of military power. Even when the White House tried to focus more on the strategic issues and leave tactical implementation to the Pentagon or State Department, decisions would slowly gravitate back to the Situation Room. Given that the president would be the one held accountable by the public, press, and Congress, the incentives usually were for the White House to take more control, not less.

The tendency to hoard power could be exacerbated by personalities, especially high-intensity ones who clashed with the famously "no drama" presidential style. That was certainly the case during the debate over Afghanistan, where the Obama team's difficult relationship with the diplomat Richard Holbrooke—a mentor of mine—became for many a metaphor for White House meddling and mistrust.

It's true that the White House mishandled Holbrooke by isolating him and undercutting his position and, in doing so, feeding his insecurities, which only made the problem worse. As a consequence, the Obama team never found a way to take full advantage of his considerable talents—something that, in retrospect, they regretted. Holbrooke's crucial patron, Hillary Clinton, understood the strains he could put on the process and worked to mitigate them. But the claim that the president doesn't like and cannot work with forceful, high profile (and sometimes high maintenance) personalities is overblown—consider the success of Clinton, Joe Biden, John Kerry, Robert Gates, and Leon Panetta.

Beyond individuals, there is also a structural imperative for the White House to dominate foreign policymaking, especially when the president is trying to execute a strategic move. A firm hand on the tiller is required to implement a policy that is sustainable and precise, and that really can only come from the White House. Moreover, some of the most delicate tasks require such secrecy and agility that they can only be managed by a tight circle at the White House (the diplomatic opening to Cuba in 2014 is a prime example).

There is also a fundamental constitutional point. Since the president is the only person who actually got elected, the idea that rigorous White House oversight is "meddling" or a "process foul" is odd. In many ways, a president can't win: act decisively, and you are criticized for going it alone and not including your advisers (e.g., the decision to go to Capitol Hill during the Syria red line episode); consult widely and exhaustively, and you are criticized as dithering (e.g., the months-long Af-Pak strategy review process); engage deeply on issues and refine options, and you are accused of micro-managing (e.g., any number of episodes involving the use of force). However the White House does not have the capacity, or often the expertise, to oversee everything, despite the compelling incentives to do so. There are numerous examples of the White House over-steering the process, allowing small details to overwhelm the big picture and getting too involved in decisions it would have been better off staying out of.

THIRD AND FINALLY, Obama's effort to transition American foreign policy from its overriding focus on the wars in Iraq and Afghanistan to a broader conception of strength and interests revealed a fundamental dilemma—one of communications. Put simply, it is very hard to articulate a future of optimism while explaining a foreign policy of limits.

A key premise behind shifting from the "long war" to the Long Game was simple common sense: even when America is most powerful, there are constraints on what it can do. That's why it cannot overextend itself, especially militarily. Yet this is difficult to communicate without being criticized as defeatist or as denying America's inherent greatness. Obama often pushed back against the criticism that acknowledging limits was somehow new. After all, when was it the United States determined everything?

The truth is such a golden age never existed.[18] Following the Second World War, when the United States enjoyed what historians describe as a "preponderance of power," China collapsed to Communism, half of Europe fell under Soviet control, and America sent half a million soldiers to the Korean Peninsula to fight to a draw. During the Kennedy and Johnson years, the world sometimes seemed close to nuclear war and the United States could not save its ally, South Vietnam. During Reagan's presidency, the United States could not stop Communist uprisings in its own backyard in Central America. Even when America was criticized for being a "hyperpower"—in the years following the fall of the Berlin Wall and before the 9/11 attacks—it struggled to bring peace to the Balkans and failed, even after Bill Clinton's strenuous efforts, to conclude a deal between Israel and the Palestinians.

Past administrations have also had difficulty talking about limits. In the 1970s, Jimmy Carter's secretary of state, Cyrus Vance was pilloried for warning that the United States should "always keep in mind the limits of our power and our wisdom." And during the Clinton administration, a senior State Department official, Peter Tarnoff, ignited a Washington firestorm by arguing that the United States had limited resources and lacked leverage to solve every problem, and because of competing demands at home, it could not allow itself to become overextended abroad.[19] Recalling these lessons, most conclude that instead of acknowledging limits, it is best to remain silent about them, talking (and often acting) as if they don't exist.

But Obama wanted to be forthright that there will always be constraints on what America can do. "[We] can't, at any given moment, relieve all the world's misery," he has said. "We have to choose where we can make a real impact."[20] In Obama's view, speaking openly about these limits is not the same as conceding America's decline. In fact, it is the opposite: understanding limits is key to sustaining America's power and leadership for the long-term.

That's why Obama described the Afghanistan and Iraq decisions the way he did, returning to the theme of "nation building at home." In this way, the main restraint on America's global leadership was its flagging domestic health. This was not acknowledging weakness; it was acknowledging reality. It was time, Obama insisted, to "turn the page" from the era that had been defined by Iraq and Afghanistan—the long war—to tackle challenges at home.

The problem is that no matter how appealing domestic renewal seems, it is often heard as the sound of retreat. Obama's August 2010 speech announcing the end of the combat mission in Iraq illustrated this dilemma. Addressing the nation from the Oval Office, Obama struck a somber tone, speaking of sacrifices and uncertainties. While he pledged that the United States would "honor commitments" abroad, it sounded as if it was something America would only do because it is obliged to do so, not because of its interests. Leadership seemed to be more of a burden than an opportunity.

This shows the challenge of defining foreign policy in negative terms—outlining what the country should not do, warning of the pitfalls to dodge—rather than in ambitious ones. How should a country seize opportunities while resisting temptations and avoiding short-sighted mistakes? Obama found himself wrestling with this through-out his presidency, perhaps most famously with his admonition that his foreign policy could be summed up by the phrase "don't do stupid stuff."

LOOKING BACK, ONE of the most effective descriptions at the time of America's aspirations in the context of limits came not from Obama, but Hillary Clinton. Listening to Obama's August 2010 Iraq speech, the secretary of state lamented that it was a downer. She thought that rather than speak to the country's hopes and opportunities, it went too far in setting a mood of pessimism and despair. She believed the message needed more "lift."

There was no daylight between Obama and Clinton in their views on the importance of domestic renewal and extracting the US military from Iraq. Nor was there any meaningful difference on understanding the reality of limits and the importance of avoiding bad choices. But Clinton worried that this kind of talk could go too far, and that all the emphasis on renewal at home would be perceived as a sign of withdrawal. She warned the president that the idea that the administration was accepting a reduced role for the United States was getting traction abroad. "When you're down on yourself, and when you are hunkering down and pulling back," she later told Jeffrey Goldberg, "you're not going to make any better decisions than when you were aggressively, belligerently putting yourself forward." A big part of the problem, Clinton said, "is that we don't even tell our own story very well these days."[21]

In her own speech at the Council on Foreign Relations just a few days after Obama's August 2010 Oval Office address, Clinton tried to tell this story. She did not deny the importance of restraint—after all, every nation must operate within limits. But she emphasized that the United States has the fewest limits of any nation globally, and argued that the way the world is changing presents not just challenges but important opportunities as well because of America's capacity for innovation, its openness, and the respect it enjoys. Clinton called this a "New American Moment," one in which "global leadership is both a responsibility and an unparalleled opportunity."

This assertion of confidence offered a more uplifting tone. However, some analysts assert that when compared with Obama, Clinton's rhetoric reveals a deeper disagreement about America's role in the world.[22] This overstates the differences between the two. Obama and Clinton agreed that there were real, growing constraints on American power—whether because of the shifting global landscape or urgent demands at home—and they shared the core belief that with the kinds of policies Obama had laid out as his affirmative agenda during his first years in office, American leadership could be renewed. In fact, Obama's rhetoric in his last State of the Union address in 2016 echoes Clinton's call that, compared to any other country, this is America's moment.

CHAPTER 4

A CASCADE OF CRISES

After the Obama administration's first two years, there was a renewed sense of confidence that the United States could drive the global agenda. While there were plenty of unexpected crises—including natural disasters such as the 2010 Haiti earthquake, terrorist threats, and ongoing tensions with North Korea—and managing the wars in Afghanistan and Iraq was hardly simple, there seemed to be more control over the foreign policy rudder. Obama and his team had weathered early tests, steadied the ship, and felt able to chart a forward-looking course. Rather than just reacting, the administration had succeeded in laying out an affirmative agenda. At the midpoint of Obama's first term, the foundations for the Long Game seemed established.

That sense of control changed abruptly with the political upheaval that began in Tunisia in late 2010, which soon spread across the Arab world. Although we did not fully appreciate it at the time, the events of early 2011 ushered in a sustained period where the United States found itself responding to events, causing many to doubt the effectiveness and willingness of America to lead. The cascade of crises was unceasing. In a way, there have been two eras of Obama's foreign policy: before 2011, and after.

The unraveling of the existing order in the Middle East—the so-called "Arab Spring"—fundamentally challenged Obama's approach, bringing to the surface issues that would define the rest of his presidency: how to define America's core interests in such a vital part of the world; what tools it has to shape events; when, where, and how America should use its military power; and how the United States manages tensions between its values and interests. Despite Obama's best efforts to rebalance US global engagement and forge policies that represented the diversity of America's interests and foreign policy instruments, the Washington commentariat and many around the world still looked to his handling of the turmoil in the Middle East as the most consequential test of his leadership.

HOPE SPRINGS

It started with very misleading optimism. The Arab Spring was an historic moment not seen since the collapse of Communism over two decades earlier. Many of us working in the White House and State Department at the time saw it with the same sense of amazement and hope. The changes sweeping the Middle East after January 2011 reinforced Obama's belief in the power of brave individuals to take control of their destinies and to transform a tired, corrupt political order. Importantly, the demands for greater political freedoms and economic opportunity were coming from the bottom up, within Arab societies, not through solutions imposed from the outside.

Initially, this political earthquake seemed to serve American interests. By creating more equitable and just systems of governance across the region, the White House believed that the Arab Spring could help the region solve its own problems. This also seemed to directly contradict the extremist narrative, as regional change was being sparked not by violent jihadists calling for a return to the 7th Century, but peaceful protestors demanding greater political freedoms, openness, and accountability.

THE ARAB SPRING coincided with my move from Hillary Clinton's State Department to the White House, where in February 2011, I started as the NSC's senior director for strategic planning. My first week on the job was dominated by the events in Egypt, as millions of Egyptians took to the streets and President Hosni Mubarak's thirty-year reign came to an end. With each day the drama seemed to spread—after Tunisia and Egypt, we saw the same demand for change and threat of unrest in Libya, Bahrain, and Jordan.

The debate about how to react to the Arab Spring rested on the most enduring and well-examined fault line of American foreign policy: whether our approach should be driven by interests or values, choosing between policies focused on promoting stability or demanding reform. Inside the administration, these debates were often seen as breaking down along generational lines, with older officials like Clinton and Gates counseling caution while younger advisors like Ben Rhodes and Samantha Power pressed for a bold change of course. While there were certainly differences of emphasis and timing, the perceived divide was often exaggerated. We saw the choices between interests and values as false ones, for the United States had to uphold both.

Obama's approach to the Arab Spring was driven mainly by his sense of pragmatism. He did not believe the United States could or should stand in the way of the changes that were sweeping the region, but he saw that it was in America's interests to see this transformation evolve in an orderly way. This was what Obama was thinking when he encouraged Egypt's leader Hosni Mubarak to step aside in early 2011. He hoped calling for a smooth transition would help defuse tensions.

Also, by getting behind what was happening in the streets, the US might preserve some influence over Egypt's future.

DURING THESE TUMULTUOUS early months of 2011, Obama saw a need to do "some truth-telling" about how things got to this point and what the United States needed to do next. Obama thought America's historic interest in regional stability had enabled these problems to fester. He wanted to put America firmly on the side of regional change and speak to the aspirations of the millions who were demanding it.

He also wanted to explain how long and difficult this process would be—and to emphasize the United States still had enduring friends and interests in the region that it would continue supporting. He needed to temper expectations, making clear there were no easy answers and that the United States could not dictate solutions to the Middle East's problems. The president intended to push back against the notion that there was some elegant solution he was missing— that, as he put it, all we needed was for a modern-day Henry Kissinger to go out there and start pulling strings. It was a complicated, cave-at-filled script that he had in mind.

Obama was itching to give this kind of speech. It was an opportunity to take a step to further the ideas he had first expressed in Cairo in June 2009. He liked the high stakes, at one point observing that this "is in many ways my international race speech," referring to his historic address in Philadelphia on race relations during the 2008 campaign. Although those of us in the White House diligently worked with our colleagues across the government to come up with fresh ideas, Obama knew what he wanted to say.

In one of the meetings to discuss the speech, he mused (with a wry hint of sarcasm) about what he would say if he were writing an essay about these events in the *New York Review of Books* or the *Financial Times*. The president said he wanted to speak about the underlying causes of the unrest, which he saw principally as auto-cratic governments trying to stay in power, using the lack of an Ar-ab-Israeli settlement as an excuse not to reform, and drawing on the sectarian divides between Sunnis and Shia. He also thought it important to talk frankly about the difficult trade-offs the United States had to manage.

"We can acknowledge that some of our interests are not exactly pure here," he said, referring to America's reliance on the region's energy supplies, "and that these equities need to be weighed in terms of how to proceed." Usually American policymakers tried to obscure such policy contradictions, but Obama believed we needed to go to the pain and confront them head-on. "The conventional wisdom has been that we don't talk about the things we can't solve," he said. "I don't buy that."

Obama pulled his themes together in a speech delivered in May 2011 at the State Department. As intended, his message broke the mold. While other senior officials had spoken hard truths about the region—earlier that year Hillary Clinton had delivered an important address in Doha, Qatar warning that "the region's foundations are sinking into the sand"—it was unusual for a president to speak so bluntly.

Obama called for a broad change of approach in America's engagement with the Middle East, placing emphasis on the centrality of political and economic reform. While Obama reiterated America's enduring security interests, he acknowledged that grievances had accrued among ordinary people that "only feed the suspicion that has festered for years that the United States pursues our interests at their expense." The speech was heralded for its sharp diagnosis of the problem and willingness not to pull punches. It was also widely interpreted as a dramatic swing away from his customary caution and pragmatism—one commentator later described it as a speech of "uncharacteristic exuberance."[1]

THIS ATTEMPT TO reorient decades of US policy presented at least three practical problems, some of which we only fully appreciated with time.

The first, and the one we did worry about at the moment, was that America's actual resources to support political and economic reform fell far short of our stated aspirations. We knew we needed to avoid the "Cairo trap," referring to the dashed expectations of the 2009 speech, raising hopes for a new beginning but with little tangible follow-through.

So we pressed hard to come up with some innovative policies, and discovered some good ideas. But we never could muster enough money to generate real leverage or develop a Middle East Marshall Plan. This was especially true when compared to the amount of money those less interested in such comprehensive reforms (the Saudis, for example) were willing to dispense.

The timing was terrible. At a moment when the president and Republicans in Congress were locked in a fierce battle on the budget and deficit spending, the idea of some massive assistance program for the Middle East was a nonstarter. The consequence was that the promise of Obama's soaring embrace of such change was not matched by sufficient action. Therefore, in the eyes of many, the administration again got caught over-promising yet under-delivering.

The second challenge was that alongside the frustrated aspirations of some, from others we faced anxieties and fears of US abandonment. Such a bold call for change made America's closest partners in the region very nervous—especially the Jordanians, the Saudis, the Emiratis, and the Israelis. They were invested in the status quo and wanted to keep it. When considering Obama's commitment to stand with those who wanted to upend the existing order and his willingness to withdraw support from those like Mubarak who had been a key ally for decades, America's friends wondered what this meant for them.

These countries feared the Muslim Brotherhood and other Islamists would fill the vacuum, giving the advantage to aspiring regional powers like Iran or terrorist groups like Hamas (and soon, ISIS). Marc Lynch, one of the most thoughtful and sympathetic observers of Obama's Middle East policy, later described the approach as "visionary but incoherent." The administration, Lynch accurately describes, "struggled to grasp the fact that the old order under attack was a US-backed regional order, defended by US allies concerned, above all, with keeping themselves in power."[2] This deep sense of uncertainty about what the US wanted made it harder to reassure regional partners—and later, these anxieties would only be exacerbated by the US approach to Syria and Iran.

Finally, the emphasis on reform failed to keep pace with events once the regional order unraveled further and faster. As the instability spread beyond our expectations, the administration instinctively hunkered down, focusing more on protecting America's core security interests (like safeguarding against external aggression against our allies or partners, maintaining the free flow of energy, and fighting terrorism). Although we never believed we could control events, we increasingly found ourselves watching as bystanders.

Toward the end of his Arab Spring speech, Obama made mention of three places that, unintentionally, foreshadowed the challenges to come. Despite all the unknowns, he wanted to recall the reasons to have hope. He cited the examples of the Libyan city of Benghazi, at that moment protected by US and allied planes; young people cramming Egypt's Tahir Square to demand political change; and the protestors in Syria, braving bullets while chanting "peaceful, peaceful." In May 2011, these examples symbolized potential, and our cautious optimism seemed reasonable. Yet it was in these three places most of all—Libya, Egypt, and Syria—where our hopes for the Arab Spring cratered.

LIBYA AND THE
"IMMACULATE INTERVENTION"

President Obama was not happy. When he sat down with his top advisers in the Situation Room late the afternoon of March 15, 2011 to discuss the looming humanitarian catastrophe in Libya, it soon became clear that he only had half-baked options.[3]

When the Libyan people began to rise up against Muammar Qaddafi, the threat to civilians made the situation different than that in other Arab Spring countries. We believed that if we allowed this rebellion to be crushed violently, it would slam the brakes on the momentum of regional political change, and worse, show that dictators could stay in power if they were brutal enough. Reports were pouring in from all corners—diplomatic and intelligence assessments from the United States and Europe, press stories, and eyewitness accounts—of arbitrary arrests, torture, and killings perpetrated by the regime. Given Qaddafi's past as a sponsor of terror (as well as his increasingly bizarre, madman behavior), the world rallied to pressure him to relent. In late February, the UN Security Council unanimously approved a resolution calling for an immediate end to the violence, imposing an arms embargo on Libya and sanctions against the Qaddafi family as well as key regime members.

But things only got worse. Qaddafi's actions and chilling rhetoric made clear to those of us in Washington—and importantly, the rest of the world, even the usually skeptical Russia and the typically fragmented Arab League—that he would not step aside without a fight. Many senior government figures started to defect from the regime (including the Libyan Ambassador in Washington), fearing what was to come. If the uprising continued, Qaddafi's forces would eventually regroup and rout the rebel forces with the benefit of superior arms. Qaddafi went to the airwaves and pledged "no mercy," threatening that his troops would go house to house looking for "traitors" and "capture the rats." As Qaddafi's forces bore down on Benghazi, a city of 700,000 people, the world saw a slaughter in the making.

THE ADMINISTRATION HAD been deliberating what to do about Libya for weeks, and had come under greater pressure to intervene to prevent what many feared would be genocide. Almost everyone agreed that we should do something—the question was at what risk and cost. By March, key American partners—especially the British and the French, and even the Arab League—were calling for military intervention.[4]

The NSC meeting on March 15 opened with a customary review of the latest intelligence, and the picture was grim. Our intelligence showed Qaddafi's forces on the move. This was corroborated by what our allies were telling us, what journalists were reporting, and firsthand accounts we were getting from the field. The British and the French were ready to offer a UN Security Council resolution authorizing the establishment of a no-fly zone, and were seeking American support. There was growing pressure from home as well: two weeks earlier, the Senate had unanimously passed a resolution urging the UN to protect civilians from attack, including through a no-fly zone.

But no one inside the Situation Room believed a no-fly zone would actually solve the problem. Qaddafi's threat came mainly from tanks and troops on the ground, not from his aircraft in the skies. A no-fly zone seemed attractive to many because it was a way to appear decisive and take action without carrying many risks. But it wouldn't stop the siege of Benghazi.

"It's just a show to protect backsides, politically," Obama later said of the idea, giving politicians comfort that they could not later be accused of inaction. He fumed that after weeks of deliberations, the only policy his advisers had come up with was little more than an empty gesture. The choice the president had before him was unappealing: to refuse to support the British and French proposal, or to agree and participate in something he knew would not work. He said he wanted to see the group again later that night, "and by the time I come back, I want some real options."[5]

After the meeting ended, the White House team stayed behind to figure out what to do. We only had a few hours and needed to come up with something. Denis McDonough, who was then deputy national security advisor and knew the president's moods as well as anyone, feared a "major blow-up" when he returned. As we kicked around ideas—everything from attacks on Qaddafi's forces to an attempt to evacuate thousands of innocents from Benghazi, what we dubbed the "Dunkirk Option"—only three choices emerged: do nothing and let the Europeans proceed on their own; join the Brits and French in a symbolic no-fly zone; or enlarge the military objective to protect civilians by attacking Libyan forces on the ground, which would require a more robust intervention and therefore more risk.

When the president and his cabinet officials considered these options several hours later, it became clear that the United States could not stand aside. The circumstances were the inverse of those that had led to the intervention in Iraq nearly a decade earlier: the threat was imminent, the intelligence undisputed, and the world was clamoring for America to do something. In fact, our European allies had made it clear that they would move with or without us.

Under these circumstances, Obama said, the US could not simply act like Russia and China, hanging back and shirking responsibility. He feared that if we stood aside and watched our allies flounder—or worse, a massive humanitarian catastrophe unfold—it would do grave damage to American leadership. "I'm as worried as anyone about getting sucked into another war," he said. "But if Benghazi falls, we'll get blamed. We can't underestimate the impact on our leadership."

BUT CHOOSING TO act did not mean that the United States should go "all-in." Despite his sense of urgency, Obama did not believe that Libya was a vital national interest. He sympathized with the arguments of Defense Secretary Gates, who warned that getting involved would be a diversion from more important commitments and not worth the costs and trade-offs.

Gates argued that intervention risked getting the United States into a morass. With just a few months left in office (he had already announced his intention to retire), the defense secretary expressed his frustrations openly, especially angered by those he recalled "blithely talking about the use of military force as though it were some kind of video game." Keenly focused on the resources that would have to be taken away from Iraq and Afghanistan to conduct a new military campaign in Libya, Gates asked pointedly: "Can I just finish the two wars we're already in before you go looking for new ones?" In his memoirs, Gates says he considered resigning over the decision to intervene.[6]

The secretary of defense appealed to the president's cautious instincts. Obama conceded the decision was a close one—Gates recalls Obama telling him it was a "51–49" call—and shared concerns about the United States getting in too deeply. While the president believed that what happened in Libya did matter to the United States, it mattered *more* to the Europeans and Arab world, and he wanted to structure America's role accordingly. "[This] is not so at the core of US interests that it makes sense for us to unilaterally strike the Qaddafi regime," he later explained.[7]

So the president proposed an innovative hybrid approach, widening the goals but tightly scoping America's involvement. Instead of a no-fly zone, the United States would take on a broader mission of protecting civilians by attacking Qaddafi's forces on the ground (some called it a "no-drive zone"). The US military would lead at the beginning of the intervention, rolling back the immediate threat to

Benghazi and taking down Libya's air defenses, which would set the conditions for the allies, led by NATO, to act. Then, we would continue to help our partners by providing "unique capabilities" such as intelligence assets, refueling, or precision-strike munitions. But we would not seek to dominate the strike missions, and would not put American troops on the ground.

The president came up with the idea himself. He later observed that he was not entirely surprised his advisers had failed to come up with this option; bureaucracies tend to drive toward either-or choices. "What the process is going to do is try to lead you to a binary decision," Obama said. "Here are the pros and cons of going in. Here are the pros and cons of not going in. The process pushed towards black or white answers; it's less good with shades of gray."[8]

Obama sought to develop a new model that differed from the typical post-Cold War military intervention—as in the Balkans or Iraq—in which America's allies often seemed like little more than window-dressing on a US-dominated operation. Now the allies wanted to step up, and the president was happy to let them. "We need to get the international community invested in this to do something meaningful," he said. Obama saw this crisis as an opportunity to show how he believed countries could work together, relying more on America's uniqueness than on its dominance.

For the next seven months, America and its allies bombed Libya, conducting nearly 10,000 airstrikes. The immediate humanitarian nightmare we all feared was averted. In August 2011, rebel forces stormed Tripoli and overthrew Qaddafi's regime, and that October, the self-declared "King of Kings" met his ugly demise when he was found on the run, hiding in a sewer pipe, and killed by rebel forces.

The operation was viewed as a resounding victory for the NATO Alliance. As the analyst Gideon Rose later put it, it was an "immaculate intervention."[9] Although some of NATO's flaws were on full display (such as the widening gap in military capabilities between the United States and its allies, especially in the Europeans' ability to sustain their operations), NATO had proven its worth by providing the leadership and organizing structure for the operation. This seemed to be an exemplar of how America could divide the labor with its partners. The entire campaign cost just over $1 billion (which at the time was what the United States spent per week in Iraq or Afghanistan), and the allies conducted nearly 90 percent of the airstrikes.

The Libya War was designed straight out of the Long Game playbook. Because Libya was not a vital interest, the United States needed to be careful not to allow its involvement to overwhelm other priorities. America would lead, but do so in a way that only it could, expecting partners to carry a large burden. This looked like a new kind of American leadership, one that was both decisive and inclusive, balancing competing interests and managing trade-offs and risks. Some championed it as a model—striking a sensible balance between the arguments of the so-called "realists" who believed that Libya was not worth it, and those "interventionists" who asserted that the United States needed to go all the way.

Yet to claim success is very hard when considering the chaos plaguing Libya in 2016, when the greatest concern is that it is becoming a hotbed for terrorists. As Obama now admits, Libya is "a mess" and, when measured against our hopes, the intervention "didn't work."[10]

In hindsight, it is tempting to see the effort as an abject failure, one that may have been successful in the moment but ultimately contributed to a whole host of problems, from the proliferation of Libya's substantial conventional weapon stockpiles to the rise of extremists groups, thousands of refugees flooding into Europe, and the violent breakdown of order in the Middle East. President Obama has said that what happened in Libya following Qaddafi's overthrow is one of his greatest regrets—and that he draws lessons from it when considering US military interventions elsewhere.

Could the ruin of Libya have been avoided? Critics assert that the way Libya has turned out reveals the fundamental flaws in Obama's approach. Consider the different arguments: Had the US gone in differently—being less willing to cede control to allies— then maybe we could have averted disaster. Or perhaps the administration should have been more willing to help postwar Libya, taking greater risks by being forceful with Libya's post-Qaddafi leaders or committing US troops to lead an international peace-keeping force. Or maybe Obama failed by not being more willing to sue for peace and negotiate with the Qaddafi regime, sacrificing the goal of political transition in the interest of leaving some semblance of order in place. Finally, some say that, in the end, Robert Gates was right all along: this only could have been prevented by not intervening at all.

WOULD EVERYTHING HAVE been better if the US had simply stayed away? It is tempting to think so. While such arguments can be seductive in hindsight, they are out of touch with what policymakers confronted at the time.[11]

Sitting in the White House, we had overwhelming evidence of Qaddafi's intent on mass slaughter. This was not a case where there was a lack of knowledge about what was going on; instead we were inundated with information that only grew more troubling with time. Moreover, there was nothing in Qaddafi's background—from his past support for terrorism (to include the killing of Americans) to his eccentric, paranoid rants—that gave us any reason to give him the benefit of doubt. The only way to know for sure if Qaddafi meant what he said would have been to let him go into Benghazi and see what happened—which we viewed as an unacceptable and immoral risk.

Some have attributed Obama's decision to intervene to the influence of an unlikely alliance between Hillary Clinton, Susan Rice, and Samantha Power. But this grossly overstates his susceptibility to such pressures. When those stories first started circulating—most notably a March 2011 *New York Times* column by Maureen Dowd characterizing this as the "fight of the Valkyries"—eyes rolled in the White House, including those among the heroines Dowd heralded. The idea that the president was a passive player being shoved around by advisers got the story wrong, and it obscured the key point.

The most important factor in the president's decision to intervene was not pressure from insiders, but the urgency of events on the ground combined with the advocacy and actions of America's allies in Europe and the region itself. Compared to most other conflicts, what made Libya unique was that so many countries around the world not only supported bold action—they were clamoring for it. If the US had opted out, the allies might well have acted anyway—recall the first airstrike was launched from a French plane. So the US played a critical role in bringing the world together and coordinating the effort.

Obama often spoke about this kind of leadership, noting that its logic was laid out explicitly in *The Audacity of Hope*. Beyond matters of self-defense, he argued that the United States should take the time and seek to build a coalition. This does not mean giving a veto to the UN Security Council—a body Obama described as one that "in its structure and rules too often appears frozen in a Cold War-era time warp." Nor does it mean "that we round up Great Britain and Togo and then do what we please," with other countries hanging back as the US does all the work. As Obama explains, taking the time to build a coalition has multiple benefits—it allows the United States to carry a "lighter load" and to "look before we leap," asking the toughest questions ahead of time. It also helps uphold the global "rules of the road" and gain legitimacy. "Multilateralism regulates hubris," he later said.[12]

It's important to remember that in the spring of 2011, Obama was criticized more for acting *too slowly* to confront Qaddafi than for acting at all. At the beginning of the crisis, we were hamstrung by the fact that we needed to get American diplomats and citizens out of the country—there was a lot of reluctance to ratchet up the pressure until they were safe. Nevertheless, Obama got hammered by critics who argued he was dithering and not doing enough to stop Qaddafi, or too passive and letting the Europeans take the lead.

Looking back, the tougher question is not whether the US should have intervened, but if it could have done so more effectively. Did the US miss opportunities to end the war sooner or on different terms? And did it mishandle the postwar, failing to give Libya a greater chance to achieve stability?

How to define success was one of the biggest challenges. Obama intervened in Libya while making explicit that the *military* objective was not Qaddafi's departure. But the United States, Europeans, and Arab League had all signed on to regime change as the broader political goal that they would seek to achieve through other means—pressure, isolation, and diplomacy. Once in, it was hard to reconcile these limited military goals with the maximalist political objective that Qaddafi must go.

The civilian protection mission—and the difficulty of defining what exactly needed to happen for those innocents to be "protected"—put the policy on the slippery path of mission creep. This mattered in terms of the targets hit (such as Qaddafi's palaces, military headquarters, and other instruments of the regime's authority) as well as the assistance the coalition provided the opposition. The military campaign evolved into more than preventing Qaddafi from threatening civilians. It became about helping the opposition win. As

Gates recalled, we maintained the fiction that the operation was only about degrading Qaddafi's command and control, but "I don't think there was a day that passed that people didn't hope he would be in one of those command and control centers."[13]

Although the US-led airstrikes were indispensable to enabling the opposition, perhaps we should have been willing to provide even more military support by deploying special forces on the ground or more weapons to assist the opposition (as we only later learned the full extent of what our partners like the French and Qataris had done). Doing so may have shortened the conflict and given us valuable leverage over the various militias after Qaddafi's ouster.

But it is hard to reconcile a more robust American military role with the goal of not "owning" the Libya War outright. After all, as the conflict dragged on, many partners were tiring and would have taken advantage of American escalation to head for the exits. For example, Norway, one of the leading strike partners whose planes had destroyed Qaddafi's residence in Tripoli, pulled out because of strains within its governing coalition, and several other key countries found themselves running low on ammunition and having difficulty sustaining their aircraft.[14]

Moreover, American military escalation would likely have required obtaining authorization from Congress. Obama had justified US involvement on an unusual, and controversial, legal theory that such a limited, "unique capabilities" operation was not the kind of "hostilities" that required congressional approval. Since we had (wrongly) assumed that the bulk of the US military role would be over in just weeks, we did not seek an explicit authorization from Congress. Some believed this argument was already tenuous, but it would have been impossible to defend if we had started doing more. And since most of Capitol Hill had soured on the operation, it was unlikely the administration could have mustered enough support to escalate even if it wanted to.[15]

IF MILITARY ESCALATION wasn't the answer, could we have intensified diplomacy and done more to cut a deal on Qaddafi's departure? As the military campaign dragged on, and as concerns mounted about keeping the military coalition together (and as the Europeans started to run out of ammunition), we were very focused on what more we could do to negotiate an end.

There was no shortage of global envoys trying. Despite a plethora of efforts by a motley crew of diplomats—including from the United Nations, an African Union initiative, a Russian chess player, and several others who purported to speak for the regime—Qaddafi showed no signs of leaving. The longer he refused to leave peacefully, the more likely his end would be a violent one.

My own direct but brief experience with the Libyans suggests a negotiated outcome was unlikely. Although we were initially wary of talking directly to the Qaddafi regime for fear of undermining other negotiators and allowing him to exploit any differences, several months into the bombing our allies were telling us that Qaddafi was misinterpreting our unwillingness to engage him as a sign of ambivalence about his future. So we decided to make a direct overture (it was supposed to be a secret but the Libyans soon leaked it to the press). In a July 2011 meeting with Qaddafi's representatives in Tunis, I joined the assistant secretary of state for the Middle East, Jeff Feltman, and the exiled US ambassador to Libya, Gene Cretz, to make one last attempt to offer a way out if Qaddafi stepped aside.

Meeting for nearly three hours at the seaside residence of the American ambassador to Tunisia, we went round and round with the Libyan delegation (which included Qaddafi's chief of staff and interpreter, who had become one of the strongman's trusted advisors) on everything from the origins of the crisis and who was to blame to the nature of the opposition and the regime's future. We had fundamentally opposing narratives about what was happening; whereas we saw Libya as another chapter in the Arab Spring with an indigenous revolt against a crazy dictator, they saw a foreign intervention un-justly overthrowing the existing order. So instead of exploring the terms of a deal, the Libyans blustered that the rebellion was driven by "foreign agents" and al-Qaeda, and that the United States should be "protecting" them instead of bombing them.

The Libyans seemed in genuine disbelief, thinking that since the reopening of ties in 2003, the United States would be their uncondi-tional friend. They were understandably concerned about their well-being. "You bombed my office at 2am!" one of them shouted at us. After the war, some of these Libyan officials admitted that at no point during the bombing did Qaddafi's family or inner circle think they would be defeated—that, in the words of one of Qaddafi's clos-est confidantes, they suffered from "supreme arrogance and miscal-culation." As Gene Cretz, who knew the Libyans as well as anyone in the US government, recalled, "[T]here was never a serious offer from Qaddafi to step down from power. I firmly believe that none of those characters around him ever had the gumption to raise the issue with him personally."[16]

ALTHOUGH NEGOTIATIONS PROVED fruitless, perhaps we could have pushed for a ceasefire without conditions, deferring the question of Qaddafi's future. This would have been similar to the 1999 NATO air campaign in Kosovo, which was also aimed at protecting civilians and ended with Milosevic still in power (only to see him overthrown in a revolution the following year); or the 1998 "Operation Desert Fox" air campaign in Iraq, where the US military bombed Iraqi tar-gets for four days but deferred Saddam Hussein's fate for the future. Gates later argued, "I think if we could have prevented a massacre in Benghazi and basically held there, we would have been better off."[17]

However, neither the Libyan opposition nor some of our Euro-pean and Arab partners would likely have accepted this approach. Even if the United States had ended its support for the bombing, with Qaddafi still in power the rebels would not have stopped fighting (nor would their most fervent supporters like Qatar, the United Arab Emirates, and even the Europeans have cut the opposition loose). Moreover, there was no reason to trust Qaddafi's regime to negotiate in good faith and uphold their end of any bargain.

Therefore, even if we had ceased bombing and allowed Qaddafi to stay in power, the war likely would not have ended—and it is reasonable to think we would have seen even more bloodshed in Libya as a result. It is hard to imagine Libya (and by extension, the region) being worse than it was by 2016, but that may very well have been the case had Qaddafi, like Assad in Syria, remained at war with his own people.

COULD WE HAVE done more to prevent Libya's postwar troubles? Nobody thought determining a post-Qaddafi future would be simple. After all, the uncertainty about what would come next was the main reason the administration hesitated to intervene in the first place. We understood the risks all too well. As Obama said at the time, "it is a huge challenge to get a country rebooted."

However we also believed that, especially compared with places like Iraq and Afghanistan, Libya had a lot going for it. It had a relatively small, homogenous population (fewer people than Tennessee) with a professional class; rich energy supplies; proximity and close ties to Europe; and a vast amount of international support and enthusiasm to help. There was reason to hope that, with some concerted yet modest assistance, Libya could lift itself out of the swamp decades of Qaddafi's rule had left. We were wrong.

In preparing for postwar Libya, we were determined to maintain the "unique capabilities" approach that had defined the US role in the military campaign. This would not be post-Saddam Iraq or post-Taliban Afghanistan, where the United States would effectively run the country. The administration did not want to "own" Libya; the president said he wanted to "cabin" the US role. But restraining our system's momentum to do so was not always easy.

SINCE A POLITICAL transition was always a goal, we started planning for post-Qaddafi Libya even before the air campaign started. This included working with our allies and the Libyan opposition to prepare them to take charge. Yet one unexpected challenge was the bureaucratic machine for postwar efforts that had been developed in Iraq and Afghanistan. Having been caught entirely unprepared for postwar reconstruction in those countries, the US had amassed vast experience in how to do nation-building, with thousands of experts and significant resources ready to offer assistance. The bureaucracy's muscle memory was for the United States to go in big, offer the Libyans help on everything, and if necessary be ready to do the job for them.

But the president remained determined not to allow Libya to morph into a massive American-led effort, draining resources and attention. This was reinforced by many in Congress, who resisted our modest requests for assistance for Libya (demanding that the Libyans pay for everything themselves) and, after becoming very skeptical about the war, would have erupted if the president had decided to put a postwar US force on the ground unilaterally.

More importantly, even if we had wanted to go in heavy, we would have had to override the wishes of those we were trying to help. Outsiders engaging in nation-building is not what the Libyans wanted. Fiercely independent and proud, they saw this as their struggle, not ours. As my former colleague Ben Fishman, who was the White House point man on Libya, recalls, "While the Libyans were extremely grateful for NATO's contribution to their revolution, they were adamant from the outset of the transition that they themselves should determine the country's future."[18] We did not fully understand Libya and only slowly perceived its endemic dysfunction.

Because of years of diplomatic isolation—the US did not have an embassy in Libya from 1980–2006—there were few experts on Libya either in or out of government. We had not grasped how weak its institutions were or appreciated the internal disunity that, as Robert D. Kaplan explains, was the "underlying cause behind Qaddafi's unruly tyranny."[19]

POSTWAR LIBYA PRESENTED a difficult conundrum we could never resolve: the Libyan people and their new leaders simultaneously insisted on doing things their own way while demanding that we do more to help. Often the Libyans did not even know what they wanted, but weren't interested in us telling them what to do. We looked to the United Nations to help chart a path forward, yet even it tread a careful path and was limited by Libyan demands to do things on their own.

Libya also illustrates the limits of what outsiders can accomplish without a significant military presence to provide security, logistics, and organizational support. Libya was never going to be Iraq or Afghanistan or even Bosnia or Kosovo, with thousands of foreign troops deployed to keep the peace and a massive international civilian presence to manage things. Contrary to the assertions of some who criticize Obama's "small footprint" approach and desire to keep American troops out, there was never a realistic option for establishing an international peacekeeping or post-conflict security mechanism. Indeed, there were no viable candidates to lead or comprise such a force. Despite a lot of talk, the Europeans never stepped up to help in the way Obama expected. And even if they had, the Libyans didn't want it.

Even with these limitations, for a time the security situation seemed manageable. Senior US officials, including Hillary Clinton and Secretary of Defense Leon Panetta, traveled to Libya to encourage the interim government. Numerous European leaders also visited

Tripoli for a victory lap. The United States and its partners diligently worked with the new leadership in Tripoli to help with reforms in key areas like energy, justice, and security.

But letting the Libyans "own" the process meant we had to grapple with inexperienced decision-making, where even the most mundane tasks, like getting contracts signed or money deposited into bank accounts, proved exceedingly difficult. Their leaders were disengaged and often absent, spending a lot of their time in places like Qatar. Looking back, the Libyans weren't in a position to absorb huge amounts of our assistance, and the militias weren't interested in giving up any of the authority they had grabbed. We also struggled with such thorny issues as obtaining the necessary legal protections for our personnel working in Libya (with echoes of the Iraq SOFA negotiations that were happening at the same time).

There were some successes. With the international community's assistance, in 2012 Libya held its first democratic election in fifty years. Perhaps most important, the United States worked with the Libyans to address two urgent security concerns: to find, secure, and destroy leftover chemical weapons from Qaddafi's undeclared arsenal; and to help secure thousands of shoulder-fired anti-aircraft missiles that we worried could be a threat to civilian airliners (although we could not ever account for the whereabouts of all of them).

Such early progress proved fleeting, but lulled many officials in Europe and the United States into believing that things would be messy but manageable. Reflecting on this period of time during a speech to the UN General Assembly in 2015, Obama said "our coalition could have and should have done more to fill a vacuum left behind." This reflects Obama's disappointment—which he would privately express in more biting terms—with the Europeans who were the most enthusiastic about getting involved and left many promises unfulfilled.

Perhaps we were also too deferential to Libyan sensitivities about interference in their internal affairs, and should have pressed them much harder across the board, especially to set policies on disarming and demobilizing militias and reincorporating them into a reformed military structure. But our leverage was limited; we could not compel them to act. And being more assertive could have backfired to the point where we lost our influence entirely.

The practical consequence of a "small footprint" approach was that there were too few American personnel there to do the work. We had limited facilities on the ground—our embassy compound had been ransacked and so new offices and housing had to be built. With security as an overriding concern, our diplomatic and development experts competed with security personnel for limited slots. By the time Ambassador Christopher Stevens arrived in Tripoli in the summer of 2012, just a handful of diplomats were working at the Embassy, and they were far outnumbered by security personnel.

With such a precarious security situation, the only way our diplomatic footprint could have been larger is if we had added even more security personnel or assumed more risk. It seemed the main purpose of our efforts had transformed from helping rebuild the country to protecting and sustaining the US presence itself. This made it excessively difficult for diplomats to do their work (the few who were there were barely able to leave the heavily-fortified embassy compound) and to get any additional traction assisting the Libyan government.

Whatever limited willingness there was to accept risks evaporated after Ambassador Stevens and three other Americans were killed by terrorists in Benghazi in September 2012. Then, in 2014, the United States and most other countries closed their embassies in Tripoli as renewed civil war loomed. So with no presence on the ground, the United States effectively picked up its toolbox and went home.

BECAUSE OF LIBYA's geography and penchant for exporting instability (as well as, one can still hope, its potential for opportunity), its
future still matters to the United States. But the implications of the
Libya intervention and its aftermath for the future of American leadership—and the exercise of American power—far outweigh the
country's intrinsic importance to our interests.

The Libya intervention does not undermine Obama's Long Game
approach, but it does expose its inherent limits. More of a tragedy
than a policy failure, Libya shows that while the United States can
act to address some problems, it cannot solve all of them, and often
the best one can hope for is incremental progress.

Consider again the policy alternatives at the beginning and end
of the Libyan War. Even with the benefit of hindsight, it is hard to
see how America's position would have been enhanced if Obama had
decided to stay away from Libya and let the allies intervene alone by
putting up a no-fly zone that no one thought would work. The likely
outcome would have been the massacre of thousands and a civil war
boiling over. At the same time, it is difficult to conceive how American interests would have been better served if the administration had
overridden the objections of the Libyans and the international community and deployed ground troops to try to enforce a peace.

THE FEROCIOUS DEBATE over what happened in Libya has hindered American leadership in at least two ways.

First, in practical terms, it is very difficult to exercise influence if
one is unwilling to take some risks on the ground. "The killing of
Chris Stevens had the effect of helping the terrorists acquire greater
power," one administration official later explained.[20] Leadership requires presence. Yet the shameless and cynical way that Obama and
Clinton's critics used the Benghazi attacks to score political points
with their rank and file undermines the ability of the United States
to practice the kind of bold, assertive leadership these partisans

purport to uphold. There will always be a difference between calculated risk and recklessness. However, if our political debate conflates the two, then America's approach to the world's problems will be driven by fear, not confidence. If the lesson for future presidents is that the United States should shy away from risk altogether and pull back to avoid tragedies like Benghazi—as it has done in Libya—its global influence will be diminished, and the "foreign policy breakdown" will have won.

Second, the debate about Libya also hinders American leadership in a more subtle, yet pernicious way. Obama's approach towards Libya meant the United States would play a role using its unique assets but would not dominate the operation from beginning to end. This still reflects American "indispensability," using its special strengths to manage and lead a diverse coalition that gets the most out of its partners. Obama said that Libya represented "precisely how the international community should work, as more nations bear both the responsibility and the cost of enforcing international law." However, this kind of nuanced leadership is difficult to capture in a phrase and, as the administration learned, too easy for critics to caricature.

"LEADING FROM BEHIND." Unfortunately, those three words came to sum up more than the Libya campaign. They became the bumper sticker critics would use to describe Obama's "weak" way of using American power. It is a simple phrase that once uttered was remembered by everyone, seeming to capture everything critics thought misguided about the president's foreign policy. Other recent presidents had been tagged with similar awkward phrases: think George H.W. Bush and the "vision thing," Bill Clinton and "foreign policy as social work," and George W. Bush and "mission accomplished."

But as stated by an anonymous Obama "adviser" to the *New Yorker* journalist Ryan Lizza, "leading from behind" was just a very sloppy way of making an important, if subtle, point. Inside the White House, we knew right away that the phrase would instantly become fodder for the critics, and that the larger point would soon be lost. It would have been better—and more accurate—if whoever had uttered the phrase had tacked on two more words: "the scenes."

For what the United States did in Libya was an example of "leading from behind *the scenes.*" While the US military played an indispensable diplomatic, military, and intelligence role in the Libya campaign, we were willing to let others shoulder more of the outfront burden. In fact, it was not something we were simply willing to do—it was something we believed was in our *interest.* Obama later said that he wanted to act in a way that prevented "free riders" and allies who would just "hold our coat" while we did all the work.[21] And importantly, such leadership is something only the US is capable of exercising.

Like a director of a Hollywood movie, it was the United States operating behind the scenes to organize the effort, assign the roles, set the schedule, supply the resources, and orchestrate the action. Other countries could be the actors, but they looked to us for direction. In the Libya War, a US admiral commanded the NATO Alliance, another US admiral commanded the air campaign, and the US secretary of state was the main driver of the diplomatic effort to hold the coalition together.

By letting others share or dominate the spotlight occasionally, this was by definition a more subtle exercise of leadership. And it is arguably the most important aspect of leadership. Success comes not from doing everything alone or hogging the stage, but for bringing the effort together into a coherent whole. After all, at the Academy Awards, actors aren't the ones hoisting the final trophy for best picture; it is the director and producer that do.

Obama's critics claim that this is not leadership, but cowardice and abdication. Yet in many ways Obama is following an overlooked American tradition that has been embraced by some of our most-admired presidents. For example, Dwight Eisenhower's "hidden hand" leadership displayed a similar style. Ike was wary of the tendency for the United States to try to bully others and do everything. Drawing on his military experience, he believed, "A platoon leader doesn't get his platoon to go that way by getting up and saying 'I am smarter, I am bigger, I am stronger, I am the leader.' He gets men to go with him because they want to do it for him, because they believe in him." What's most important, Eisenhower observed, is to get out of the "business of saying we are out in front, [that] we know all the answers."[22]

In her memoirs, Hillary Clinton dismissed "leading from behind" as a "silly phrase." Looking back on Libya, she explains, "It took a great deal of leading—from the front, the side, and every other direction, to authorize and accomplish the mission and to prevent what might have been the loss of tens of thousands of lives."[23] No other country could have played such a multidimensional role, using the mix of diplomatic, political, military, and intelligence tools that only the United States has. This is the definition of strength: to bring the world together to solve a specific problem, achieving goals that the United States could not—or should not—get done alone.

EGYPT AND THE LIMITS OF LEVERAGE

Libya presented a test of America's leadership through military power, alliance management, and small-footprint postwar reconstruction efforts in a country that had been a sworn enemy just a few years earlier. The response to the turmoil in Egypt is a case study in how the administration struggled to address a different set of challenges—testing America's leverage and influence in how it uses its military and economic assistance in a country that for decades has been a regional ally and a recipient of billions of American taxpayer dollars.

Egyptian President Hosni Mubarak's sudden departure in February 2011 set off an earthquake both in the region and Washington. For decades, the US-Egypt relationship had been a cornerstone of America's Middle East policy, built on years of close diplomatic cooperation and substantial military assistance, undergirded by $1.3 billion per year of guaranteed support for Cairo as a result of the 1978 Camp David Accords and Egypt's peace treaty with Israel. With Mubarak relegated to history's dustbin, the American relationship with Egypt now faced a difficult balancing act: how to continue to encourage and shape Egypt's internal evolution toward greater political freedom and economic opportunity while, at the same time, upholding our core security interests.

Both of these goals were essential to Obama's policy in the region. Yet the tensions between the two proved very difficult to reconcile. In his May 2011 speech Obama had stressed the importance of fundamentally changing the American approach, but what did that mean for a stalwart ally like Egypt?

For a year after Mubarak's fall, circumstances did not force us to confront this tradeoff directly. The US worked to support the interim leadership led by Egypt's powerful Army chief, Field Marshal Mohammed Tantawi, as he led his country toward its first democratic election for president. Then in June 2012, everything changed when Mohammed Morsi, a Muslim Brotherhood leader, was elected. For decades the Muslim Brotherhood had been brutally repressed and forced to live in the shadows; it rejected the existing regional security order, especially peace with Israel. Now one of its leaders was Egypt's president. America's key allies in the region, many of whom considered the Muslim Brotherhood a terrorist organization, were appalled.

DURING THIS TIME the United States tried its best to play it straight and support the new leadership in Cairo. Confronted by massive economic and security challenges and with no experience governing, Morsi and his team were quickly overwhelmed. As a way to help, we offered advice on everything from economic policy and social reforms to how to structure their system for more effective national security decision-making.

From a military perspective, we saw this moment as an opportunity to reshape US security assistance to achieve mutual interests, focusing on such areas as border security, maritime security, and counter-terrorism. We wanted to work with the Egyptian military to wean it off obsolete weapons systems largely irrelevant to modern-day threats.

Like many of our Arab military partners, the Egyptians prioritized expensive weapons like jet fighters and tanks—even if such capabilities weren't especially helpful against threats like terrorists in the Sinai. Our Egyptian counterparts were not enthusiastic about moving away from such "legacy" capabilities, suspicious that our insistence on such reforms was actually code for downgrading the relationship. They prized their special status from so many years of guaranteed assistance and close cooperation. Moreover, their resistance to change also reflected the entrenched interests of the country's military and security services in the so-called "deep state."

By mid-2013, the situation in Egypt was on razor's edge, and basic order seemed at risk. Morsi and his team made mistake after mistake, blaming everyone else for their problems. The economy was in tatters and the security situation getting worse. I visited Cairo on several occasions for talks with Egyptian military leaders, and I remember thinking that the country seemed ready to explode.

We were especially worried about terrorist threats from Sinai, as there were regular attacks on Egyptian security personnel, tourists, and the international peacekeeping forces (including several hundred Americans) there to monitor the peace agreement with Israel. Sinai had always been a kind of Wild West of Bedouin smugglers and bandits, but the situation had become far worse with such instability emanating from Cairo, massive economic dislocation and the influx of weapons from Sudan and postwar Libya, all of which contributed to the rise of jihadi groups there.

The Israelis were alarmed. They had suffered several attacks on their border, yet the Egyptians did little to thwart them. Under the "cold peace" Egypt and Israel enjoyed under Mubarak, the two sides had regular contacts and coordinated security efforts in Sinai. Morsi ended that dialogue, and whenever we pressed him to do more to control the situation, he dismissed the problem as overblown. The Israelis made clear to us privately that they would not sit back and allow a jihadi-infested Sinai to become a threat—and if they were attacked and Morsi still refused to act, they would take matters into their own hands.

By the summer of 2013, the situation in Egypt was getting desperate, and the military was poised to step in, topple Morsi, and impose order. Washington went into full crisis mode (coinciding with these events were our rising concerns about Syria, and the August 2013 chemical weapons attacks). While there was no denying Morsi had made a mess of things, we did not want to see a counter-revolution by force. The administration's message to the military leadership was clear: stay in the barracks and out of politics.

Because decades of the close cooperation had built strong trust between the two countries' military establishments, it fell principally to Secretary of Defense Chuck Hagel (who had replaced Panetta in early 2013) to convey this message to then-Defense Minister General Abdel Fattah al-Sisi. A year earlier, the Egyptian general had been Morsi's pick to lead the powerful army, vaulting over many more officers senior to him (in the early days, there were worries that he was too close to Morsi). But now he seemed ready to move his president out. Over the course of many phone calls, Hagel asked al-Sisi not to intervene, urging that he instead help Egypt move toward political reconciliation. Hagel cautioned al-Sisi not to follow the example of Mubarak, warning that any move by the Egyptian military—especially violence against pro-Morsi protestors or the Muslim Brotherhood leadership—would inevitably impact Egypt's relationship with the United States, including our willingness to continue unequivocal support for the Egyptian military.

Al-Sisi listened patiently to our concerns. But he remained unconvinced. He said they could no longer suffer Morsi's incompetence, and worse, he asserted the Muslim Brotherhood was in bed with Hamas (which was true) and al-Qaeda (which was not). Al-Sisi saw Egypt in an existential struggle, with the country's very survival at stake. He openly worried about its becoming Islamist like Iran or chaotic like Syria, and seemed desperate for the administration's support. "Do not turn your back on us," he would plead, and asked several times whether America is "with us in the war on terror or not?"

When the military stepped in and removed Morsi from office and put al-Sisi in power—and then took violent action against pro-Morsi protestors, killing over a thousand people and injuring many more—US-Egypt relations fell into its greatest crisis since the 1970s, and the Obama administration faced yet another formidable test.

IN RESPONSE TO the military's ouster of Morsi, many inside the administration and in Congress wanted to punish the new regime swiftly, with some arguing that we should cut off all military assistance. Bringing the curtain down on the relationship did not make much sense to me—while we needed to respond, this would have eliminated what little leverage we had. Moreover, despite our disappointment with al-Sisi's decisions, we were still better off with Egypt as a security partner than without it—Egypt was simply too big to throw overboard.

Recognizing this, Obama wanted to strike a balance, deciding to show his displeasure by canceling a major military exercise and withholding certain items of military assistance—F-16 fighters, Apache helicopters, kits to make Abrams tanks, and Harpoon anti-ship missiles—while continuing to fund the sustainment and maintenance of Egypt's existing military hardware. By doing this, we hoped to generate some leverage to influence the new regime's decisions and get Egypt back on a democratic track.

In an intensive effort of defense diplomacy that lasted several months, Hagel and al-Sisi continued to spend many hours on the phone (I listened in on every call, and tallied nearly thirty hours total), where the Egyptians heard the rationale for these steps and what we wanted to see happen. While not pleased, they accepted that the administration needed to take these actions to address our concerns about the removal of Morsi and violence against protestors—as well as to head off even more severe consequences being proposed by some members of Congress.

But Cairo's patience wore thin. As the months went by, the Egyptians became increasingly agitated, especially as concerns about instability in the Sinai and along the Libyan border became more urgent. They argued that the United States was withholding capabilities, including the Apaches, needed to confront these threats. Complicating things further, our other close regional partners—none of whom were sad to see Morsi go, thinking he was a stooge of Iran—were very supportive of al-Sisi. The Saudis and the Emiratis poured money into Egypt, and the Israelis praised al-Sisi's forceful actions in the Sinai and tough moves against Hamas. Our military colleagues in Tel Aviv claimed that their security coordination with Cairo was as good as it had ever been, and they were incredulous that we seemed ready to throw it all away.

While Egypt's frustrations with us mounted, they resisted engaging in the more comprehensive discussions we sought about the long-term reform and revision of the security relationship. They also made known that they would look elsewhere for support, making several high-profile overtures to their old Cold War patrons in Moscow. While we never believed Egypt saw Russia as a particularly appealing partner, it made sense for them to hedge their bets and was a reminder to us that Cairo had options of its own.

IN OUR EFFORTS to reform the US-Egypt security relationship, we were hindered by a unique funding practice known as "cash-flow financing." Little understood, but critically important, cash-flow financing is how the United States has provided security assistance to only two countries: Israel and Egypt. Essentially, it works as a credit card, allowing these countries to finance the purchase of American weapons with money advanced to them.

The Egyptians have long valued cash-flow financing. Beyond the prestige, it has allowed them to modernize their military and purchase major weapons over the course of several years (with the additional exception of Israel, every other country that receives US defense assistance has to spend its money year-to-year, making it harder to finance the acquisition of such large systems). By enabling the Egyptians to move away from Soviet-made hardware and by implementing the Camp David peace with Israel, this has served American interests.

But the problem with cash-flow financing has been how it limits the United States—we couldn't simply cut off the assistance even if we wanted to, because Egypt had already spent our money. This model became unsustainable given the political winds that were buffeting both sides. Put simply, we concluded the US-Egypt security assistance program needed to be fixed to be saved.

IN THE SPRING of 2015, President Obama decided to allow delivery of the weapons we had withheld for a year and a half. Withholding the assistance was not getting us anywhere—if anything, it had become counter productive. What little leverage we had over Cairo was diminishing. Obama believes policies should work, and this one wasn't. Although the administration was right to withhold some assistance in response to the Egyptian military's violence against protestors, this policy did not create the incentives we had hoped.

But the decision was not simply caving in. Importantly, Obama announced steps to overhaul the assistance relationship by focusing it on critical areas such as counter-terrorism and border security. The fine print of the president's decision, which most analysts skimmed over, was even more far-reaching: beyond restoring the assistance, it also set in motion changing the way the money has been provided by phasing out cash-flow financing. Essentially, this means taking away Egypt's credit card and instead giving it a debit card, so the weapons purchases will be taken out of Egypt's annual defense allocation. This may sound like an arcane accounting issue, but by putting the US on a path out of a financial straightjacket, this move represents the most significant shift in the security relationship since 1979.

It will take several years to implement, and will cause plenty of heartburn in Cairo and among American defense contractors, who had come to rely on the steady income. But to preserve the relationship in an era that will bring more turbulence, future presidents need greater flexibility in how they can manage the assistance. This doesn't mean a reduction of America's interest or staying power or even resources. At $1.3 billion a year, Egypt will still receive far more military assistance than any other country after Israel. But the shift, while painful and complicated to implement in the short term, puts the assistance relationship on more sustainable footing (and for the US, a more advantageous one).

CRITICS HAVE HOWLED at the Obama administration's handling of Egypt from all directions. As Ben Rhodes put it, "We're in that sweet spot where everyone is pissed off at us."[24] By continuing the security relationship, some claim the president finally bowed to reality. In their eyes, a military relationship with Egypt is so critical that not only should the US sustain its assistance untouched, it never should have suspended its support in the first place.

Others assert Obama caved to political pressure and turned his back on democracy—and the ambitions he made in his May 2011 speech. They argue we should fundamentally change our relationship with Egypt, perhaps ending (or at least severely curtailing) the military assistance that has been the cornerstone of the relationship for over three decades in the interest of making bold demands for democratic reform.

A third group criticizes the policy's execution, asserting that it left the US with the worst of both worlds: by first suspending the assistance, and then finally letting it go forward, the administration hurt both its credibility in democracy promotion and Egyptian confidence in the United States, hemorrhaging influence along the way. Moreover, this flip-flop created another irritant with countries like Saudi Arabia, the UAE, and Israel. By trying to strike a middle path—which failed to generate any new leverage—the administration ended up creating more problems than it solved.

All three of these critiques are justified. It is in the US's interest for Egypt to be strong and secure, and for its military to be modern and capable. And it is in the US's interest for Egypt to pursue democratic reforms and create a more open society based on freedom of expression and the rule of law. While Egypt faces a host of internal problems—its alarming economic plight, demographic youth bulge, and rising insecurity from terrorist threats will be huge challenges for years—the US should want Egypt to be a leader and a stabilizing force in a deeply troubled region. So the question for the US is how best it can position itself to have any influence over the choices Egypt's leaders will make.

Of course, this has to be about more than military assistance (and the US has fallen woefully short on economic help). Yet because of the Egyptian military's primary place in that country's governance and society, and central role of US-Egyptian military ties in the overall relationship, such assistance remains the critical tool of American influence. Although this experience also shows we should not overstate the leverage it gives. As much as Egypt values our support, it is not enough to compel them to do exactly what we want.

That is why President Obama's decision to resume the military relationship—while at the same time fundamentally changing the ways it is financed and spent—was the right one. This effort to modernize the relationship is key to ensuring that US-Egyptian security ties, which have served American interests for many years, remain an investment worth making for the Long Game.

CHAPTER 5

THE TIDE OF WAR

No issue has tested the Long Game more than Syria. Nor has any foreign policy dilemma proved more vexing or demoralizing for those of us who played a role in shaping and implementing it.

What started in 2011 as another Arab Spring ember ignited into a regional inferno. In her memoirs, Hillary Clinton accurately described Syria as a "wicked problem": it defied easy solutions, and all the choices were bad. "Do nothing, and a humanitarian disaster envelops the region," she wrote. "Intervene militarily, and risk opening Pandora's Box and wading into another quagmire, like Iraq. Send aid to the rebels, and watch it end up in the hands of extremists. Continue with diplomacy, and watch it run headfirst into a Russian veto. None of these approaches offered much hope of success."[1] And over time, the choices only became worse.

Looking back on the course of the Syria crisis, it is tempting to see this only as a story of lost opportunities, serial missteps, and inept decision-making. The outcomes have been truly horrific—with more than 300,000 killed, millions of refugees, the rise of the Islamic State, and a disintegration of regional order that the world will be grappling with for at least a generation. This might seem to be a clear failure of American policy. But when one weighs the possibilities for greater US action alongside competing goals, and the demands of managing trade-offs and risks, it is more accurately a cautionary tale of the limits to American, or anyone else's, power.

"MANAGED TRANSITION"

Early on, the administration settled on the objective of seeking Bashar al-Assad's departure from office. This was initially seen as reflecting the momentum of the Arab Spring, and we thought that Assad would go the way of Mubarak. As the violence spiraled, the administration concluded that Assad's departure would remove the essential driver of the conflict.

Therefore, the more difficult question has been how to achieve this goal while avoiding major risks and exceedingly high costs—developing a policy that, in the totality of American interests, is balanced and sustainable. To listen to the critics, getting Assad to go should have been easier. They argued that because Assad had stubbornly clung to power, Obama either had no strategy to loosen his grip, lacked the fortitude to bring it about, or had given up on the goal altogether.

Yet setting a political objective is not the same as designing a policy to achieve it. Simply because the United States could not wave a wand and make Assad disappear did not mean Obama lacked a strategy. In fact, "Managed Transition" best describes the Obama approach to Syria's future—although the phrase neither qualified as a compelling bumper sticker nor was it ever codified in a strategic document. Obama himself did not use the phrase publicly until the fall of 2015, more than four years after he first said Assad had to go. The United States wanted Assad out, but it wanted the leadership transition to proceed in a way that would not lead to even greater chaos and bloodshed. The policy debates inside the administration (as well as in the public debate about Syria) resided in the fundamental, and uncomfortable, tension between the two words "managed" and "transition."

There has never been any doubt that the United States has the power to bring about a transition in Syria. Since 9/11, decapitating brutal regimes was something it had a proven track record of doing quite effectively. But none of those transitions were particularly tidy. After the regimes had been toppled by American military power, the result was further instability, and in the cases of Afghanistan and Iraq, a massive sacrifice of US lives and resources to try to help those countries get back on their feet. While Obama wanted Assad to be gone, he did not want to repeat the mistakes of the past. In discussions at the White House and inside the Pentagon, we knew we could use military force to end Assad's regime, and discussed many ways to do so. Yet we always got stuck on the question of what would come next. In these kinds of situations, Obama later said, "we have to refrain from jumping in with both feet."[2]

That is why there was such emphasis on having Assad's departure be "managed." The best outcome would be for Assad to leave as part of a negotiated settlement, in a way that would allow a transitional government to take hold and basic order to be preserved. We wanted to give the Syrian opposition a stake in the outcome and establish the context for the international community to provide support. We didn't want the entire government to implode and create the kind of chaos we saw in Iraq. We wanted to be sure that in any transition, our core security interests would be met—especially, up until mid-2014, ensuring that chemical weapons would remain secured. So by pressuring Assad through economic, political, and military pressure, we hoped to achieve his departure through diplomacy.

The problem was that Assad never seemed tempted to leave. This surprised us—early in the crisis, most officials believed Assad lacked the necessary cunning and fortitude to stay in power. He was being kept afloat by the lifeline from his principal backers, Russia and Iran. Perhaps, like Saddam and Qaddafi, he was just delusional about his popularity and the nature of his enemies. Whatever the reason—and it was likely a combination of factors—a managed departure seemed far away. As things in Syria got worse, the conversation turned to risking more forceful steps to bring about a transition.

WE WERE ALWAYS dangling between the horns of the policy dilemma; whether one placed more emphasis on "managed" or "transition" determined the moves you advocated and the risks you could live with. We considered steps to bring about a quicker, less-managed transition—hoping the regime would topple by increasing the pressure or intervening directly with military force—we kept returning to the consequences and the costs we would then have to carry.

At the Pentagon, the two military options we considered most carefully were to create a "no-fly zone" over Syria and a "buffer zone" or "safe area" inside Syria, along the border with Turkey. These also happened to be the most popular ideas among commentators and our regional partners. Both seemed appealing. Eliminating Assad's air power would remove a crucial military asset, and a safe zone would be a place for internally displaced Syrians to shelter and perhaps serve as a base from which the Syrian opposition could operate. Yet as we explored these options beyond the first move, the questions became much more difficult, as it was hard to see how they would actually solve the core problem—or prevent further escalation.

Creating a no-fly zone seemed easy enough in theory, but grounding Assad's air force seemed unlikely to be decisive. The US military had maintained a no-fly zone in Iraq for over a decade after the first

Gulf War, but this did not ease concerns about Saddam's effort to develop WMD. In Bosnia in the 1990s, the NATO-enforced no-fly zone did not prevent ethnic cleansing on the ground. In Libya, a no-fly zone would not have prevented the regime's forces from fighting. So if one wanted to use American air power to make a difference, it would have meant a similar kind of "civilian protection" mission as we had in Libya, a substantial undertaking few advocated.

The "safe area" concept was even more uncertain. Our Turkish colleagues were particularly enthusiastic about this idea—which they called a "safety belt"—arguing that it would be a way to relieve the tremendous Syrian refugee crisis they were grappling with (which would, of course, eventually explode into Europe). We started talking seriously with the Turks about this idea in the fall of 2012, establishing a formal military working group to explore the possibilities.

In meeting after meeting, Turkish officials presented us with detailed maps about where such safe areas could be located and how they could be configured. We pursued these discussions at great lengths over many months. But they always got hung up on the same issues: how we would enforce these areas, how they would be administered, who would provide the troops, and what would happen if they came under attack.

As one of my White House colleagues put it at the time, a safe zone would be like a "tethered goat"—if attacked, and it almost certainly would have been, we would be obliged to defend it. The lawyers asked what legal authority we would have to do this (since there was no chance we would get a UN authorization given Russian opposition, and a safe zone would technically violate Syrian sovereignty). No one wanted American troops to protect a safe zone and, unsurprisingly, no other country came forward with a credible commitment. Although there were assertions that other countries would step up to help if only we took the first step, there was little evidence that this would be true—it was hard to escape the implication that, in the end, the United States would again be left holding the bag.

MOREOVER, FOR THE first several years of the crisis, concerns about Syria's chemical weapons stockpiles colored every aspect of the administration's discussions about how much it could ratchet up the pressure on Assad. We viewed chemical weapons as his most lethal trump card; if we pushed too hard he could unleash havoc. Or, if the regime suddenly collapsed with its state institutions hollowed out, as had happened in Iraq and Libya, then the weapons could easily become vulnerable to theft. We had visions of the massive looting in Iraq that had taken place after the fall of Saddam in 2003, except instead of museums and government buildings, this time it would be chemical weapons sites. In the effort to get rid of Assad, we did not want to create an even more terrifying security threat with chemical weapons on the loose—something that we rightly would have been held responsible for.

Although the administration stressed the importance of Assad's departure as the political objective, during 2011-14 chemical weapons were seen as a higher priority for America's security interests. This presented a dilemma. After the deal with Russia to remove the chemical weapons, the regime was a necessary silent partner in relinquishing its stockpiles. When that process was complete in mid-2014, the largest obstacle to putting more pressure on Assad was removed, as we no longer needed his regime to help get the chemical weapons out.

The deal to get chemical weapons out of Syria also taught different lessons, shaping both the US and Russian approach toward the conflict in the years to come. In Washington, this showed that Russia had leverage over Assad, and that when pressed it would use its influence to get the regime to relent. Yet Moscow took away something else: that Assad was indispensable to get anything done inside Syria.

THROUGHOUT THE SYRIAN crisis, President Obama has resisted any proposal that would have led to the United States owning the problem outright. He was as candid about this in his public statements as he was clear to his aides behind closed doors. When asked in a 2013 interview how he weighed what to do about Syria, the president recited the kinds of questions he had consistently raised privately: "Would a military intervention have an impact? How would it affect our ability to support troops who are still in Afghanistan? What would be the aftermath of our involvement on the ground? Could it trigger even worse violence or the use of chemical weapons? What offers the best prospect of a stable post-Assad regime?" Describe for me specifically what will work, the president would demand, and if you can make a case we can get this done, we'll do it.

Obama believed that while acting might provide short-term satisfaction, in the end it would do more harm than good. It was not that Obama was seeking to avoid military intervention at all costs, but because he was cognizant about the implications for his overall global strategy. Such decisions are not made in isolation from other interests. With deeper intervention, Obama warned in 2014, "there was the possibility that we would have made the situation worse rather than better on the ground," and US involvement would have meant "we would have the fourth war in a Muslim country in the span of a decade."[3]

The logic of Obama's concerns was compelling—and he had been warning about it since he first ran for president. Writing in *The Audacity of Hope*, he was very clear about the "script" the United States needed to avoid. Once the US intervened in such conflicts, it would "spur insurgencies based on religious sentiment and nationalist pride, which in turn necessitates a lengthy and difficult US occupation, which in turn leads to an escalating death toll on the part of US troops and the local civilian population. All of this fans anti-American sentiment among Muslims, increases the pool of potential terrorist recruits, and prompts the American public to question not only the war but also those policies that project us into the Islamic world in the first place." This was the clear lesson of Iraq, yet many critics chose to ignore or dismiss it, as though the conflict had never happened. Puzzled by this amnesia, Obama agreed with Secretary Gates, who said in a 2011 speech that anyone who advised sending a big land army back into the Middle East "should have his head examined."[4]

So we found ourselves in an uncomfortable box—we wanted Assad to go, but not if the cost entailed significant military intervention. As we sought a managed outcome, with diplomacy slowly plodding along, one grappled with the painful realization that a political transition away from Assad was not coming anytime soon. Meanwhile, Syria was burning.

HISTORY'S GHOSTS

To help understand how many officials in the Obama administration—including me—approached the Syria crisis, one must pause to take a brief historical detour. For in many ways, the roots of the debate about what to do in Syria go back to the 1990s debates about the Balkans—starting with the Srebrenica massacre more than two decades ago.[5]

In July 1995, Bosnian Serb forces killed nearly 8,000 innocent Muslim civilians in Srebrenica, a small valley town in eastern Bosnia. This massacre—the worst atrocity in Europe since World War II, one that occurred while UN peacekeepers stood by fecklessly and NATO refused to intervene—shamed the international community, and its lessons have loomed over the debate about American military intervention ever since.

Srebrenica became a brutal symbol of the price of inaction. Had the United States and its allies intervened sooner, the tragedy could have been prevented. As a stunningly self-critical 1999 report by then-UN Secretary General Kofi Annan concluded, "The cardinal lesson of Srebrenica…is that a deliberate and systematic attempt to terrorize, expel, or murder an entire people must be met decisively with all necessary means."

Like the failure to act in order to prevent the Rwanda genocide the year before, Srebrenica was a stain on America's power and reputation. It also exposed the limits of the international system to forge collective action, even in the face of genocide. But the terrible event galvanized the United States to intervene in Bosnia, launching airstrikes and negotiations that led to the 1995 Dayton Peace Accords. Once America acted through a combination of force and diplomacy, it ended a war and renewed US leadership. The lesson seemed clear: the United States should never again stand by idly in the face of evil.

This bitter legacy directly influenced the post-9/11 debate about whether to invade Iraq in 2003. The painful memory of Srebrenica is one of the reasons the Bush administration received support for going to war against Iraq from many Democrats (myself included) who saw confronting Saddam as necessary, at least in part, by upholding the "responsibility to protect."

From a strategic and humanitarian perspective, the case to intervene in Iraq seemed even stronger than in the Balkans. Saddam Hussein had already proved his willingness to massacre civilians (the slaughter of Kurds in the 1980s and the Shia after the 1991 Gulf War offering the most stark examples), and his military was a far greater threat than that posed by Bosnian Serbs. Therefore, the argument went, the United States needed to stand firm and not hide behind dithering allies or a weak UN, as it had in Bosnia in 1995. As George Packer observed in 2002, Bosnia had turned many liberals into hawks.[6]

So in March 2003, the United States did in Iraq what many believed it waited too long to do in Bosnia (and did not do at all in

Rwanda): it used force to prevent a dictator from further terrorizing innocents—a risk that seemed worth taking to protect our common interests and uphold our values.

Yet the disaster that unfolded in Iraq taught a competing lesson. Intervening in such conflicts can unleash havoc that the United States is neither prepared nor willing to handle, and impose costs that harm other interests at home and abroad. Iraq's legacy was another "never again": that America should not topple governments and occupy countries without a clear sense of what it wants to achieve and what sacrifices it is willing to endure.

In significant ways, the lessons of the Balkans and Iraq then shaped the Obama administration's thinking about the 2011 intervention in Libya. Again, there was an impulse to act decisively to stop a looming humanitarian catastrophe, which we described as a "Srebrenica on steroids." But we also had concerns about what would come next if we intervened and the very real possibility of enveloping the United States into a protracted conflict like Iraq.

The decision to intervene created deep divisions within Obama's national security team and was a rare instance where his two heavyweight advisers—Hillary Clinton and Robert Gates—ended up on opposite sides. In trying to bridge these differences, Obama sought to apply the lessons of both Srebrenica and Iraq, threading the needle between taking urgent military action to save lives while preventing the United States from getting sucked into another morass.

The Libya intervention prevented a massacre and helped bring down a dictator, and for a moment it appeared to offer a more hopeful lesson. Yet now, when Libya suffers from insecurity and chaos, no one takes pride in what that country has become. Obama believes that things would have been worse had the United States not intervened, but has expressed regrets about what has happened in Libya since Qaddafi's demise. When considering using force elsewhere, the experience of Libya forced him to ask: "Do we have an answer for the day after?"

THE COMBINED EXPERIENCES of Bosnia, Iraq, and Libya infused the debate over what to do about Syria, yet the lessons were often difficult to reconcile. The conflict comprised the worst elements of the others—with hundreds of thousands of innocents slaughtered, a ruthless dictator, extremists, refugees, and weapons of mass destruction—and no easy answers. Sitting in the Situation Room debating what the United States should do, the presence of the historical ghosts was palpable—after all, most of us had forged our careers in the intense policy battles of these previous interventions. Their contradictions shaped the difficult policy compromise that defined American policy toward Syria.

My former White House colleague Philip Gordon has summarized the dilemmas of intervention this way: In Iraq, the US intervened and occupied, and the result was a costly conflict whose consequences America will grapple with for a generation. In Libya, the US intervened but did not occupy, and the result is chaotic instability. And in Syria, the US neither intervened nor occupied, and the result has been catastrophic for the Syrian people and the region.[7] Yet to complete (and further complicate) the picture, one cannot overemphasize the importance of Bosnia, where US dithering failed to prevent a genocide, but its belated intervention ended a war.

Policymakers often turn to the past to navigate the present, both to learn lessons and avoid mistakes. This has been especially true with the Syria crisis—when debating what to do, history loomed large. "A president does not make decisions in a vacuum," Obama told Jeffrey Goldberg. "He does not have a blank slate."[8] We would often recall the costs of inaction and the good that can come when the United States takes risks and asserts leadership. But we also forced ourselves to remember how easy it is for the United States to lose its way.

America has the power to act, but the challenge is how it should do so while heeding the lessons of the past. Alas, on Syria, history did not provide a short cut.

CONTAIN AND MITIGATE

Getting rid of Assad, as important as that would be, was only one piece of the strategy. As the administration labored to bring about a transition through pressure and diplomacy, we also were focused on ensuring that the crisis did not grow into something far worse. Unfortunately, history will show that, at best, we were only partially successful.

If "managed transition" was the political objective, an additional goal could be summed up by another mantra, this one never uttered: "contain and mitigate." Like a doctor dealing with a particularly advanced cancer, we were seeking to ease the side effects and prevent the disease from metastasizing while searching for a lasting answer—we needed to create the time and space for a managed transition to occur.

While Syria could not be fully "cured" anytime soon, we believed it was in our interest to contain the conflict from threatening our close partners who bordered Syria—especially Israel, Jordan, and Turkey—and to prevent wider regional instability. And we also sought measures to mitigate the worst aspects of the Syria crisis, whether that meant addressing the humanitarian emergency caused by millions of displaced people or ameliorating the tremendous suffering of those still left inside Syria.

Humanitarian support was the most visible manifestation of this strategy. As of late 2015, the US had provided over $4.5 billion in relief for those internally displaced inside Syria and the refugees flooding into neighboring countries.[9] Given the insecurity inside Syria and the fact the US government had no presence there, an elaborate system was established to get the support to those in need (working with series of local middlemen).

BUT THE VITAL tool to implement "contain and mitigate" was, notably, the very thing the administration's critics accused it of not using enough of: the military. This came in two ways.

First, we "hardened" Syria's neighbors. This meant, starting in 2012, deploying various American military assets to reassure our partners, build their capabilities to address any spillover, and deter Assad from attacking them. For example, the United States stationed Patriot anti-missile systems in Jordan and Turkey (and each required several hundred troops to operate and protect). We also deployed a squadron of F-16s to Jordan, which regularly trained with Jordanian forces and flew missions to make clear to Assad that America had Jordan's back. Between 2012 and 2015 the United States also provided approximately $3.6 billion in military assistance to Jordan, especially to help it address critical needs like intelligence and border security. By 2015, the military had about 2,200 troops stationed in Jordan—a number that, while not secret, the Jordanians had asked us to keep quiet for fear that it would provoke Assad.[10]

Second, the administration tried to make the opposition more cohesive and capable. This policy unfolded slowly, consuming countless hours in White House meetings, with every detail closely examined, parsed, and debated.

The challenge was immense. The Syrian opposition was a disjointed and ragtag bunch, with poor leadership, little organization, and bitter internal rivalries. They were also getting pounded relentlessly by Assad's military. Although Syria was awash with weapons, the opposition was outgunned by the regime, who through the course of the conflict used its full arsenal—airpower, heavy armor, SCUD missiles, and chemical weapons—against them. Russia and Iran provided substantial support. To try to shore up the opposition, many regional players—especially the Saudis, Qataris, and Turks—flooded resources into Syria in the hope that with more money and guns, the opposition could at least stay on its feet, and eventually turn the tide against Assad.

While the conflict raged on, and the steady stream of weapons and cash continued to flow into Syria, concerns mounted that the wrong elements of the opposition—the extremists, some affiliated with al-Qaeda—were being strengthened. Yet the United States was not in the game. Why were we so slow? Part of the reason stemmed from a lack of understanding about who the opposition was and worries that if we provided military assistance, it would end up in the wrong hands.

But other questions that many had—especially in the White House—were about effectiveness, accountability, and risk. Would providing assistance actually work? It was one thing to provide arms and resources, but would the opposition know what to do with them? How could we be sure that the opposition would not end up using the weapons in the wrong ways—to commit human rights abuses or war crimes? And would arming the opposition put us on a slippery slope toward large-scale intervention?

During 2012, the administration deliberated these questions exhaustively. Over time it made incremental decisions to provide some support that balanced these risks. For example, after starting with humanitarian assistance and medical supplies, the United States eventually began to provide the opposition with "non-lethal" combat support like communications gear, body armor, and medical supplies. As much as we credited ourselves publicly for such steps, we knew this still left us playing at the margins. So by the summer of 2012, many senior officials began advocating that the United States do more, arguing we should build a full-scale program to equip and train the opposition.

In her memoirs, Hillary Clinton describes how she and then-CIA Director David Petraeus began discussing this idea and advocating for it. My boss at the time, Secretary of Defense Panetta, also wanted us to step up (as did I). We believed that while arming and training such a force might not prove decisive, it would at the very least provide a psychological boost to the opposition and give Assad reason to doubt his future. Just as important, it would give us more influence over the opposition's direction; we worried that the support from countries like Saudi Arabia and Qatar was ending up in the hands of extremists, and without some "skin in the game," we had little leverage with our partners.

By the fall of 2012, Petraeus had a plan to vet, arm, and train opposition fighters, and he and Clinton took the idea to the president.[11] Yet Obama remained unconvinced that such an effort would have the intended effect. He was concerned about the nature of the Syrian opposition, believing we needed to know more about it before providing lethal support. That argument left us in a chicken/egg situation: we could learn a lot more about the opposition if we were trying to recruit and train them, but we could not start doing so because we knew too little.

Fundamentally, at that time the president believed there were too many open questions, and that such a modest step was not worth the risk of putting us on a slide away from contain and mitigate and toward deeper American involvement. In his assessment of the trade-offs, the significant downside of entanglement outweighed the modest upside of limited training. As Clinton recalled, for Obama, getting involved "in any way in another sectarian civil war in the Middle East was not what he had in mind when coming into office."[12]

WHILE OBAMA DECIDED not to proceed with the training effort in the fall of 2012, the planning continued to mature. And just several months later, in the summer of 2013—after reports of the chemical weapons attacks—the White House announced that the United States would provide direct military assistance to the rebels.

Numerous press accounts reported this new policy as the beginning of the effort that the president had decided against months earlier.[13] The White House simply described this as, in the words of Ben Rhodes, "military support" to the armed opposition that "is going to be different in both scope and scale in terms of what we are providing to the [Syrian armed opposition] than what we have provided before."[14] The administration's most strident critics, led by Republican Senators John McCain and Lindsay Graham, called the decision to provide lethal assistance "long overdue."

Still, it would not be enough. Despite the president's decision to increase the "scope and scale" of military support for the opposition, a year later little had changed on the ground. If anything, the opposition seemed in even worse shape. So in the spring of 2014 the administration decided to ratchet up its efforts even further, embarking on a much larger program for the US military to equip and train the Syrian rebels against terrorist organizations, not the Assad regime. Run by the Defense Department, this program would be large-scale—aiming to train as many as 5,000 fighters by the end of 2015—at a hefty price tag of $500 million.

Obama announced this effort in his May 2014 speech at West Point, and its ambition and scope were news to us at the Pentagon. It also surprised the Congress, who would have to write the check. As the US set out to build the program, many members of Congress raised serious concerns about the price tag and how the training would work (raising the same questions we had been asking ourselves). As much as Congress had been advocating for arming and training the rebels, once a program was proposed, it proved not to be very popular.

So why did the president shift from initial reluctance in 2012 to pursue such a program to less than two years later deciding to embark on a much larger, more expensive US military effort? I think for two reasons. First, our experience providing military support to the opposition had improved our understanding of what was possible. We now had better answers for the president's questions about how precisely this would work. After the smaller effort began in 2013, we proved we could find and train fighters who were at least moderately capable in the fight, scoring some battlefield successes.

And second, the president's risk calculus changed. Whereas arming the Syrian opposition had once been seen as something that could jeopardize our larger interests, now Obama concluded that "contain and mitigate" would not work without it because of the growing threat from violent jihadi groups—most notably, ISIS. Everyone agreed there needed to be "boots on the ground" in Syria, but since the US, Europeans, and Arab countries would not provide any beyond small numbers of special operations forces, there was no alternative to training Syrians.

There was still plenty of reason to doubt whether this would be effective. But we hoped that with significant resources and the US military in charge, the chances of success would make the risks worthwhile. Regrettably, our doubts proved well-founded.

THE TRAINING DEBACLE

The spectacular collapse of the US military program to equip and train the Syrian opposition—with the revelation in September 2015 that just a handful were still in the fight—was as depressing as it was shocking, especially for those of us who had believed in the effort, lobbied for it, and had a hand in building it.[15]

Reflecting on other US experiences with such endeavors, perhaps we should not have been so surprised—it was clear Obama, while certainly disappointed, felt somewhat vindicated by the doubts he had been expressing all along. "I've been very skeptical from the get-go about the notion that we were going to effectively create this proxy army inside of Syria," he told *60 Minutes* in October 2015. Here again, given how important training local forces remains to US strategy in Syria and Iraq, it is useful to reflect on our recent history—and the lessons we should draw.

Working to arm, train, and sustain insurgent or indigenous forces is hardly new, and history offers a few cases showing that it can be effective. The program to strengthen Afghanistan's mujahideen rebels against the Soviets is usually held up as the shining example for how this can work. But that is also a mixed result—after all, one can draw a direct line between the arming of Afghanistan's Islamic fighters in the 1980s and the rise of al-Qaeda terrorism in the 1990s and 2000s. And history is littered with many more examples of when similar efforts have failed or backfired. Think of the Bay of Pigs in the early 1960s. Or the South Vietnamese Army after US forces withdrew in the early 1970s. Or the Nicaraguan Contras in the 1980s.

This checkered record was certainly on President Obama's mind, and he made no secret of his skepticism. "I actually asked the CIA to analyze examples of America financing and supplying arms to an insurgency in a country that actually worked out well," he said in a 2014 interview. "And they couldn't come up with much."[16]

Recent experience provided further reason for caution. In Iraq, thousands of American troops occupied that country for nearly a decade, and the US spent billions of dollars training the Iraqi security forces. Despite some successes, those efforts could not prevent a large chunk of the Iraqi army from rapidly collapsing in the spring of 2014 as ISIS stormed Mosul and hurtled toward Baghdad.

In Afghanistan, another country the United States and its allies have occupied for over a decade, building the Afghan Security Forces has been a key pillar of our strategy. Yet as Afghan forces have been out on their own against the Taliban, they have been struggling even to maintain a stalemate. Obama's surge of troops into Afghanistan did help provide security and achieve the core goal against al-Qaeda, but it is unclear how enduring that will be. When judging how the Afghan forces will hold up after more coalition forces leave, it is safe to say the jury is still out (which is why a smaller contingent of US and allied forces will likely stay there for years).

AMERICA'S EXPERIENCES IN Iraq and Afghanistan illustrate that standing up local security forces—or, in Pentagon parlance, "building partner capacity"—is hard enough when we are all-in; as the cases of Libya and Syria show, it is even harder when we're not.

In 2013 in Libya, the United States and key partners like the United Kingdom and Italy embarked on a major effort to train a "General Purpose Force" to help strengthen the government against the militias. This effort fell flat, as the Libyans were unable to come up with competent recruits and promised resources (they had agreed to reimburse us for training them). While the British and Italians actually trained a few hundred troops—only to see them return to Libya and instantly disband—Washington's part never even got off the ground before the instability in Libya made it impossible to proceed (and even these efforts were blemished: for instance, the Libyan recruits had been expelled from the UK after some of them rampaged through an English village and assaulted women; and an earlier attempt to train Libyans in Jordan faltered after a group of them set fire to their training facility).

Having worked on the Libyan training program and the early stages of the Syria effort, I know no one ever believed success would come quickly, if at all. In both cases, we had a limited or nonexistent presence on the ground to administer the work, making essential steps like finding and vetting recruits difficult. Given insecurity, the training would have to be done elsewhere, complicating things immensely (we were planning to train Libyans at an unused base in Bulgaria, and Syrians in Turkey). And even if we had successfully recruited and trained forces, neither Libya nor the Syrian opposition had a capable military command structure they could plug into, raising the question of how these forces would be led, fed, and sustained over time.

Despite such limitations, there was enough reason to try, and in both cases we had reason to hope for success. Libya had a government at the time that was desperate for international help, which promised that the recruits were ample and ready, and pledged full financial support. President Obama was keenly focused on this policy, and pushed the bureaucracy hard to make progress. In the much tougher situation in Syria, the United States had crucial help from partners like Turkey and Saudi Arabia, who also promised to find thousands of recruits, provide locations for the training, and help pay for the effort.

There was also no question the US military was well suited to do this. After years honing its skills in Iraq and Afghanistan, the military developed an impressive capacity to train partner forces, learning a lot of valuable (and hard) lessons along the way. This is what made these setbacks particularly sobering. When it comes to building capable forces in such situations, one can have all the will, skill, money, and allies. But still that is no guarantee. "Is it possible to build an indigenous force that will actually take control of its own destiny?" asked Army General Martin Dempsey, who before becoming chairman of the Joint Chiefs had spent two years training the Iraqi security forces. "I don't know."[17]

Would it have made a significant difference if the US had started training earlier? Even those like me who advocated providing military assistance to the Syrians in 2012 must concede that it might not have changed much. Once the administration decided to provide direct military assistance to the armed Syrian opposition just a few months later, in 2013, it proved not to be enough, leading us to embark on a large-scale, Pentagon-led effort a year later. And then when that failed in 2015, the US returned to a more modest, small-scale effort, providing weapons and guidance from special operations forces.

As Hillary Clinton said in a 2014 interview, long before the military training program collapsed, "I can't sit here today and say that if we had done what I recommended…we'd be in a demonstrably different place."[18] After all, if our massive investments of time, resources, and troops to train forces in Iraq and Afghanistan have delivered mixed results at best, one should have reasonable expectations of what a far more modest investment under more limiting circumstances will bring.

This does not mean that we should throw up our hands and quit. Nor does it mean—as the administration's critics assert—that such failures stem simply from lack of leadership or gross incompetence, and that only if different people were in charge then everything would have worked as planned. Washington finger-pointing aside, the challenge is far tougher.

A core pillar of Obama's Long Game strategy toward the vast swath of crises stretching from Mali to Afghanistan has been to create capable partners to help do the work with us, to expand our reach without stretching us too thin. Obama outlined this policy explicitly in his May 2014 speech at West Point, where he described the goal of creating a "network" of partnerships to deal with these threats.

Yet as the president himself acknowledged, there is good reason to be skeptical this will work. There are no silver bullets: success requires having a large reservoir of patience, resilience to setbacks, and greater appreciation for the limits of what we can do. In some instances, progress will be painfully slow. In other instances, we will be better off scaling back our ambitions to achieve more focused, modest results.

THE ISIS CRISIS

The summer of 2014 witnessed a dramatic and sudden shift in the administration's approach to Syria and the broader crisis in the

Middle East. Driving this change was the rise of the Islamic State in Iraq and Syria, or ISIS (or in Arabic, Daesh). The rise of ISIS posed an acute threat to American interests, changing the calculus about what would be required even to achieve "contain and mitigate." That's why the president decided to launch the Pentagon train-and-equip program. And that's also why he decided to do what his critics (and some senior advisers) had been advocating for years: conduct American airstrikes in Syria and insert special operations forces on the ground. A year after the red line, the United States military was back in Iraq and waging war in Syria.

From the early days of the Syrian war, we had worried that an extremist threat such as ISIS could emerge. Fueled by foreign fighters from Europe and financing from the Gulf, jihadis were gaining ground. We also understood the threat such extremists posed in Iraq. In the spring of 2014, when the Iraqi cities of Ramadi and Falluja fell, the US worked with the Iraqi government to give it support by expediting weapons shipments. Then in June 2014 ISIS captured the northern Iraqi city of Mosul, home to over a million people. Islamic militants were racing toward Baghdad and threatening the Kurdish region.

ISIS's capability surprised us. So did the rapid collapse of the Iraqi Army. We did not appreciate how severely it had deteriorated since 2011. Part of the reason was the fact that the US military was no longer at its side—which not only impacted the Iraqi army's ability to maintain readiness, but also made it harder for us to see how weak it had become.

Another reason we were caught off-guard was that at the time, most of Washington and the world's attention was captivated by the crisis in Ukraine. Russia's military intervention in Ukraine and annexation of Crimea had upended the European security picture and took attention away from the crises in Syria and Iraq. (A small but personal example of this: in March 2014, I testified with other senior officials before the Senate Foreign Relations Committee in a hearing that was supposed to be about Iraq and Syria, but senators spent most of their time asking us about Ukraine).

The sense of urgency changed after Mosul. ISIS now had its hands on millions in cash from captured Iraqi banks, along with heavy armor and vehicles and tons of weapons from overrun Iraqi Army depots—most of which had been provided by the US after its forces withdrew. With Iraq seemingly on the brink of collapse and Syria only getting worse, Obama decided it was time for the US to get more involved directly. The goal was to disrupt, degrade, and ultimately defeat ISIS, so it would not be a threat to us, our allies, or regional stability.

The strategy to achieve this goal had several parts: direct military action by the US and its partners against ISIS, mainly through airstrikes; strengthening indigenous forces by surging trainers and special forces back into Iraq, and then into Syria; providing significant military assistance to the Iraqis and opposition fighters in Syria; taking actions to choke off what fueled ISIS (foreign fighters, financing, and messaging); and providing humanitarian support. By 2016, there were over sixty countries involved in various parts of this effort.

THE STRATEGY HAS been premised on three assumptions. First, Obama remained determined that the US not "own" the ISIS problem outright. That's why there is such emphasis on strengthening partners in Iraq and building them in Syria, as well as bringing European and Arab countries into the effort. That does not mean, however, that the United States steps aside and lets others do the work alone—direct American military action is a vital component.

The second assumption is that the strategy will take time. Success must be measured in years, not days. Patience is key to sustainability. Embedded within this is the belief that, despite the real dangers ISIS poses, fundamentally time is on our side—that the progress the US and its partners can make will outpace ISIS.

Obama sees ISIS as a potent threat, but not an existential one. Sometimes his description of this has been too glib, depicting the threat in a way he certainly regrets (such as once characterizing ISIS as the "JV team"). But the underlying point is valid. ISIS is a huge concern, but it does not threaten the basic security of the United States, like Nazi Germany during World War II or the prospect of nuclear annihilation during the Cold War. It is not a serious ideological rival like Soviet communism. It is not winning mass support in the Middle East.

The fact that terrorists are turning to less sophisticated, albeit sensational attacks like mass shootings (which have been happening all too often in America by those who have nothing to do with ISIS), shows how they can adapt. However, as the respected terrorism analyst Peter Bergen observes, the chances are around five thousand times greater for an American to be killed as a result of gun violence unrelated to terrorism than from a terrorist attack.[19] For Obama, the greatest threat that ISIS poses is that in responding to it, we lose sight of the Long Game—whether that means "owning" the problem by occupying large swaths of the Middle East or by giving into anti-Muslim xenophobia and undermining our values and civil liberties here at home.[20]

But it is important always to interrogate the assumption of time, especially as ISIS evolves and finds other havens to operate from. Time is required for balance and sustainability, but time can also allow things to get worse and make the problem harder to solve. Strategic patience can become strategic constraint.

For example, time allowed the Russians to intervene directly in Syria in the fall of 2015, complicating the strategy immensely. After the November 2015 terrorist attacks in Paris and the March 2016 bombings in Brussels, senior US officials found themselves asking whether they in fact had enough time to implement the current approach, or whether the US needed to recalibrate and do more. This does not mean throwing out the strategy for a new one, but it raises the question of whether the US should accelerate its inputs, with more direct military action and increased effort to build the capacity of partners on the ground.

THIS LEADS TO a third assumption shaping the strategy. From a policymaking perspective, one of the core challenges the administration has faced in fighting ISIS has been finding the right tools to fit the problem. ISIS has no regard for borders—we understood that the problem between Syria and Iraq was contiguous. It is more accurately thought of as "Syriaq," in which the lines on a map are meaningless. However, the ways we use our tools to fight ISIS are not always the same. In both places US airpower is an important component, and direct military action is degrading ISIS capabilities and destroying its leadership. And in both we need a more capable military partner to confront ISIS on the ground, taking back and holding territory.

Although these efforts operate under a common military banner—"Operation Inherent Resolve"—it is a struggle to implement a one-size answer. In Iraq, the government could be part of the solution, while in Syria the government was part of the problem.

That's why the administration established what it called an "Iraq First" strategy. The Baghdad government was imperfect, but one we could cooperate with; we could share intelligence, coordinate airstrikes, provide lethal assistance, and deploy US troops to help train the Iraqi security forces. The US is working with many other partners—including the British, French, Danish, Australians, and Dutch—who are also on the ground with troops to help train and equip the Iraqis, and join in the air bombing of ISIS. We face very different circumstances in Syria, and therefore a far more difficult challenge. Neither the United States nor our partners has a substantial presence on the ground (although the US military, and that of some European countries, are slowly increasing the presence of special forces).

OPPORTUNITIES MISSED?

Given the threat ISIS poses and how horrific the situation in Syria has become, one must constantly ask what the US could have done differently. Aside from a full-scale intervention, were there alternative courses in Syria or Iraq? The short answer is yes. Yet one must acknowledge that these alternatives would not have been easy, may not have worked, and risked making things even worse.

In addition to arming the Syrian opposition earlier—even though experience shows this likely would not have been dispositive—four possibilities stand out.

The first is whether the rise of ISIS could have been avoided if US troops had stayed in Iraq after 2011. Assuming we could have solved our disagreements with the Iraqi government (or chosen to trust them), it is hard to say whether a few thousand troops primarily on a training mission could have prevented ISIS. Some critics, like Senator John McCain, vehemently believe it would have made a decisive difference. Yet over 100,000 US combat troops could not prevent the rise of the early incarnation of ISIS, al-Qaeda in Iraq. In fact the US presence was a magnet for terrorists.

However, if the US had found a way to keep a small residual force in Iraq, we would have had greater insight into how badly the Iraqi Security Forces were deteriorating, at least giving the administration more time to react. This would not have been risk-free—American troops would have been without legal protections and also likely remained terrorist targets. When US troops returned to Iraq in 2014, they did so within an entirely different context, with a new Iraqi government asking for help and openly inviting the US in. Unlike 2011, Obama believed he had an Iraqi partner he could work with (and the same is true in Afghanistan, where an enduring presence will remain). By 2016, around 3,600 American troops are in Iraq, and they will likely stay for some time.

Second, the US could have initiated airstrikes earlier in the crisis, just as it was prepared to do in order to deal with the specific threat from Syria's chemical weapons. Beyond the red line episode, we had come close to initiating strikes several times in 2013-14, only to pull back. If the United States had acted then, it most certainly would have been alone. From the sidelines many urged us to get in the fight, yet no countries were willing to join—even France, who had been with us to enforce the red line, was unwilling. At one point the US had approached Arab partners with the idea for them to invoke "self-defense" and ask us to act against Assad on their behalf, but no one would do so. This is in contrast to when the anti-ISIS campaign started in 2014, when an Arab coalition and a few Europeans joined the US military in conducting airstrikes.

Since August 2014, US and coalition forces have bombed Syria every day—as of this writing, over 3,700 strikes—without any con-sultation or coordination with the Assad regime (there have been over 7,600 coalition airstrikes in Iraq), hitting more than 22,000 tar-gets combined. To put it another way: where the United States flew, it owned the airspace. Given this, in retrospect perhaps conducting airstrikes in Syria was not the grave risk that we feared.

Once the US began attacking ISIS, Assad's air defenses never even challenged American aircraft. Perhaps his unwillingness to con-front us was because we were bombing his enemies; maybe the rea-son was because by that point his forces were degraded and exhausted. Given how rapidly the situation in Syria spiraled out of control—and how hard "contain and mitigate" proved to implement—we should have tested Assad earlier.

Third, once the US started conducting strikes in August 2014, it could have taken greater risks in the targets it hit, which could have done more to make Assad wonder whether eventually he would be next. The political and legal basis for the air campaign was that it was against ISIS, not Assad. But even within those parameters, the US could have chosen targets that were near Syrian positions, or operated closer to regime-controlled territory while warning Assad not to engage us. We found that in the places we were bombing, Syrian planes mostly stayed away, establishing a de facto no-fly-zone over parts of the country. So we could have widened the aperture of the strikes to areas where the regime was fighting the moderate opposition. This would have increased the pressure on the regime—but it also would have exposed us to such risks as civilian casualties and escalation.

Obama acknowledges that perhaps he does not do enough to exploit ambiguity, but remains very skeptical that one can do so while maintaining escalation control. Since it would not be in our interest to escalate, he did not want to put Assad in the position of calling our bluff. Senior military officials were also firmly against this idea. Like the president, they asked what would come next, warning of the threat to US pilots and the likelihood of civilian casualties. Yet while we were all wary of mission creep, so was Assad; we should have run the risks and done more to eat away at his sense of security, perhaps gaining some leverage.

Another idea we should have explored more seriously was the "discrete" use of force at regime targets—not some massive, "shock and awe" air campaign, but precise, tit-for-tat actions against things Assad valued (such as his presidential helicopter fleet, or a favorite residence). This could have been done without attribution. For example, it has been widely reported that on multiple occasions the Israelis proved successful at taking actions against regime targets to eliminate specific threats without escalation. They never claimed credit, but Assad knew what had happened and got the message.

THE ADMINISTRATION'S INCREMENTAL approach to military involvement in Syria was driven by a desire to avoid mistakes. Thinking of the lessons of the Iraq War—and the imperatives of the Long Game—not doing "stupid stuff" made sense (after all, who actually supports doing "stupid stuff?").

But it is worth asking whether the costs of incrementalism have been worth it, and whether by acting in these relatively modest ways—starting the Syrian training a few months earlier, maintaining some presence in Iraq after 2011, initiating airstrikes sooner and, once the bombing began, being a little more creative with targets—the US could have avoided (or at least had a better chance to "contain and mitigate") the massive Syrian refugee crisis or wielded more influence over Russia not to escalate as it did in 2015. None of these steps would have been the kind of game-changer many critics suggest, but even a modest improvement would have been good enough. And in retrospect, they were probably achievable while not undermining the president's larger goals.

Finally, one must ask if the administration erred by focusing so much on Assad's departure—and if, as with Qaddafi in Libya, Obama set for himself the kind of a rhetorical trap he tries hard to avoid, placing too much emphasis on the fate of a single leader, and would have been better off with more flexibility.

As the crackdown in Syria intensified in 2011, the administration initially resisted pressure to call for Assad to step down. Part of this stemmed from the fact that we held on to the hope that Assad would relent on his own. After all, during the previous few years we had experienced a warming in relations with Syria and had just returned the US ambassador to Damascus. In these early days, Assad was still considered by some as a reformer, or at worst an amiable dunce, and hardly viewed as a vicious madman in the mold of Saddam or Qaddafi. By the spring of 2011, the administration had spent two years trying to negotiate a deal between Syria and Israel, and when the protests first erupted it was still considering whether the "Syria Track" of the Middle East peace process was viable.

Such hopes were extinguished by the summer of 2011, when it became clear we had underestimated Assad's brutality and concluded that the opposition would never take a deal with him still in power. Once the administration decided that Assad needed to "step aside," but do so in a way that was managed, it recognized that it would create a gulf between expectations and reality.

The president still believes that calling for Assad's departure is about asserting America's moral authority, and the idea that "if you weren't going to overthrow the regime, you shouldn't have said anything" strikes him as a "weird argument."[21] Yet looking back, some of Obama's top advisers wonder whether they had moved too fast to call for Assad to go—asking if the US would have been better off (and perhaps have had more policy flexibility) if it had stayed silent on the question. Some of my former colleagues now say that, as a practical matter, the US needs to steer away from this kind of "Roman Coliseum" impulse, in which American officials render a thumbs-up or thumbs-down verdict on other leaders.

However even if the administration had remained on the fence about Assad, the opposition inside Syria, as well its regional patrons, would not have. It is for that reason that the Assad regime is the essential driver of the conflict, and why one can't pretend that Assad is part of the solution. Which brings us back to the original dilemma in Syria: the question is not whether Assad should go, but how—and who should take responsibility for the outcome.

WHEN DESCRIBING AMERICA's role in the world, Obama has often pledged that the "tide of war is receding." He has also frequently declared the war in Iraq as "over" and committed to bring the US military role in Afghanistan to an "end." So as American military forces returned to Iraq in 2014 and intensive US airstrikes continued, many argued that Obama had been finally mugged by reality.

Critics asserted that they had been right all along, deriding Obama's past declarations of wars ending as his own "mission accomplished" moment. Most commentators use Syria as the single prism to interpret Obama's approach to the world. As the columnist Roger Cohen argues, "Syria is the question the Obama Doctrine must answer if it is not to be deemed modest to the point of meaninglessness."[22]

Considering the scope and scale of America's military campaign against ISIS in Iraq, Syria, and elsewhere, it is true the tide of war is still with us. In retrospect, some of Obama's declarative rhetoric suggested starker conclusions than actually existed. Each day, thousands of US military personnel take the fight to ISIS, whether by conducting direct military action or by supporting partners and allies on the ground, often at great risk. Given that Obama's strategy is premised on sustainability and patience, this battle will be conducted far into the future. He has always been clear about that fact.

This is where Obama is misunderstood—and, by some, purposely misportrayed. He has never believed in complete US withdrawal from the Middle East or renounced the importance of military power. In words and actions, Obama has made clear his commitment to America's interests and partners in the region, and to defeating ISIS. But he is equally determined not to ruin the country in the process or let the problems of the Middle East become the singular obsession of American foreign policy.

The key is not to allow the "long war" to return as the organizing principle for America in the world, causing everything else—our other interests, our values, our resource decisions—to be swallowed up. This fight must always be waged in the context of the Long Game.

CHAPTER 6

THE BEAR ROARS BACK

When the Russian military escalated its involvement in Syria in September 2015, unleashing a brutal air assault on behalf of the Assad regime, many saw this as a fundamental failure of Obama's approach to Moscow. Coming less than two years after Russia's illegal takeover of Crimea, and amid its ongoing military support for separatists in Ukraine and escalating military threats to America's European allies, the Kremlin's moves stoked tensions between Russia and the West that were reminiscent of the Cold War.

During Obama's first term in office, the "reset" had paid dividends. Over the course of several years, the United States and Russia were able to achieve genuine successes where their interests converged. In 2010, the two countries worked together in the UN to impose the toughest sanctions ever against Iran. They also signed and ratified the "New START" treaty, eliminating a third of their nuclear weapons as a result. They cooperated on shoring up a key supply line for American troops in Afghanistan—the "Northern Distribution Network"—enabling the United States to reduce its reliance for access on a volatile Pakistan. The two countries also increased trade and foreign direct investment, and the United States helped Russia enter the World Trade Organization. And on Libya, they worked together to allow the UN Security Council to authorize the use of force against the Qaddafi regime; Russia's abstention was the first time a Kremlin leader had allowed the UN to authorize a humanitarian intervention (of course this would come back to bite us, as Vladimir Putin was clearly determined never to let such a thing happen again).[1]

But the reset was never mistaken for a honeymoon. Meaningful cooperation existed alongside a pile of disagreements and troubling Russian behavior. Official Russian attitudes about the United States remained laced with grievance and blame, claiming that NATO presented a threat and that Moscow had been repeatedly lied to about the alliance's true intentions and in fact viewed Russia as an enemy (which was, at least up until 2014, not true). Russia also used the reset era to modernize its military and address the shortcomings that had been exposed in the 2008 Georgia War—cutting its bloated ranks and investing in rapidly deployable forces. To display its might, Russia conducted several large-scale exercises involving tens of thousands of troops and featuring provocative scenarios that included a war with NATO-like forces and a simulated nuclear strike on Warsaw.

At the end of 2011, Russian President Dmitri Medvedev announced he would step aside and let Putin, who had been prime minister, return to the presidency. Obama had developed an easy relationship with Medvedev. They were close in age and both lawyers who favored a coolheaded and practical approach. Medvedev seemed to care about his relations with the West and wanted to improve them, and the United States was happy to oblige. There was no question that Putin, even if behind the curtain, remained the country's most powerful person, but we had sought to get as much done with Medvedev as possible.

As Putin reemerged from the shadows, things quickly soured. After Russia's parliamentary elections in December 2011 were marred by reports of fraud and voter intimidation, Putin publicly blamed the United States (specifically, Hillary Clinton) for fomenting public protests. Putin's return as president in 2012 created a heightened atmosphere of conspiracy, resentment, and suspicion with the West, as well as more repression at home. The reset was over.

As THE SITUATION with Russia grew worse, especially after Ukraine exploded in 2014, critics were quick to allege that the reset was a token of American accommodation that Putin had been able to exploit. Yet such assertions don't hold up to scrutiny.

In the quarter century since the Soviet Union collapsed, America's interactions with Russia have followed a familiar cycle. Presidents enter office believing that relations are adrift, so they seek to renew ties and enhance cooperation. But over time tensions rise, engagement ebbs, and critics declare that the initial approach was naïve. This was true for Bill Clinton, who closely cooperated with Yeltsin in the 1990s, only to be later criticized for "losing" Russia; and George W. Bush, who claimed to have looked into Putin's soul in 2001, only to see this ground lost with the Russian invasion in Georgia. Obama's experience followed the same rhythm.[2]

Obama's alleged "weakness" did not drive Putin's aggression. After all, Putin still rolled into Georgia despite years of the Bush administration's supposed "toughness." Moreover, the downturn in relations began almost immediately after Putin reassumed office, with the Obama administration signing sanctions legislation into law, speaking out forcefully about Putin's domestic crackdowns (especially against democracy organizations and those calling for LGBT rights), and canceling planned summits. At the Pentagon, our own modest efforts to develop productive military-to-military relations—exploring joint projects such as counter-terrorism—fizzled out, as the Russians showed little interest and we weren't going to chase them.

Considering what the reset achieved—fewer nuclear weapons; greater international action against countries like Iran, North Korea, and Libya; critical supply routes to American troops in Afghanistan—the US got a lot out of it. It behooves those who believe the reset policies were foolhardy to answer whether we would have been better off without such achievements, or how they could have been otherwise accomplished.

The reset with Russia was always thought of as a temporary measure, a kind of diplomatic phase, not as a lasting new era in the relationship. If the administration erred, it was in allowing the reset to be oversold and, after Putin returned to power in 2012, being too slow to declare it over. As Hillary Clinton recalled, "the reset was not a reward; it was a recognition that America has many important strategic and security interests, and we need to make progress where we can."[3]

RUSSIA'S INVASION OF Ukraine in 2014 and its illegal occupation of Crimea precipitated the worst European security crisis since the demise of the Soviet Union. The Russians attempted to redraw an international border by force, supported rebel groups with military equipment and personnel, and worked to undermine a sovereign government in Kiev. The conflict would cost around 8,000 lives by 2016, and its onset sparked deep worries about what might come next. Would Russia try to take over all of Ukraine, or invade the Baltics, sparking a direct confrontation with NATO? While we were not shocked that Putin felt compelled to do something once his client regime in Kiev had collapsed, we were very surprised that he went as far as he did, gobbling up Crimea and fomenting a violent rebellion in Ukraine's east.

In response, Obama pursued a policy that was firm but precisely calibrated. He warned that escalation would provoke a broader

crisis and give Putin exactly what he wanted: a confrontation between two great powers akin to the Cold War (here it is important
to recall the origins of the Ukraine crisis had nothing to do with
the United States or NATO—it started over steps to bring Ukraine
closer to the European Union).

Even before the Ukraine crisis, Obama never doubted that the
United States had to stand up to Putin. In one meeting soon after
Putin returned as president in 2012, Obama told us the main challenge is to put him in a box to stop making mischief. Yet he struggled with how to send this message in a way the Russian leader
would understand. The president said we have to look him in the
eye—knowingly referring to George W. Bush saying in 2001 that he
had "looked into Putin's eye" and "got a sense of his soul"—and
make clear that if he acted out, there would be consequences.

While many Washington commentators (and some administration officials) clamored for the United States to respond more forcefully, especially by doing a little more military saber-rattling, Obama
resisted. The day after Russia invaded Crimea in early March 2014,
Obama told his national security team that it needed to "right size
our response to actual interests, rather than be side tracked by the
chattering classes."

The heart of this debate within the administration was about the
nature and extent of Russia's threat. Some officials, especially those
in the military, believed Russia was one of the greatest threats the
United States faced. Its military capabilities, combined with its nefarious intentions, could do great harm to American interests.

Obama did not dispute this fact, but saw Russia fundamentally as
a country driven more by weakness than by strength. It was, he said,
a "regional power with a strong military." That did not make Russia
unimportant—it could still do great damage, and history shows that
declining, weak states are more prone to risky behavior and instability
than stronger powers. In considering his options, Obama said he did

not want to make decisions defensively, as though Russia were "ten feet tall," and was wary of turning even small conflicts into old-school superpower showdowns. He also believed that Putin's Russia would not change anytime soon—under the Russia constitution Putin could serve as president until 2024—so the US needed an approach that would endure.

Therefore, the strategy Obama devised to address the Ukraine crisis and the Russia challenge had three components: to punish Russia, to reassure our allies, and to support Ukraine.

FROM RESET TO RESOLVE

The first part of the strategy was to put Russia into the penalty box. This began with relatively easy moves—cancelling planned trips and meetings and severing military contacts, eventually leading to disinviting Russia from high-profile international fora such as the G-8 leaders meeting. Although symbolic, such actions were necessary. We never expected that canceling a meeting would force Putin out of Ukraine, but it certainly would not make him happy. Putin was one of the most image-conscious leaders on the planet, both for himself and his country; he did not spend tens of billions on the 2014 Sochi Winter Olympics just because of his love of sport.

The more tangible punishment came in the form of economic sanctions against dozens of individuals and institutions inside Russia, including the government figures and private sector cronies closest to Putin, such as his chief of staff. By making it hard, if not impossible, for influential Russian leaders to travel, access their money, or do business, the sanctions raised the costs on those calling the shots in Moscow.

Importantly, the sanctions were imposed together with the countries of the European Union, which made their bite far more painful. At the time, many in Washington asserted that the Europeans were too concerned with their deep economic ties to Russia and would never stand with us, chiding Obama for waiting for the Europeans to act (one should note that at every turn, Washington pundits have predicted the Europeans would fold, but they have held firm). But our view was that it was worth taking the time to act in concert with our European allies—both because the sanctions would be more effective and because it would send a strong message of transatlantic unity. Putin wanted to control Ukraine, but the far bigger prize would be to divide the United States from Europe. We needed to stick together.

Obama wanted to ensure that Putin had a way out should he choose to take it. Throughout the crisis, Obama referred to this as the "off-ramp." He wanted to make Russia face a stark choice. If Putin had a change of heart and decided to resolve his issues with Ukraine in a way that upheld the basic rights of sovereignty, independence, and self-determination that the Ukrainian people should enjoy, the United States and the West would welcome Russia back into the fold.

Critics wailed that any discussion of an "off-ramp" was a sign of weakness. But if we did not want to make confrontation inevitable, we needed a way to deescalate the crisis and make clear to Putin there was a path out. Moreover, Obama saw the "off-ramp" as an essential way to strengthen America's hand. If Putin took the offer and relinquished his support for the rebels and returned Crimea to Ukraine, all the better. But in the more likely scenario that he would stay the course, the United States would be in an even better position to rally the world behind a strong response (the logic being that in order to maintain support for tougher measures, we needed to make sure Putin was perceived as the one at fault). It was the same logic the Obama administration applied to the Iranian nuclear threat.

The "off-ramp" was necessary for another reason—to control escalation. Obama recognized that there was an asymmetry of interests in Ukraine, with Russia willing to gamble more. Put simply, Moscow had more at stake. As Obama reportedly said in one meeting, "if I wanted to invade Canada or Mexico, no one could do much about it."[4] If both sides engaged in a tit-for-tat exchange of escalatory policies, inching closer to direct confrontation, this would not be in the US's interest (or Europe's, and especially not in Ukraine's). And concerns about escalation were foremost on Obama's mind when it came to the question of how to help Ukraine defend itself.

THE STRATEGY'S SECOND component was to reassure our European partners, especially with American military power. We needed to make clear to Europe that we had its back.

The heart of the transatlantic security alliance is the mutual pledge to defend one another—that an attack against one is an attack against all—enshrined in "Article Five" of the 1949 NATO Charter. In the days after Russia's takeover of Crimea, the US and other European partners deployed fighter jets, ships, and troops to front-line NATO states bordering Russia, making clear to Moscow not to test our willingness to enforce Article Five.

Obama reaffirmed this pact in a speech during a September 2014 visit to Tallinn, Estonia. In many ways, that address can be read as a bookend to Obama's first speech in Europe, in Germany, over six years before. As a candidate in Berlin, Obama's audience was a rapturous crowd desperate for change. As a president in Tallinn, Obama now spoke to a nervous audience, desperate to hear that the United States stood by them against Russia. He reaffirmed that "solemn duty," stating clearly that the United States would defend the territory of every NATO ally. "If you ever ask again, who will come to help, you'll know the answer," Obama said.

The words were important, but reassurance had to be more, which raised the question of whether and how much more the United States and Europe would step up. The Ukraine crisis generated a surplus of breathless talk about frayed alliances, a vacuum of leadership, and European jitters about American withdrawal. Yet on this score the reality turned out to be better than it seems. While some see the Ukraine crisis and the threat of a resurgent Russia as exposing fundamental weaknesses in the transatlantic security alliance, NATO's response has revealed more of the alliance's strengths than its shortcomings. In fact, events since 2014 have brought about the most significant shift in the transatlantic security relationship since NATO's entry into Afghanistan after 9/11.

It began with the military component. Since the end of the Cold War, American troops have been flowing out of Europe due to smaller budgets and to deal with priorities elsewhere. But from the moment the Ukraine crisis erupted in 2014, US and allied forces have been streaming back into Europe, maintaining a persistent land, air, and sea presence in NATO's eastern front-line states.

For the United States, this includes a persistent rotational presence of troops in Poland and the three Baltic countries of Latvia, Estonia, and Lithuania. The US military is also prepositioning war-fighting equipment like tanks and artillery in those locations—a possibility that an infusion of $1 billion in additional funds from the Congress in 2014, known as the "European Reassurance Initiative," made possible. And in 2016, the administration decided to quadruple its defense spending in Europe—from $789 million to $3.4 billion—with emphasis on strengthening the most vulnerable European partners. The debate is no longer whether the US military should maintain such a robust force presence in Europe, but how large and specifically where it should be.

Along with the stationing of troops, the American and European militaries have pursued an aggressive sequence of major military exercises. The most significant series of American military training in Europe since the end of the Cold War took place in 2015. That summer, approximately 15,000 troops from 19 NATO countries participated in

"Allied Shield," an exercise to enhance interoperability, readiness, and responsiveness. And in the summer of 2016, as many as 12,000 US troops took part in a Polish-led military exercise, dubbed "Anaconda." Such efforts enhance NATO countries' capabilities to work and fight together, making clear to Russia that the alliance's commitment to collective defense remain steadfast.

Beyond these immediate responses, the Ukraine crisis jump-started NATO's discussions about building more military muscle. For years, US defense leaders had been hectoring their European partners to increase military spending, warning of the dangers of a "two-tiered" alliance of NATO haves and have-nots. Too often, this was perceived as more of a theoretical debate against some future, ill-defined foe. But the egregious display of Russian militarism in Ukraine, and later in Syria, caused many NATO partners, particularly countries like Germany, Poland, and the Baltics, to finally step up and invest more in defense (however welcome, this still remains only a modest step forward as too many NATO members still lag behind).

Perhaps most important has been the shift in the debate about the purpose of NATO itself. Until the Ukraine crisis, some wondered if NATO was still relevant at all—questions that seemed to be asked every few years since the end of the Cold War. For example, ahead of the 2014 NATO Summit in Wales, we worried that one of the dominant questions would be what the Alliance's purpose would be after its drawdown from Afghanistan. Yet the crisis in Ukraine (as well as the exploding crisis to Europe's south and the insecurity emanating from North Africa) clearly demonstrated NATO's enduring relevance, galvanizing the US and the Europeans to do more to protect themselves. Vladimir Putin did more to make the transatlantic alliance relevant than any US policymaker could have wished.

THE THIRD PART of the strategy was to support Ukraine. Since 2014 the United States has pledged billions of dollars to help reform and rebuild the Ukrainian economy. It has also provided strong political support, showering the new Ukrainian leadership with high-level visits and attention. Nevertheless, in Washington, the chief metric of support has been the degree to which the Obama administration is willing to provide military assistance.

The context is important. Ukraine was not a country the United States had a particularly close military relationship with. The military was deeply corrupt, and Russia was its closest partner. Ukraine's defense industry, which between 2009–2013 was the eighth largest arms exporter in the world, was closely tied to Russia. During the democratic protests in Ukraine, we were concerned the Ukrainian military would intervene on the side of the Moscow-backed government and crack down on the protestors. Both the secretary of defense and the chairman of the Joint Chiefs called their Ukrainian counterparts to warn them not to intervene, and to their credit, they kept their forces off the streets. Yet after the Russian-backed government fell and the new leadership came to power, we were still wary.

When the new government in Kiev took power, Ukraine's leaders made clear that they wanted our help to make their military more capable and professional. The administration responded by designing a reform program to help them in three ways, starting with providing Ukraine assistance to meet basic needs for its military operations against Russian-backed insurgents. Washington was the first to respond to Ukraine's requests for help, and with over $750 million committed by 2016 in security and technical assistance, it remains by far the single largest donor. This support included rations for deployed military forces and vehicles like Humvees, communications gear, night-vision goggles, helmets, body armor, and surveillance equipment for the border guards.[5]

Such efforts have been criticized as too little and too slow—especially since the US was not providing weapons. Moreover, Washington's careful process and elaborate rules for sending military assistance make quick delivery frustratingly difficult. However, in less than a year, the United States had jump-started its military relationship with Ukraine, committing exponentially more than it had provided in the entire previous decade combined. In the early months of the crisis, we had no budget for Ukraine, so every dollar we used had to be taken from somewhere else. As one of my Pentagon colleagues memorably put it at the time, we were left looking for loose change between the budgetary couch cushions.

That quickly changed. In 2013, the United States spent less than $10 million on security assistance for Ukraine; in 2016, it allocated over $300 million.

Beyond immediate needs, the Ukrainian military required help through training and exercises. NATO and Ukraine had worked together since the mid-1990s, and Ukraine had hosted military exercises with the US and European allies. But prior governments in Kiev, especially under the Moscow-backed regime, never gave priority to NATO interoperability (having compatible equipment and common methods and standards), and they starved the military of proper equipment and training. Since 2014, Ukraine's new leadership has wanted to develop a military oriented toward the West. To do so, the Pentagon started training Ukrainian troops, including a National Guard and special operations forces. It has also built a robust exercise program—including such initiatives as the September 2014 "Rapid Trident" exercise, involving over 1,200 NATO troops on Ukrainian soil. This has helped the Ukrainians improve their ability to defend themselves—and sends an unmistakable signal to Moscow.

Finally, and perhaps of most long-term importance, the United States has embarked on a program to help Ukraine reform—and in some cases, rebuild—its defense institutions. They need advice on how to spend their defense budget more wisely; plan for a new navy (which was swallowed by the Russians in Crimea); and to grow and empower a generation of non-commissioned officers. Ukrainian defense leaders are quite candid that the biggest obstacle to reform is a military mind-set that remains largely oriented toward the Soviet way of doing things, so they want assistance in improving military education.

IS "MORE" STRONGER?

Despite these moves to punish Russia, reassure our allies, and provide Ukraine with political, economic and military support, Obama's response is seen as another example of chronic indecision and weakness. Critics blame the reset as the original sin that gave Putin the incentive to act aggressively, asserting that Obama has compounded the problem by responding tepidly to Putin's annexation of Crimea and support for the rebels in Ukraine's east and by allowing Moscow to gain the upper hand in Syria.

Most critics' arguments can be summed up with two words: "do more." They believe the United States should have been more tough with Russia from the beginning. They believe the United States should have done more to support Ukraine. They believe the United States should have been more involved in the diplomacy to help bring an end to the crisis. They believe the United States should have done more to reassure our NATO partners. And in Syria, they assert the US should have done more to push Russia back.

But what would a policy of "more" look like, and would it have been more effective?

As THE FORMER US ambassador to Russia Michael McFaul points out, Obama's actions are comparable to Ronald Reagan's response to the Soviet-backed crackdown against solidarity in Poland in 1981, when the United States also imposed stiff sanctions on Moscow (but with one big difference—the Reagan administration acted unilaterally, leaving the Europeans incensed). Obama's response was far more robust than George W. Bush's reaction to the Georgia invasion in

2008, Lyndon Johnson's response to the Soviet intervention in Czechoslovakia in 1968, or Dwight Eisenhower's actions after the Soviet invasion of Hungary in 1956.[6]

Most importantly, one wonders how Putin is benefiting from his behavior in Ukraine. Yes, Russia has occupied Crimea and holds sway over seven percent of Ukraine's territory in the East. Both are unacceptable and pressure must stay until they are reversed (and the US should not accept Russia's annexation of Crimea, just as it never accepted the Soviet Union's annexation of the Baltics).

Yet overall, Russia is not stronger as a consequence of Putin's actions. At a time when many Russian officials believe they need to be diversifying their economy, it is contracting at 4% in 2015 numbers. The ruble is at an all-time low. Russia is more isolated in the world community than it has been since the Soviet era. Russia is subject to sanctions applied not just by the United States, but also by its closest trading partners in Europe. And while Russia was once Ukraine's main partner, now the Kiev government is rushing closer toward Europe and the US.

When considering the strategic ledger, it is not clear how Russia has the upper hand. But commentators seem stuck on what McFaul calls the "myth of Putin's strategic genius." Obama is incredulous at critics who say Putin has been outwitting him: "I'm always struck by the degree to which people buy this narrative," Obama says.[7]

Russia's 2015 military escalation in Syria—and sudden deescalation in March 2016—only poured fuel on this fire. Moscow's motivation in Syria is simple: to protect Assad. In Putin's mind, he's defending a basic principle against "outside intervention" to bring down an allied government—as he has angrily watched what has happened over the last 15 years to former Russian allies like Serbia, Iraq, Libya and Ukraine. While the scale of Russia's military role in the Syrian conflict became far greater—with more than four thousand troops and fifty combat aircraft involved—it was hardly new. Russia has been there from the beginning of the crisis as one of

Assad's only allies and chief weapons suppliers. Russian military personnel have been on the ground throughout (after all, that was key to the safe removal of Syria's chemical weapons).

Seen this way, Putin's moves have been driven primarily by fear and weakness, not confidence and strength. He saw his only ally left in the Middle East on the ropes, and therefore Russia had to come to its defense. "The fact that Putin had to send his own troops and own aircraft and invest in this massive military strength," Obama said, "it was a testament to the weakness of Assad's position." Russia wants to maintain the only military outpost it has in the region, anchored by a key naval facility in Tartus, Syria. Beyond that, Obama asked, "what is it that Russia thinks it gains if it gets a country that has been completely destroyed as an ally, that it now has to perpetually spend billions of dollars to prop up?" [8]

With military escalation, Russia showed it could put some points on the scoreboard. Putin's actions have maintained the status quo and saved Assad (so far). But at what cost?

As in Ukraine, it is hard to see how this improves Putin's strategic position. His endgame is hard to discern. Perhaps, some argue, Putin just wants to be geopolitically relevant. Or he has his eyes on a bigger prize: by stepping in where the United States has refused, Russia is trying to fill a leadership vacuum in the Middle East.

However, Putin's open alliance with Iran, Hezbollah, and Assad only isolates Russia in the region. Going after the very Syrian opposition that countries such as Saudi Arabia, Qatar, the UAE, and Turkey have expended tremendous resources in trying to supply—and propping up a regime that is Israel's sworn enemy—is hardly a winning strategy to become the dominant outside power in the region. Moreover, it seems likely that Russia's continued support for Assad will continue to boomerang back on Moscow by making it an even more enticing target for Sunni extremists, as the October 2015 terrorist attack on the Russian civilian airliner over Sinai made clear.

While Russia's military escalation has bolstered Assad, it has only made Syria worse—and thus increased refugee flows to Europe, which Putin likely sees as a positive side effect (some have called this Putin's "militarization of migration," although this probably gives him too much credit for strategic intent). In response, Obama has avoided a knee-jerk reaction and instead practiced strategic patience.

Many foreign policy pundits seemed to be fixing for a fight with Putin. And given his behavior, such a fight is tempting. Yet as in Ukraine, by acting defensively Putin got himself into a situation that will continue to be costly. "Putin acted in Ukraine in repsonse to a client state that was about to slip out his grasp, [and] he improvised in a way to hang on to his control there," Obama told Jeffrey Goldberg. "He's done the exact same thing in Syria, at enormous cost to the well-being of his own country."[9]

This is why, in Syria as in Ukraine, Obama has been determined to make America's response to Russia meaningful yet proportional. He doesn't see it as a return to the Cold War of two countries of equal clout or capability, which is exactly the kind of status Putin craves. "This is not some superpower contest," Obama has said. "And anybody that frames it in that way isn't paying attention to what is happening on the chessboard."[10]

THE OBAMA ADMINISTRATION has also grappled with whether to "do more" to enable Ukraine to stand up against Russia. This was the crux of the heated debate over whether the United States should provide weapons to Ukraine that came to a head in 2015.

Simply put, the Ukrainians were outgunned. They suffered severe losses in the early days of the fighting, and with the Russians on the side of the separatists, it was never going to be a fair fight. In the initial days of the crisis the Ukrainians gave the Pentagon long lists of what military equipment they wanted, which seemed to be just about everything—from blankets to fighter jets. When we asked them to prioritize what they needed, we would often get different answers depending on which officials we spoke with. While we agreed to provide nonlethal support and start training (the latter more important over the long-term), our deliberations became knotted over the question of lethal assistance.

This was one of the few occasions I can recall in the Obama administration in which just about every senior official was for doing something that the president opposed. He had many reasons. Because Russia would simply counter with even more of its own assistance to the rebels, the president was skeptical that providing lethal support would make a huge difference in changing the military balance. And he was most worried that such support would escalate the crisis, only increasing the bloodshed or, worse, giving Putin a pretext to go further and invade all of Ukraine. Such concerns were shared by key European governments, especially the Germans (who were vital to the sanctions and diplomacy) but even the usually hard-line Baltic countries, who feared Russian retaliation.

Obama supported the Ukrainian leaders, yet I think he has never been entirely comfortable with them. In deciding whether the US should do more, he wants to know whether the Ukrainians were truly committed to reform. This was often hard to see. Obama and the new Ukrainian president, the former candy tycoon Petro Poroshenko, had a difficult first meeting in Warsaw in 2014, and his concerns about the Ukrainians were compounded when Poroshenko visited Washington in September 2014 and gave a speech before Congress criticizing the administration for not giving lethal assistance. I remember reflecting at the time that Poroshenko had received some bad advice from his allies in Washington if he thought that the best way to get the administration to do more would be to belittle the support that he was getting.

Obama also worried about the potential unintended consequences of providing lethal assistance. After the MH-17 civilian airliner was shot down over the skies of Ukraine by Russian-backed separatists in July 2014, killing nearly 300 civilians, Obama privately pointed out that this kind of thing can happen when you provide lethal assistance to a group that you don't entirely control (the same argument applied about whether to support the Libyan opposition in 2011 or the Syrian opposition in 2012).

The president said it was unlikely that Putin intended for a civilian airliner to be shot down, but that his support for the rebels had, in fact, led to it. Obama knew that he too would be accountable for the way that any assistance the US provided would be used. That said, this was not an ironclad rule. At the exact moment in the summer of 2014 that we were carefully considering every last ounce of assistance we'd be providing to the Ukrainians, and whether any of it could risk escalation or misuse, we were vigorously trying to resupply the Kurds in Iraq, another non-state actor, with thousands of tons of ammunition and weapons to assist them in their fight against ISIS.

I came to believe that it made sense to provide Ukraine with some lethal capabilities, such as Javelin anti-tank missiles (although I too was initially worried about escalation, I concluded that the risks were manageable). But at the same time, I never thought providing lethal assistance would be the decisive step that some of the proponents claimed, especially those outside government. Such weapons would take care of some Russian-supplied armor, raising the costs for Moscow and boosting Ukrainian morale. However, given the time it takes to procure and deliver such assistance, as well as the limited quantities under consideration, they would not have altered the military balance substantially.

Sometimes the desire to control escalation went too far, causing the White House to litigate every step we could take to support the Ukrainians. One such episode from the spring of 2014 bordered on the comical. After we had decided to provide non-lethal military assistance to the Ukrainians, the question was how we would get it there. The quickest route would be via military aircraft, but senior

White House officials were concerned that the image of US military cargo planes with their "grey tails" could be provocative to Moscow. After hours of meetings on this subject, we finally decided to transport the materiel by trucking it into Ukraine overland. It seemed a bit too cautious, but problem solved.

A few weeks later, I arrived in Kiev for my first visit to conduct defense talks with the Ukrainian leadership (I flew commercial). After we landed at the airport and were taxiing toward the gate, I looked out the window and was surprised to find sitting on the runway two hulking US Air Force C-17s, with their grey tails in full glory for all to see. It was the communications and security advance team for Vice President Biden, who was scheduled to stop in Kiev a few days later. In all our earnest deliberations back in Washington about how to deliver nonlethal assistance, no one stopped to think that the mere fact the vice president was traveling to Kiev could create the very "escalatory" image that we were supposed to avoid. If the Russians noticed, they didn't care.

CRITICS ALSO HAVE clamored for Obama to "do more" to reassure America's Eastern and Central European allies, who justifiably worry that they are next in Putin's crosshairs. These allies know that most of the reassurance measures and the funding for them are temporary. With President Putin expected to stay in office into the 2020s, Europeans want to secure a more lasting American commitment. To be sure, there is more the United States can do here—such as adding to the troops and military capabilities it has already deployed, or making its "persistent" rotational troop presence a permanent one.

But the challenge for President Obama has been—as it will be for his successor—how to do "more" of this while simultaneously addressing other global priorities, especially addressing the security needs in the Middle East and executing the rebalance to Asia amid resource constraints. In the three most important strategic arenas for the

United States—Europe, the Middle East, and Asia—our partners are anxious about the future, and all want more of the US. But they have maximalist desires that are impossible for the US to meet equally. Just as the world is asking for more, the dynamic in Washington leaves us with less. Obama has tried to reassure partners by balancing these competing demands and trade-offs in a way that is sustainable. Once again, doing more of everything is not a strategy.

FINALLY, THERE IS the argument that in Ukraine the US has ceded too much control to the Europeans (especially the Germans) and should have asserted more leadership in the diplomacy with the Russians. The United States has been an active and essential player behind the diplomatic scenes. But for at least three reasons, Obama was determined to avoid getting drawn into the direct US–Russian negotiation over Ukraine.

First, he believed that doing so would give Putin exactly the superpower status he wanted. Second, he believed that having the Europeans in the lead would send a stronger message of unity, in particular, because the Europeans had greater economic leverage over Russia. Moreover, having German Chancellor Angela Merkel in charge would increase the chances that the European Union member states would support and sustain tough sanctions, with Germany corralling and pressuring other countries (which is what happened). And third, there was a question of bandwidth. It was hard to reconcile the time and energy required to lead the diplomacy on Ukraine with the demands on the United States elsewhere around the world, especially after ISIS took over much of Iraq and Syria in the summer of 2014. For all these reasons, the division of labor seemed sensible—and most likely to bring the desired result.

TO SUM UP, one can see how Obama's response to the Ukraine crisis, Russia's escalation in Syria, and Moscow's challenge generally is another example of the Long Game. The steps taken so far against Russia have been more robust than those of most of Obama's predecessors when faced with similar circumstances. These moves have been aimed at achieving a sustainable support relationship for Ukraine that will show benefits over time. They have been designed to reassure and bolster our NATO partners in a way that is balanced and sustainable. The US has shown a willingness to let the Europeans lead in diplomacy, while working vigorously behind the scenes to husband its diplomatic resources for other demands around the world.

When comparing Russia's recent behavior in Ukraine and Syria alongside the US approach, one sees two starkly contrasting approaches to wielding influence—and very different perceptions of what it means to be "strong." With Russia's military incursions, Putin is trying to protect a sphere of influence and create facts on the ground. Yet as Obama has often put it, Syria is not a great "prize," and Russia's actions leave it reviled and isolated in the region and around the world. The fact Putin "invades Crimea or is trying to prop up Assad doesn't suddenly make him a player," Obama says.[11] While such actions may create the veneer of strength in the moment, leading some to conclude Obama has been outfoxed and outmanned, it is difficult to argue that Russia's decisions improve its position for the future.

As leaders, Obama and Putin could not be more different. If Putin has his own version of the long game, it is hard to observe. He is no great strategist. He doesn't play chess—he plays checkers, or maybe just rolls the dice, all with an almost cartoonish machismo. Few believe that's a recipe for future success. Yet still critics urge Obama to be "strong" and make the kinds of choices that would cause him to be, well, more like Putin.

CHAPTER 7

PLAYING ALL
FOUR QUARTERS

Of all the issues Obama inherited, he was most determined to test a new approach with Iran. The position the United States found itself in at the beginning of his first term illustrated one of the most troubling of George W. Bush's legacies: by acting in a way it thought "tough," refusing even to try to talk with Iran, the Bush administration left the US with little leverage and few tools to halt Tehran's efforts toward developing a nuclear weapon. The "axis of evil" rhetoric sounded strong, but had only served to back the United States into a corner.

When Obama came into office, Iran had the wind at its back. There were many reasons: the Iraq War had taken out Tehran's main enemy, Saddam Hussein, only to replace his regime with a sympathetic, Shia-led government. Iran's coffers were flush with oil revenues, which it poured into modernizing its military and projecting its nefarious influence throughout the Middle East. Iran was fueling its main proxies—Hezbollah in Lebanon and Hamas in the Gaza Strip—each of which posed a grave threat to Israel.

Iran's nuclear capabilities were barreling forward unchecked. When the Bush administration came into office in 2001, Iran did not have any centrifuges for enriching uranium, one of the two pathways to make enough nuclear material for a bomb. By 2003, it had around 100 centrifuges, and by 2009, it had over 5,000. Iran denied that this kind of crash development was for weapons, an assertion few believed—after all, it kept most of its nuclear infrastructure hidden from the world in hardened bunkers buried deep inside remote mountains. If Iran got a nuclear weapon, it would be a game-changer for the Middle East, threatening America's closest partners and potentially setting off a regional nuclear arms race. While these concerns were widely shared around the world, most saw the US policy as the main obstacle to addressing the issue.

Without a US-led diplomatic process to pressure Iran to come clean and cease its nuclear weapons activities, Obama found his options limited. Each carried substantial risks: he could gamble that the status quo would lead Iran to change its mind (which we thought was a fantasy); he could accept an Iran with nuclear weapons (which would be deeply destabilizing); he could use military force to set back Iran's program (something we were neither sure would work nor adequately prepared for at the time); or he could try to change the game by trying a new approach (which might not work).

Faced with these choices, the president was determined to make a major push on Iran. Yet while the administration agreed on what it wanted to achieve, the way to get there was very complex, and Obama's strategy shaped nearly every aspect of his foreign policy. Robert Gates accurately describes the diplomatic and military play to deal with Iran's nuclear program as a kind of national security black hole, "directly or indirectly pulling into its gravitational force our relationships with Europe, Russia, China, Israel, and the Gulf Arab states."[1]

THE DUAL TRACK

The US needed to manufacture some leverage, so Obama pursued a "dual track" policy of engagement and pressure. Each part of the strategy was essential to the other, requiring careful choreography and following an intricate logic. It was based on a core assumption: by refusing to try to engage Iran in meaningful discussions, the United States had allowed Tehran to gain the upper hand by portraying Washington as the problem, making it harder to rally the world to bring meaningful pressure.

Therefore, instead of being a sign of a weakness, engagement was the key ingredient to gaining strength: by engaging, the United States would put the onus on Iran and test whether it was serious in proving its nuclear efforts were for peaceful purposes. If it was (which we doubted), all the better, and we could proceed with negotiations. If it wasn't (which we expected), then we would be able to use its intransigence to expose its true intentions. That would give the United States critical leverage to go to our partners—especially in Europe and Russia—to join us in making Iran pay a price for not cooperating. In this way, engagement was a form of pressure required to reposition the US, now giving it the upper hand.

For decades the United States had had its own economic sanctions against Tehran, but without the rest of the world aboard, the Iranians had not felt the pinch. They needed to face a meaningful choice. A higher price might force Iran to change its calculus and come to the table, or it could live in greater isolation with its nuclear ambitions frozen in place. But if that didn't work, then we could fall back on the option of using force—which by then the US military would have had more time to train and prepare for—with greater legitimacy and support because we had first tried the diplomatic route.

This was a quintessential Long Game play—and to use one of the sports analogies Obama likes, it required playing all four quarters of the game. Patience and thick skin were needed to see it through, as critics would pick apart every move and try to throw the strategy off course. Success would not come instantly; with progress coming incrementally, at any given moment it would often be hard to see if the strategy was working or not.

ENGAGEMENT WAS THE first step, one Obama took just minutes after being sworn in as president. In his first inaugural address, he offered an "outstretched hand" to foes like Iran. From that point forward, Obama worked to show that the United States was willing to talk, pursuing a series of unprecedented moves. He took to the airwaves and spoke directly to the Iranian people; sent letters to Iran's supreme leader with an offer to improve relations; and for the first time in decades allowed senior diplomats to meet alone with their Iranian counterparts to discuss possible solutions. Predictably, the Iranians resisted such overtures, responding to Obama with their customary anti-American bombast and rejecting steps designed to test their claims about their nuclear program's true intent.

Along with using Iran's belligerence as a way to create leverage, Obama also sought to expose Tehran's deception. For years the US intelligence community had been monitoring the construction of what was suspected to be a secret nuclear enrichment facility deep in a mountain near the Iranian city of Qom. The Iranians had lied about the existence of such a facility, and once the intelligence agencies had enough confidence in their evidence (a process they spent a lot of time carefully completing, lest they repeat their failures in Iraq), the administration decided to blow the whistle.

In September 2009 Obama joined with his counterparts from the UK and France to expose the revelation, sending a shockwave throughout the world and throwing Tehran back on its heels. Even those who tended to give Iran the benefit of the doubt, such as Russia, were surprised and angered. Exposing Iran's deceptions, combined with Iran's failure to respond to Obama's engagement overtures, had laid the groundwork to increase the pressure.[2]

Tom Donilon, the national security advisor who played the central role designing and implementing this approach inside the White House, described this as the "simultaneous multivector pressure strategy." While this label did not exactly roll off the tongue, it accurately described the diversity and relentlessness with which the United States squeezed Iran as a way to gain leverage.

ECONOMIC PRESSURE WAS the key vector. By the end of 2009 the Obama administration had launched an intensive diplomatic effort to impose new international sanctions against Iran. These measures, which Secretary Clinton dubbed "crippling sanctions," added up to an unprecedented framework of commercial and financial penalties. Imposed with the authority of the UN Security Council, they closed Iran's oil spigot and made it harder for Tehran to conduct business and banking worldwide.

Securing this global consensus took months of painstaking negotiations. Many of America's partners were skittish about taking these steps because of the financial costs they would suffer, in some cases losing billions of dollars in trade. Clinton worked tirelessly on this effort, cajoling and arm-twisting large powers such as Russia and China as well as appealing to smaller countries like Uganda and Lebanon. Looking back, this was the most successful US-led effort to bring the world around such a tough, costly, and risky policy in two decades, since the George H.W. Bush administration built a coalition against Saddam Hussein in 1990.

These steps had a profound impact on Iran's economy, which contracted severely. Inflation spiked by more than 40 percent, and the value of the Iranian currency plummeted. Oil exports fell by more than half, costing Iran tens of billions of dollars. Foreign investors and big multinational companies fled. Prices skyrocketed. As evidence of this pain, Iran's leadership dropped its usual defiant assertions about their resilience and began to complain about the injustice of such an "economic assault."

With this achievement, the United States finally had the upper hand. As Clinton later reflected, "During the Bush years Iran had managed to play the world's great powers against one another and avoided serious international sanctions for its misdeeds. The Obama administration changed that."[3] But leverage from sanctions, however crippling, would not be enough. We needed to add military pressure as well.

OBAMA HAD ALWAYS made clear that for the "dual-track" strategy to succeed, the prospect of military force had to be real. "All options on the table" became the shorthand phrase Obama used over and over to make this point. While we hoped that diplomacy and sanctions would be enough to end Iran's nuclear threat, we needed the kind of insurance only military force could provide. The United States aimed to make clear that it could not accept merely "containing" Iran's nuclear threat, but would take necessary steps to "prevent" it. Iran had to understand that if diplomacy failed and they would not give up peacefully, the US military had other ways to take care of the problem.

This was more than a matter of semantics. Iran, and concerned partners like Israel and the Arab Gulf states, parsed each word uttered by the president and every other senior American official, looking closely for any sign of weakness. They wondered whether the leader who was working so hard to get the US out of wars would be willing to risk starting another. Complicating things further, they listened to senior American military and intelligence officials warn of the negative consequences of military action against Iran. While truthful, such statements planted seeds of doubt about whether the United States would ever pull the trigger.

The president and his senior team went to great lengths to express his resolve to take military action, repeatedly asserting the "all options" mantra. Obama stressed this was not a "bluff." The United States needed to show its partners in Israel and the Gulf Arab states that it would be there for them. But words of resolve could only take things so far; he knew that the United States had to demonstrate resolve, which started with ensuring it had the military capability in place to execute any option he ordered.

THE PROBLEM WAS that as late as 2010, we were not ready. Although over time the US military could certainly muster the capacity to set back Iran's nuclear weapons ambitions, thus far it had neither readied the capability nor developed the adequate planning and processes to act quickly in the event that the president decided that diplomacy had failed or because something forced our hand (like an Israeli strike). As Defense Secretary Gates recalled, "There had been no discussion in either the Bush or Obama administrations...about momentous decisions that might be required within minutes if serious shooting broke out in the Gulf."[4]

During his first year in office, Obama directed the Pentagon to get ready for such a contingency, making clear that if he ever decided to strike, he did not want to be told it would take months to plan and prepare. Gates also sounded the alarm that the administration needed to think through how it would respond to contingencies such as an Iranian attack on US interests or an Israeli attack on Iran. How would the administration respond to an Iranian provocation? Would it back up Israel if Israel launched a surprise attack? For months Obama's senior team pored over such questions, the result being what the Pentagon called a series of "break glass" plans to handle them.[5]

In addition to issues of planning and procedure, we needed to do more to ensure the military option was not an idle threat. This required having operational capabilities both to deter Iran from lashing out and, critically, to destroy Iran's nuclear facilities if so ordered. Maintaining the necessary forces in the region—or military "posture"—required a lot of tough resource decisions. One of the ironies of reducing the American military presence in Iraq was that it became harder to ensure the US maintained enough firepower nearby to deal with Iran. The White House was intensely focused on what we described as "setting the theater," often pushing the Pentagon to keep certain capabilities—like personnel, ships, and aircraft—in place when they were scheduled to deploy elsewhere. The result was a robust enough force presence to make good on Obama's pledge that he was not bluffing.

Although the administration tended to let the American military presence speak for itself—Obama once said it wasn't "sound policy" to advertise "what our intentions are"—at times we did speak more openly about it to send a message. One important example was a December 2013 speech by then-Secretary of Defense Hagel in Bahrain.

At that time, with diplomacy with Iran getting some traction, we thought it necessary to make clear that nothing had changed in the US military posture and that "all options" remained on the table (in fact, throughout the negotiations, the Pentagon had never been instructed to change anything about its preparations against Iran). So, in an unusual step, the defense secretary specifically itemized the capabilities the US military had in and around the Persian Gulf, including over 35,000 military personnel, the most advanced fighter aircraft, and over forty naval ships (including an aircraft carrier strike group). Even with American forces out of Iraq, withdrawing from Afghanistan, rebalancing to Asia, and facing budget cuts at home, we wanted to show that the United States had some heft near to Iran. This robust footprint—which is significantly greater than what was deployed in the Middle East before 9/11—also contradicts the notion that the US has "retreated" from the region (and these numbers increased when the campaign against ISIS began in 2014).

BEING PREPARED WAS about more than having the right weapons in place. Because Iran was constantly developing new ways to hide or defend its nuclear sites (as the discovery of the Qom facility illustrated), the US military also had to keep pace by developing its own innovative means to conduct successful strikes. To do so, the Obama administration invested heavily in special weapons to penetrate Iran's defenses. The most notable of these is a fifteen-ton bomb, the "Massive Ordnance Penetrator," more commonly referred to as the "MOP." Designed to be dropped from an aircraft flying at 20,000 feet, this massive weapon had remarkable accuracy and the ability to burrow hundreds of feet underground. It was the ultimate bunker-buster.

Although many of the MOP's details were shrouded in secrecy inside the government—any information about it had to be carried around the Pentagon inside a locked bag—its existence was not a secret, and it was the subject of numerous press accounts and one could even see it in action on YouTube in videos posted by press outlets and defense industry trade publications. And it was hardly a mystery what it was built for.

Ashton Carter, who served as the Pentagon's weapons acquisition chief before becoming Obama's fourth secretary of defense, explained to a journalist in 2015 that the weapon was specifically designed for such deep underground targets, and that the investment in the "MOP was a directive from on high," meaning from the White House. "And I'm still under instructions to refine it [and] improve it," Carter said, at the cost of millions of dollars. When asked by another journalist if such refinements enabled the MOP to destroy facilities like those underground in Iran, Carter said simply, "Yes. That's what it was designed to do."[6]

While we hoped such steps would convince the leadership in Tehran not to test America's resolve, the most discerning—and skeptical—observers sat in Tel Aviv.

MANAGING ISRAELI ANXIETIES

The Israelis' discomfort with Obama's approach toward Iran was understandable. After all, a nuclear weapon in the hands of a regime that had pledged to wipe Israel off the map was an existential threat. Iran had skillfully manipulated the international community for years. In addition to nuclear weapons, Iran fueled Israel's enemies through its support of terrorist proxies and its proliferation of conventional weapons.

Yet because of divergent interests, the Israelis also didn't fully trust the administration. They worried that in Obama's eagerness to get a deal, the United States would leave them vulnerable. At times such doubts led them to consider taking matters into their own hands and attacking Iran, which on at least one occasion they were only weeks away from doing. Both governments believed in a policy of *preventing* Iran from getting a nuclear weapon, as opposed to containment, but they profoundly disagreed on how to execute it. These differences—which simmered throughout Obama's presidency but boiled over when the Israelis actively opposed the 2015 nuclear deal—defined what has been one of the most turbulent periods in US–Israel relations since Israel's independence in 1948.

The honest policy disagreement was exacerbated at the highest levels by a combustible mixture of personalities and politics. That started at the top, with the enormously complicated relationship between Obama and Israeli Prime Minister Benjamin Netanyahu. Obama believed deeply in the need to maintain a strong US–Israel relationship, and he admired the Israelis' historic resilience, especially in the face of terrorism. But he was skeptical of offering uncondi-tional support. And he neither fully trusted Netanyahu nor was impressed by his bombast. Netanyahu clearly valued close ties with the United States, but his and his team's willingness to play in US politics to weaken Obama or limit his choices—whether that meant currying favor with Mitt Romney during the 2012 election or lobbying Congress directly to reject the Iran deal—only fueled the mutual suspicion.

The long-time Middle East negotiator and former Obama White House official Dennis Ross accurately observed that inside the administration, there were two mindsets about how to handle Israel. Some believed the relationship was fundamentally competitive, thinking that Israel took from the United States but offered little in return. Others saw the relationship as fundamentally cooperative, believing that ever closer collaboration was in American interests. While both mindsets had powerful advocates, Obama's policy ended up being an unusual blending of the two, which often left outside observers (including many Israelis) confused. The result was a US–Israeli relationship that was at once engulfed in bitter distrust and, in critical ways, the strongest it has ever been.[7]

THE DRAMA AND public discord masked how extraordinarily close the US–Israeli security relationship had become. Those of us working below the political storm and in the bureaucratic trenches certainly felt this way. But more significantly, so did those who brought historical perspective. Robert Gates, who had played a key role in the relationship while working for eight presidents of both political parties, recalled in his memoirs that "no US administration ha[s] done more, in concrete ways, for Israel's defense than Obama's." Dennis Ross, who also was at the center of US–Israel policy for decades and helped shape the modern strategic relationship during the Reagan administration, observed that "the scope of the security relationship went beyond what any previous administration had put in place."[8]

It's easy (and perhaps self-serving) for American officials to make such assertions. So listen to Israeli leaders. Former defense minister Ehud Barak has said there is more "intimacy" between the two militaries than ever before. Current defense minister Moshe Ya'alon describes the relationship as "deep and intimate, and unprecedented in its scope." Ron Dermer, Israel's ambassador in Washington who has been in the middle of the most heated recent political imbroglios, heralds how the Obama administration has "upgraded security cooperation" with the Israelis. And Netanyahu himself called the two countries' defense ties a "remarkable partnership."

At the core of this is the significant security assistance the United States provides the Israeli military—well over $100 billion in total during the past few decades, and increasing in the past few years. Such support is bipartisan: in 2007 President George W. Bush agreed to provide Israel with $30 billion for a decade, which Obama has agreed to extend and will likely increase in the coming years. Annually, this adds up to over half of the total US support for foreign militaries worldwide.

This assistance provided Israel with the most advanced weapons capabilities, from precision munitions to sophisticated fighter aircraft. Israel is the only country in the region that will get the high-performance capabilities like the F-35 Joint Strike Fighter (which is the future of the US's own air force) and the first country in the world that the US agreed to provide the tilt-rotor V-22 Osprey. Perhaps the most famous example of US–Israel security cooperation is in missile defense, where the two sides have worked together to develop and finance the Iron Dome system, which has proved its effectiveness in protecting Israeli cities from Hamas rockets.

Yet the strength of these ties goes beyond money and hardware. It includes policy, such as the common interest in fighting extremists, maintaining a strong relationship with Jordan and ensuring that Israel maintains its "qualitative military edge", or "QME," in the region—which is policy-speak for the idea that Israel has the capability to protect itself, by itself, against larger-sized militaries in the region. The former Israeli ambassador to the US Michael Oren accurately describes QME as the "DNA of the US–Israel Alliance." During the Obama years, the level of consultation, coordination, and sharing on these issues between US and Israeli military and intelligence officials has been unprecedented.[9]

Ironically, the military relationship was undergirded by what many perceived to be the most brittle area of the American-Israeli partnership under Obama: the personal relations among leaders. For all four of Obama's defense secretaries—Bob Gates, Leon Panetta, Chuck Hagel, and Ashton Carter—the relationships with their Israeli counterparts have been among the closest of any around the world.

This is something I saw up close during many hours of meetings and phone calls Secretaries Panetta and Hagel had with their counterparts (and I spent more time with the Israelis than any other foreign counterparts). Panetta and Barak had worked closely together since the Clinton administration and had an easy relationship. And Hagel, who before taking office endured harsh criticism alleging a lack of support for Israel, met more often with Defense Minister Ya'alon than any other counterpart; they developed an especially warm relationship, and upon leaving office Ya'alon publicly praised Hagel as a "true friend" of Israel. This close partnership has continued under Carter (although Ya'alon had a less charitable view of Secretary of State John Kerry, exacerbated by their differences over the Israeli-Palestinian peace process).

DESPITE SUCH STRONG security ties, the Israelis worried that Iran's progress toward a nuclear weapon would outpace our diplomatic efforts to stop it. They warned that Iran's successes in defending its nuclear facilities, combined with its advances in acquiring just enough nuclear material and technological know-how, would provide what they called a "zone of immunity," in which it would be too late for the military option to work. They argued that Iran could then remain on the cusp of getting a bomb without actually crossing the line, effectively keeping the gun cocked and loaded while evading the consequences. The Israelis found the prospect of living with such an enduring threat unacceptable, and were itching to take action.

Inside the administration, there was a lot of nervous speculation about whether the Israelis would strike. Our worries became especially intense in the spring and summer of 2012, when the Israelis began talking more openly about the need to act. We sought to use our close ties to reassure them, but wondered whether this would be enough—and in several instances, we were on edge that an attack was imminent.

One such moment came in the summer of 2012, when Ehud Barak called to say he needed to come to the Pentagon immediately to talk with Secretary Panetta about Iran. The next day, Barak joined Panetta and several of us for breakfast in the defense secretary's spacious Pentagon office. In a discussion that lasted the entire day, the Israeli defense minister explained that the Netanyahu government's concerns about Iran had reached a tipping point.

The problem, Panetta recalled saying to Barak, "is that if you attack them now, you can only set them back by a few years...you'll give them a black eye. We, on the other hand, can deliver the knockout punch." Moreover, he warned Barak that an Israeli action would have the unintended consequence of undermining the effectiveness of any American military option. [10]

Barak still questioned whether Obama had the resolve ever to take action. For added insurance, he asked for the United States to give Israel the capability to do this on its own. Barak was disappointed not to get even more, but promised to return home to try to make the case for delay. In the end we averted this crisis, but knew that another one was just around the corner.

THE DUALITY OF Obama's approach to Israel—heated political competition and suspicion alongside unprecedented strategic collaboration and trust—often left it open to misinterpretation. This was especially the case when, as happened all too often, our differences exploded into public.

At times the temptation to score political points proved overwhelming, causing frictions that could have been avoided. But even when disagreements were at their most open and bitter at the political level, especially over what to do about Iran, the core security relationship never suffered. It only became stronger. The criticism that Obama sometimes mishandled the Israelis is warranted. Too often, the president and those aides closest to him let their personal pique get the better of them, leading to unnecessary squabbles and slights. But critics often overlook that what matters most for the long term—the depth and breadth of the core security partnership—has never wavered.

GULF PRESSURE

The Israelis weren't the only ones in the Middle East who were suspicious about where our diplomacy with Iran would lead. We also had a lot of work to do with our partners in the Persian Gulf, especially in Saudi Arabia and the UAE.

The strategic convergence between the Israelis and the Gulf partners over Iran was significant. They both viewed Iran as an existential enemy intent on becoming a regional hegemon. Like the Israelis, America's Gulf partners were suspicious about our diplomatic effort, preferring the United States to take military action—or, in the memorable words of the late Saudi King Abdullah Al Saud, to "cut the head off the snake." Short of this, they were looking for reassurance in two ways. First, for the US to prevent Iran from getting a weapon (without much of their help, by the way); and second—in the event we actually succeeded and achieved a nuclear deal—to assuage their fears about an Iran unburdened of sanctions. So just as Obama set out to strengthen the US–Israeli security relationship, he also pursued policies to revitalize Persian Gulf security.

Yet this, too, unfolded in a contradictory way. While Obama pressed to do more for Gulf security, and worked intensively to engage with their leaders, he also expressed great frustration with some Gulf allies for their reckless behavior (such as pouring cash and weapons into Syria and Libya with little regard where they ended up), political repression, and endemic misogyny. Obama and some of his senior aides also resented the role the Gulf countries played in US politics, sometimes blaming them for undue influence in the Washington foreign policy community (a claim that, I believe, is overblown).

Beyond maintaining America's military presence in the Middle East, the Obama administration sought to improve the defense capabilities of our Gulf partners and shift the regional military balance away from Iran. Since 2007, the Pentagon has approved arms sales worth more than $85 billion to the GCC states, nearly as much as in the previous fifteen years combined. In 2011, the administration completed one of the largest arms deals in US history, a sale of F-15 fighter jets to Saudi Arabia. In 2013, the Pentagon announced the $11 billion-plus sale of the most modern "standoff" weapons (missiles that could be fired at a long distance far out of range of counterattack) to Saudi Arabia and the UAE. In 2014, the United States and Qatar signed an $11 billion deal for Patriot missile defense batteries, Apache helicopters, and Javelin anti-tank missiles.

The US also worked to enable the Gulf states to cooperate more closely together. Compared to Europe and Asia, the Middle East lacks a common security mechanism. While there are many reasons for this (particularly in a region characterized by mutual suspicion and fierce independence), the Obama team took steps to try to enhance regional cooperation.

For example, we concluded we needed a venue where the United States and its Gulf partners could meet as a group to discuss shared security concerns. So the administration established a high-level "Security Cooperation Forum" to discuss concerns like Iran. Building on this effort, in May 2014 then-Secretary of Defense Hagel helped organize a meeting in Jeddah, Saudi Arabia, with his Gulf defense minister partners. Hosted by then-Crown Prince and now King Salman of Saudi Arabia, the event helped lay the policy foundation for the Camp David summit of Gulf leaders Obama organized in May 2015, who met again in Saudi Arabia in 2016. At these meetings, officials discussed ways to improve the Gulf partners' ability to work together on future threats, including maritime, cyber, and air and missile defense. This included proposals for them to acquire US defense capabilities by pooling resources and making common investments.

Such arms sales raised eyebrows in Israel. As a result we had to spend a lot of energy to ensure that our Israeli friends remained confident in their qualitative military edge. Secretary Gates established a joint US–Israel working group to ensure that Israel's QME was not diminished by such arms sales, and to discuss their specific defense needs to offset such concerns. These could be very difficult conversations, and we tried to convince our Israeli partners that their interests were also served by having capable Gulf countries able to deter and fight Iran.[11]

Moreover, we reminded the Israelis, if the United States did not provide such capabilities, the Russians and French (and one day the Chinese) would happily oblige, although without any concern for Israel's military edge. The Israelis conceded that while there were overlapping interests at the moment, none of the Gulf partners were Zionists. They also pointed out that the kind of change that swept away a relatively predictable leader like Mubarak could come soon to the Saudi monarchy.

In the end, the US was able to stay true to its commitments and achieve the difficult balance of strengthening both the Israelis and our Gulf partners. Combined with our own military preparedness in the region, these steps served to increase the pressure on Iran. Despite the popular narrative of American "withdrawal" from the Middle East or assertions that the United States wanted to shirk its role as the regional stabilizer, the end of the Obama years found the United States providing more military capabilities to its regional partners—undergirded by deeper security and intelligence relationships and a sustainable force presence—than ever before.

A FOURTH QUARTER VICTORY

The dual track strategy of engagement and pressure on Iran began to show progress during Obama's second term as negotiations accelerated. What began as a secret negotiating channel between the US and Iran grew into a multifaceted, multicountry negotiation that was dizzying in its complexity. Leading the charge was John Kerry, as relentless and indefatigable a diplomat as has ever led the State Department.

When the talks concluded in July 2015, the result was an historic achievement. Much has been written about the complicated diplomatic process that led to success. Whatever one's view of the outcome, it was one of the most consequential diplomatic undertakings in American history, standing alongside Richard Nixon's opening to China in 1972, Jimmy Carter's brokering of peace between Egypt and Israel with the 1978 Camp David peace agreement, George H.W. Bush's diplomacy to build the Gulf War coalition and the "two-plus-four" process to reunify Germany in 1990–91, and the US-led Dayton Peace Accords which ended the war in Bosnia in 1995.

By cutting off the pathways for Iran to acquire a nuclear weapon and placing its nuclear programs under a strict regime of inspections and monitoring to ensure that they are for peaceful purposes, the United States achieved through diplomacy what the use of force could not. Even our most optimistic assessments suggested that a military "knock-out punch" would only set Iran's nuclear programs back by a few years. And importantly, this deal was done with the support of our closest partners as well as Russia and China.

This achievement also involved a considerable amount of risk, something that is often harder to appreciate now that we know how things turned out. Obama's approach was a big gamble, of the magnitude many critics say he is unwilling to take. By engaging Iran directly—including through secret talks, which if exposed prematurely would have ignited a diplomatic and political firestorm—he staked his prestige on something that was more likely to fail than succeed. The costs of failure would have been high. But Obama judged that the costs of not trying would have been far greater.

THE IRAN DEAL was a significant accomplishment for security in the Middle East. But its implications were far greater. Obama thought the outcome validated his foreign policy approach, and believed the ways it was attacked by his critics—who rejected the agreement before even reading it—revealed the worst of aspects of the "foreign policy breakdown" in Washington.

In many respects, the strategy to thwart Iran's ambitions was the antithesis to the way the United States handled Iraq after 9/11. Both countries were aspiring regional hegemons seeking to augment their power with weapons of mass destruction (although, of course, Iran actually had an advanced WMD program, and Iraq did not). But while in Iraq the United States chose to use military force, in Iran it addressed the threat by using all of the tools in its toolbox—diplomacy, economic incentives, and military pressure and reassurance.

It also showed contrasting styles of leadership: instead of marching off largely alone as it did in Iraq, leaving disgruntled allies behind, to handle Iran the US reestablished its position, built leverage and brought the world together in common cause. In Iraq, the by-product of American policy was greater regional instability and resource-draining military occupation; whereas the outcome of the Iran nuclear diplomacy was stronger partner military capacity and a substantial yet sustainable American military presence in the region. And while the nuclear agreement did not solve all of America's problems with Iran—it did nothing to address the regime's internal repression against political opponents, its support for terrorists, its ambitions against Israel, as well as its overall efforts to destabilize regional order—the deal did establish a more transactional relationship, one that in early 2016 made it possible to deescalate crises and free imprisoned Americans like *Washington Post* journalist Jason Rezaian.

Obama relished the opportunity to draw this contrast. Such enthusiasm was on full display during his August 2015 speech at American University, which was his most detailed defense of his Iran policy. Although the speech was specifically about Iran, it contained a broader argument he has been making since his first campaign for president. There is a direct connection between his American University speech and his 2007 speech at DePaul. Obama correctly argued that many who opposed the Iran deal were the same people who had advocated for the Iraq War—and who fell back on the familiar arguments about weakness and futility of negotiations. Obama chastised those who played on fear and belittled diplomacy. It was this mindset, Obama asserted, that was "offered by the same people who have no compunction with being repeatedly wrong"—those following the "Washington playbook"—and they needed to be held accountable.

The core difference was in the definition of American strength. Obama again returned to the idea of what it meant to be "strong," calling out his critics for their "vague promises of toughness." Instead of offering a different solution, critics chose to hide behind the rhetoric of resolve, playing into fears and painting diplomacy as appeasement. "But none of those arguments hold up," Obama said, recalling the debate about Iraq over a decade earlier. "They didn't back in 2002, in 2003, they shouldn't now."

Strength isn't narrowing all of your options so all that's left is the use of force—after all, it was that kind of "strong" policy that Obama inherited in 2009, with America isolated and Iran ascendant. Strength is using all of our assets—diplomatic, economic, and military—to build a global coalition to solve a problem. Strength is having the confidence, patience and persistence to implement the strategy over many years and in the face of many obstacles.

At the end of Obama's speech at American University, he recalled John F. Kennedy's observation that the pursuit of peace is not as dramatic as the pursuit of war. But one cannot confuse drama with strength. The Iran agreement exemplifies what a Long Game foreign policy looks like. And, more than any other Obama policy, whether the deal succeeds or fails poses the strategy's greatest test.

CONCLUSION

HISTORY'S WEB

Over fifty years ago, the theologian Reinhold Niebuhr—a philosopher Barack Obama has often described as one of his favorites—cautioned about the temptation of power, the dangers of hubris, and the necessity of humility. We must remember, Niebuhr observed, that all great nations are "caught in a web of history in which many desires, hopes, wills and ambitions, other than their own, are operative."[1] Appreciating this reality is a crucial first step in understanding Obama's worldview and the making of his foreign policy.

Obama has always had a keen sense of history's web—both for the country and for himself. He sees America's role in the world as part of a broader story—one in which it must play the essential part, but alone does not have the power to dictate outcomes. To best position the US to do what only it uniquely can—bring countries together to solve problems, set agendas, and seize opportunities by channeling the hopes, wills, and ambitions of others—it must make the right strategic choices.

While Obama has tremendous faith in his convictions, he considers his accomplishments with a hint of Niebuhrian modesty. "You hope at the end of your presidency," he once reflected, "you can look back and say I made more right calls than not…and that America, as best it could in a difficult, dangerous world was, net, a force for good."[2]

So did he succeed? One measure of how Obama's record will stand in the light of history is to explore how his approach, priorities, and management style compares to those of other presidents. Another is to test Obama's policy by its own terms, measuring the Long Game strategy against the eight fundamental components of its checklist: balance, sustainability, restraint, precision, patience, fallibility, skepticism, and exceptionalism.

IKE, BUSH 41…OR NIXON?

Obama's political opponents have tried to "Carterize" him, arguing that like Jimmy Carter, he has left behind a foreign policy legacy of weakness, regret, and humiliation. Reaching further back, historian Robert Kagan cites the examples of Warren Harding and Calvin Coolidge, neither of whom are remembered as presidential greats, comparing their tepid response to the outcome of World War I when America withdrew from the world to Obama's reaction to the aftermath of the Iraq War. Some critics even stretch to compare Obama with failed Democratic presidential candidates like George McGovern or Michael Dukakis.[3]

Obama's own models are more revealing—and perhaps surprising. Steering away from the bright stars in the Democratic foreign policy firmament—FDR, Truman, Kennedy, Hubert Humphrey, or even Bill Clinton—Obama instead was most attracted to the example of moderate Republicans like Dwight Eisenhower and George H.W. Bush.

OBAMA AND EISENHOWER might seem an unlikely pair, but they share more than their passion for golf and Kansas roots.[4]

Both presidents inherited a country battered by unpopular wars they were determined to unwind. They were dubious of an excessive faith in military force to solve problems, and were wary of the idea that once unleashed, military power could be completely controlled. They were supremely confident in their own abilities, but prized modesty. They often resisted the arguments of more hawkish advisers—and dismissed most foreign policy commentators. They had testy relations with many in the press, who they saw as congenitally disposed to hyperbole and conflict. They focused on returning to a sustainable balance between an ambitious global agenda and domestic resources to support it, worried that if they didn't better match its means with ends, the country would be on the road to bankruptcy.[5]

Today, such parallels reflect a cultural mood: The Obama years coincided with a renaissance in the historical memory of Eisenhower. For example, plans finally came together to build a memorial to Eisenhower on Washington's National Mall. Several books heralding his foreign policy leadership shot onto the bestseller lists.

In his 2012 book *Ike's Bluff*, Evan Thomas writes admirably about Eisenhower in a way Obama would appreciate, praising him as a leader who "had the patience and wisdom, as well as cunning and guile, to keep the peace." Many other commentators joined in: Peter Beinart argued that "Ike would be proud" of Obama's restraint and nuance, while James Traub observed that just as Eisenhower was criticized for vacillation and kowtowing to enemies (for example, by not responding forcefully to the Soviet invasion of Hungary in 1956), Obama has been criticized for any number of non-interventions. Fareed Zakaria explained that while most great presidents are remembered for a grand project like the Marshall Plan, establishing NATO, or opening to China, others—like Ike and Obama—deserve credit for a "deliberative process of decision-making, a disciplined evaluation of costs and benefits and perhaps above all an instinctive feel for the power of restraint."[6]

Obama and his team would agree. In a 2010 speech at the Eisenhower Library in Kansas, Defense Secretary Robert Gates (another Kansan) said the United States needed to emulate Ike's example when "real choices were made, priorities set, and limits enforced." Just weeks before stepping down as secretary of state in 2013, Hillary Clinton said she often recalled Eisenhower's approach. "You know," she said, referring to the lessons of Ike's leadership, "you've got to be careful, you have to be thoughtful, you can't rush in." In Obama's 2009 speech at West Point announcing his decision to send additional troops to Afghanistan, he cited Eisenhower's guidance on the importance of maintaining balance across "all national programs," a point that critics derided as defeatist. And speaking again at West Point in 2014, Obama drew on this legacy to remind his audience of graduating cadets that "tough talk draws headlines, but war rarely conforms to slogans," and quoting Eisenhower, said, "War is mankind's most tragic and stupid folly; to seek or advise its deliberate provocation is a black crime against all men."

Although both Ike and Obama will be remembered for military restraint, they also expanded the role of modern military tools significantly. Eisenhower presided over a massive build-up of nuclear weapons; Obama innovated the military's cyber strategy. Eisenhower emphasized covert operations as an instrument of national policy; Obama vastly expanded the use of drones and the size and deployments of special operations forces. And both leaders stressed the importance of building indigenous forces that would be able to provide, as Eisenhower put it, "the maintenance of order, the safeguarding of frontiers, and the provision of the bulk of the ground capability" to fight local conflicts.[7]

OBAMA WAS EVEN more effusive about the lessons he took from George H.W. Bush. Although he framed his 2008 campaign as a necessary corrective to the actions of the 43rd president, he said at the time that he had "enormous sympathy" for the foreign policy of the 41st. "I don't have a lot of complaints about their handling of Desert Storm," Obama said of the senior Bush administration. "I don't have a lot of complaints with their handling of the fall of the Berlin Wall." On the campaign trail Obama described his foreign policy as a "return to the traditional bipartisan realistic policy of George Bush's father."[8]

Like Bush 41, Obama believed he was in a pitched battle between what he described as "ideology" versus his brand of "foreign policy realism." After all, the elder Bush (as well as his two most influential advisors, former Secretary of State James A. Baker III and National Security Adviser Brent Scowcroft) was held in suspicion by many conservatives as a non-believer, too soft on communism, often too timid to assert leadership, and too willing to cut a deal with adversaries. Although Bush 41 presided over a remarkable period of American dominance, he was criticized for squandering what Charles Krauthammer memorably dubbed the "unipolar moment."

When Bush left office in 1993, his foreign policy record was tarnished not for overreaching, but for doing too little. He was pilloried by both liberals and conservatives for failing to exercise American power more forcefully—whether that meant not finishing off Saddam Hussein after America's lightning victory in the 1991 Persian Gulf War, or his reluctance to intervene in the Bosnia conflict. Reflecting back on his son's presidency, the elder Bush sounded a lot like Obama (and Eisenhower) when he lamented to his biographer Jon Meacham about the "hot rhetoric" that can "make it easy to get headlines, but it doesn't necessarily solve the diplomatic problem." Bush 41 also regretted the "lack of humility" and the influence of the "hard-charging guys [referring to Dick Cheney and Donald Rumsfeld] who want to fight about everything, use force to get our way in the Middle East."[9]

One can hear the echoes of Baker's infamous admonition about Bosnia—that the US "didn't have a dog" in the fight—in Obama's approach to Syria. Bush was criticized for being too cautious about the changes that swept Europe after the Berlin Wall fell—saying he would not "dance" on that wall. As the Soviet Union was collapsing in 1991, Bush went to Kiev and warned Ukraine not to secede quickly—which deeply angered the more hard-line Pentagon led by Cheney and was mocked by critics as the "Chicken Kiev" speech. It is also striking to compare the Bush 41 administration's bitter disputes with the Israeli leadership—and showdown with influential political groups like AIPAC—with Obama's own disagreements with Israel and tangles with its supporters in the US. (As secretary of state, Baker became so angry with the Israeli deputy foreign minister he banned him from entering the State Department—that minister was Benjamin Netanyahu.)

It was this sense of clear-eyed caution, humility, and fierce prioritization of interests that attracted Obama and his advisers to the elder Bush and his team, and they frequently sought their counsel. Defense Secretary Gates personified this connection, having served in Bush 41's West Wing as deputy national security adviser before becoming his CIA director. Gates remained very close with the elder Bush, and enjoyed great influence with Obama. Obama also occasionally reached out to Colin Powell, who endorsed him in 2008, and probably preferred to be remembered more for his performance as Bush 41's chairman of the Joint Chiefs than as Bush 43's secretary of state.

Scowcroft was another favorite, so much so that author James Mann described Obama's closest advisers as "Scowcroft Democrats," and many spoke openly of their admiration for him. "I love that guy," Obama once said.[10] The ultimate insider, Scowcroft embodied the non-ideological modesty and quiet competence that the Obama team valued. Importantly, Scowcroft and Obama had both been early opponents of the war in Iraq. Obama's first two national security advisers, Jim Jones and Tom Donilon, stayed in regular touch with

Scowcroft, and Donilon explicitly tried to conduct the NSC process with Scowcroft's model in mind.

Obama told Jon Meacham that George H.W. Bush was "one of our most underrated presidents," handling the end of the Cold War "in a way that gave the world its best opportunity for stability and peace and openness."[11] While the elder Bush prized his retirement and never took the opportunity to offer advice (and loyally supported his sons), Obama heaped praise on the former president and took every opportunity to laud his accomplishments, awarding him the Presidential Medal of Freedom in 2011.

The similarities between Obama and Bush 41 also reveal something about today's foreign policy debate, especially among Republicans. Although Bush 41 is widely respected—and in his twilight, is the subject of popular books and admiring television retrospectives—his foreign policy approach has fallen out of fashion. In his failed 2016 campaign for president, Jeb Bush spent more time talking about his brother's foreign policy than his father's, and he had to distance himself from family stalwarts like Baker (principally because of Baker's criticism of Israeli policies on the peace process).

It is telling that a quarter-century after Bush 41's presidency, the greatest champion of his foreign policy is not a Bush, or any other Republican—it is Obama. The same is true about Eisenhower. At a moment when Republicans are reeling from the influence of the Tea Party and the rise of demagogues like Donald Trump, some political analysts (including leading conservatives) are urging the party to emulate the "modern Republicanism" of Eisenhower.[12] Yet no Republican leader today will carry the Eisenhower foreign policy mantle. Obama willingly does.

The Ike-Bush 41-Obama approach—powerful yet modest, ambitious yet aware of limits, decisive yet suspicious of impulse—tries to steer a middle path. In his speech announcing his 1980 run for president, Bush quoted a line from Eisenhower's first State of the Union address that sums up the brand of foreign policy shared by these three presidents. "There is in world affairs," Bush said, "a steady course to be followed between an assertion of strength that is truculent and a confession of helplessness that is cowardly."[13]

THE COMPARISONS WITH Eisenhower and Bush 41, while largely favorable for Obama, also suggest some less attractive contrasts.

For example, all three leaders embraced a "team of rivals" approach to picking a foreign policy team, priding themselves as comfortable enough in their own skins to have strong, high-profile players around them. However, while Eisenhower empowered the National Security Council system, and the Bush-Baker-Scowcroft team is remembered as perhaps the best ever, Obama never seemed to get his process to work as well as it could have. There always seemed to be an element of frustration that colored White House relationships with key cabinet players. After leaving office, Clinton, Gates, Leon Panetta and Chuck Hagel—who combined had well over a century of experience in Washington—all lamented how the White House handled decision-making (although they would have to concede it was nothing like the dysfunction that riddled previous administrations). The result sometimes was that the policy process would become bogged down, drawing out decisions and exposing Obama to criticisms of micro-management.

Style is another difference. Unlike Bush 41, Obama was widely perceived as never relishing the personal aspect of foreign relations. Whereas Bush loved forming friendships with leaders, energetically engaging in what was described at the time as "rolodex diplomacy," Obama is seen as aloof and guarded, often leaving him distant. Such criticisms get under Obama's skin. He cites such accomplishments as the Iran deal and progress on climate change—both of which required a lot of direct intervention with other leaders and plenty of presidential cajoling—as evidence that he has proven to have the necessary personal relationships to get things done. Although Obama has developed some strong personal ties with fellow leaders—German Chancellor Angela Merkel is perhaps the best example, because their dispositions are similarly unsentimental and technocratic—his low tolerance for theater and symbolism often made leaders think he was disapproving, in stark contrast to the eager, effusive style of Joe Biden or the deep relationships enjoyed by Hillary Clinton or John Kerry.

The sharpest difference among the three leaders is in presidential rhetoric and the expectations it creates. Neither Eisenhower nor Bush was accused of being a great orator. Eisenhower was renowned for his circumlocutions and vague statements, as was Bush for his awkward, staccato delivery and odd turns of phrase. And neither leader succeeded at framing the era during which they served—after all, Eisenhower's most remembered address was his final one (warning of the military-industrial complex), and Bush struggled with what he described as "the vision thing."

Obama had the opposite problem. He could give a good speech. Yet his conspicuously soaring rhetoric, combined with his determination to engage the battle of ideas and his confidence in doing so, sometimes left a gap between concept and action. Especially during Obama's early years in the White House, when hopes were highest and there was such hunger for a new kind of rhetoric coming from Washington, expectations for change became overwhelming. He did little to temper these hopes (something he did a lot more of in the latter years of his presidency). As a result, some of Obama's most heralded speeches and policy initiatives—like his 2009 address in Cairo, or his effort to rid the world of nuclear weapons—fell victim to over-promising and under-delivering.[14] It was an example of immodesty—albeit rhetorical immodesty—that neither Eisenhower nor Bush would have, perhaps could have conceived.

In this sense, because of his oratorical talents and policy ambition, Obama faced a more acute version of the dilemma that both Ike and

Bush 41 shared: a long-term strategy that combines balance, patience and restraint is difficult to sell. It is hard to inspire people when you are stressing what not to do, even if it would avoid trouble.

OBAMA'S FOREIGN POLICY bears some resemblance to another Republican administration, but likely one he would neither highlight nor feel flattered to be compared to.

Richard Nixon also became president at a moment when America was in deep crisis, bogged down by a controversial war, an unruly domestic environment, and a geopolitical context that saw America's power in eclipse. People were tired, and Nixon believed that the country needed to recalibrate after the exhausting Kennedy–Johnson years. He privately worried that America was headed "down the drain" and told the nation that when it came to addressing the world's problems, the United States "cannot—and will not—conceive all the plans, design all the programs, execute all the decisions and undertake all the defense of the free nations of the world." America needed to be more careful with its commitments and husband its power, helping "where it makes a real difference and is considered in our interest."[15]

Where it was in America's interest to act, Nixon was ready to, as he put it, "go for broke"—just like Obama set out to "do big things." Both believed that extracting the United States from costly entanglements would open the opportunity for bold strokes. They sought, in Henry Kissinger's words, a "new period of creativity" where the United States would tackle problems through "maneuver, originality, and imagination" and by empowering others.[16]

Nixon overcame decades of enmity and opened relations with China; Obama pursued diplomacy with Iran and Cuba. The "Nixon Doctrine" tried to get allies to do more to provide for their own defense, while Obama sought to "build partner capacity." Both tried to rein in defense spending, revitalize diplomacy, and foster what Kissinger called new "structures of peace" by strengthening regional institutions.

Nixon and Kissinger also famously centered power in the White House, executing some of their boldest moves through secret talks, and Nixon too was deeply skeptical of the Washington establishment. The Obama White House has been accused of being "Nixonian" in the ways it hoarded decision-making power and proved willing to maneuver around the system—although it had little of the paranoia and ruthlessness that characterized Nixon. And there is another key difference: while Obama suffered his share of controversies, he was never crippled by scandal (although his political adversaries have certainly tried). There is no "-gate" associated with Obama. In fact, his is the first two-term presidency since Nixon's that has not been hampered by some kind of criminal investigation that led to indictments of senior White House officials (Reagan had Iran-Contra; Clinton had impeachment; and George W. Bush had the Valerie Plame CIA leak affair).

More haunting are the parallels in how the two most controversial wars of the modern era—Vietnam and Iraq—came to an end. While Nixon achieved "peace with honor" by ending the US combat role in Vietnam in 1973, the collapse in 1975—symbolized by the chaotic evacuation of Saigon as the US-backed South Vietnamese forces retreated—was an ugly bookend to that misadventure, painfully recalled nearly forty years later, when the Iraqi Army melted away and ISIS rampaged southwards to Baghdad. Obama had ended the war in 2011 with "our heads held high," but by 2014 American troops had to go back into Iraq to keep the country from disintegrating.

IN *THE AUDACITY OF HOPE*, Obama drew attention to the worldview of another American leader, from the more distant past: John Quincy Adams. Today's foreign policy practitioners don't think much about our sixth president, but in the words of historian John Lewis Gaddis, Adams was "the most influential American grand strategist of the nineteenth century."[17]

In addition to his single term in the White House, Adams was one of America's most consequential Secretaries of State, and his foreign policy is best remembered for his statement "America goes not abroad, in search of monsters to destroy." This is usually seen as a warning against interfering in the affairs of others and as a justification for isolation. Yet Adams was no isolationist. While he believed that the United States must be a political, economic, and moral model for the world, first it needed to become stronger at home—whether that meant improving its economy or achieving greater social justice by ending slavery. He considered America exceptional, but counseled restraint because he feared overextension. To bolster US power, he advocated for territorial conquest and investments in manufacturing, education, and transportation infrastructure to unify the country. In this sense, Adams had a grand strategy—an integrated sense of objectives among competing goals at home and abroad, driven by an abiding confidence in what America could do.[18]

In broad terms, Adams's strategy looks a lot like Obama's. Obama cites Adams's influence, observing that "if suspicion of foreign entanglements is stamped into our DNA, then so is the impulse to expand—geographically, commercially, and ideologically."[19] Both presidents had a holistic view of strength, seeing "nation building at home" as a vital component of projecting influence abroad. Both focused on the limits of power and how best to manage trade-offs with finite resources. Both proved willing to take risks, but cautioned against adventurism for fear it would divert away attention and resources from long-term goals. And while both believed that the US should rarely impose its will, they shared the conviction that the country must play a unique global role as an exemplar of freedom and opportunity. Although they governed nearly two centuries apart, Adams and Obama had a firm grasp of the essentials of policy—and how to use those to pursue a grand strategy to advance America in the world.

In his own assessment of presidential foreign policy leadership, the scholar Stephen Sestanovich lumps Obama with Eisenhower, Nixon, and Bush 41 (he does not go as far back to Adams) as a "retrenchment" leader, who seeks to scale back commitments and husband national resources.[20] This is in contrast to "maximalist" presidents like Truman, Reagan, or Bush 43, who pursued a more confrontational, all-or-nothing approach that tends to leave the US over-extended. This dynamic is cyclical. Although retrenchment is popular at first, it tends to lose public support. As Sestanovich observes, these presidents' shared challenge was "how to convince the American people that their foreign policies [were] more successful, less rudderless, and reactive, than it seemed."[21] The result is that America's maximalist inclinations come creeping back, and calls for the US to assert itself more—taking greater risk and ownership—seem attractive.

The problem, however, is that maximalism in its purest form leads to foreign policy disaster—think Vietnam and Iraq—and the policies being advocated by Obama's Republican opponents is maximalism on steroids. Looking forward, we should not accept that after years of rejuvenating American power, the future promises yet another period of squandering it. As a student of history, Obama is certainly aware of this tragic cycle, and therefore is determined to put his successor in position to break out of it. This is why, with the Long Game, Obama has tried to forge a policy that is a blend of these two approaches.

THE LONG GAME CHECKLIST

In his 2009 book, *The Checklist Manifesto*, Atul Gawande explains the power of a simple checklist to enhance strategic decision-making. While Gawande's focus is on how doctors can prevent surgical mishaps or ways pilots can deal with in-flight emergencies, a checklist is also a powerful tool to assist in the assessment—and the making of—foreign policy.

Yet I am not aware of foreign policy analysts or practitioners using one. They should. Because in many ways, foreign policy practitioners and doctors have a lot in common—they must diagnose problems without the benefit of full information; their task involves a careful mix of prevention and intervention; and their choices involve high stakes. During times of crisis, I always felt that working in foreign policy must be something like being an emergency room doctor, where one must make consequential decisions at a fast pace with great uncertainty and little time to reflect. And some foreign policy problems, like some medical conditions, aren't fixable, so the best one can do is try to keep the patient alive, minimize the side effects, and remember that greater intervention can sometimes make the problem worse.

Such a checklist is not the doctrine foreign policy experts clamor for. But the core elements of Obama's Long Game do comprise a practical guide to managing American power and making strategic choices, ensuring the US remains in the best possible position to solve problems and pursue its interests. When thinking about Obama's legacy and the lessons for his successors, the Long Game checklist is a good place to start.

Balance. This is the foundation. Balance has defined Obama's foreign policy approach in multiple ways: balance between America's interests and values; balance between priorities at home and abroad; balance between our goals in different regions; balance between our priorities when seeking a certain outcome; balance between the responsibility we would assume and that we expected of others; balance among the tools of defense, diplomacy, and development we use to solve problems.

Recall the situation Obama inherited when he came into office: a foreign policy that was severely imbalanced, both in terms of the regional challenges the United States was putting its energies toward (Middle East versus the Asia-Pacific) and the tools it used (military force versus diplomacy and development). More broadly, Obama found a situation whereby almost every measure of national policy—at home and abroad—America was headed in the wrong direction.

This isn't hyperbole to score political points. What's remarkable is the amnesia many have about how things were (or perhaps just find it convenient to forget as a way to avoid accountability): an economy careening toward a second Great Depression; millions of Americans out of work; industries teetering on collapse; over 150,000 US troops at war, paid for on a credit card with an account overdue; America's prestige and moral standing at historic lows. Obama immediately acted to correct this imbalance, and whenever he had to respond to the unexpected or was pushed to do more, he remained determined not to make the same mistakes.

Inherent to the idea of balance is to accept that, as powerful as the United States is, its resources are finite. This is self-evident, but strangely remains impolite to acknowledge. The essence of a successful grand strategy is prioritizing goals, making choices, allocating resources, and managing trade-offs. By definition, strategic balance is redistributive; if you want to do more of one thing, it usually means you have to do less of something else. Yet many of Obama's critics treat it as an additive undertaking, whereby the United States can simply pile more on its plate, devoting greater time, resources, and attention whenever a new crisis emerges. They enthusiastically advise what the US should do more of, but fall silent when it comes to what it should do less.

However, foreign policy is about choices. American power can grow, but it is not endless. Recognizing this fact again makes Obama a direct descendant of Eisenhower, who made "balance" a central theme of his famous 1961 farewell address. Good judgment, Eisenhower explained, "seeks balance and progress; lack of it eventually finds imbalance and frustration."[22]

The necessity of balance can also be looked at another way—and as a reason to inspire confidence. It is a manifestation of America's special role. While Obama believes the US "can't fix everything," it remains essential. "If we don't set the agenda, it doesn't happen," he says, observing that he has never attended an international meeting where the US was not looked upon to drive the discussion.[23] Therefore balance is required because the United States must grapple with more demands, diverse goals and interests than any other global player. Despite all the talk of America's decline, no other country is as desirable or enjoys such expectations from so many corners of the world.

This has practical implications. Reflecting on the hundreds of meetings I hosted or attended with foreign officials during my time in the Obama administration, it is hard to think of many who asked for less of the United States (notably, the Chinese are the only ones who come to mind). They all wanted more of our time, our attention, our assistance, and our resources. Because the cumulative effect of these demands can make maintaining balance so hard, they can be seen as a burden. But this also presents a tremendous opportunity—when there is a problem in the world, few countries first look to Beijing or Moscow for solutions and guidance. They look to the US.

Sustainability. If something is imbalanced, it is also unsustainable; something that is teetering will eventually fall. Obama almost always thought several moves ahead, acutely focused on the second- or third-order consequences of his decisions, asking whether a policy would be sustainable beyond his time in office. The comparison he made to being a relay swimmer reveals his thinking; while it was his turn in the race he wanted to make as much progress as he could, and then be in a position to hand things off in the best possible way.

The emphasis on sustainability stemmed in large part from what Obama inherited when he entered the White House. He believed he was handed a situation at home and abroad that was fundamentally and dangerously untenable. Without a dramatic course correction, America would slide further into decline. He often stated his determination not to leave the same kind of mess to his successor; he wants to leave a "clean barn."[24]

However, sustainability is about more than not wanting to pass the buck to whomever comes next. Most foreign policy achievements are made when policies are sustained over time—think of how containment defeated the Soviet Union, or how the decades of support the US has provided allies in Asia and Europe has enabled them to thrive.

On almost every issue, Obama established policies that were more sustainable than as he found them. The American military is no longer overstretched. The economy is off the precipice, with unemployment the lowest it has been in nearly two decades. The United States is closer to energy independence (oil imports are down 60 percent from 2008 levels). It remains the underwriter of the global order, and has stronger partnerships and alliances abroad, with improved relations in Asia, Latin America, and Europe. Iran's nuclear weapons ambitions are in check. There is greater transparency in the ways the US government uses some of its more controversial national security tools, from surveillance to the use of drones, which Obama believes is essential to sustaining support for their future use.

On other issues—specifically in the Middle East and the threat of ISIS—the sustainability of Obama's course is less certain. By avoiding the pitfall of military occupation and not trying to govern large swaths of the region, Obama's intent was to build a strategy that would withstand the test of time.

It has not been about being "hands-off" or "withdrawing" America from the Middle East, turning its back on the problems there, but pursuing policies that are sustainable. This is what Obama has strived to do regarding ISIS, acknowledging that the threat will not be "defeated" during his presidency, but instead is a generational struggle. He sought to achieve what the Pentagon calls a "steady state" or "new normal" of activities. Yet the strategy relies on maintaining an acceptable level of risk—and even Obama admits that if the threat becomes too great, or if the US were to suffer a catastrophic terrorist attack, it would have to respond even more forcefully.

Restraint. Strategy is as much about what one decides *not* to do than what one does. On many questions the administration faced—especially when it involved military force—the issue was not whether the US was capable of doing something, but whether it should.

Because the United States has so much capability, it is often tempting to pretend trade-offs don't exist or are easy to manage. When problems are viewed in isolation—what one could do about Russia, or Syria, or Ukraine, or Libya, or China—it is often clear how the US could do more. But the challenge policymakers face is figuring out how to pursue multiple, and often competing, goals simultaneously. Restraint proved to be a hard sell: emphasizing what one will not do may be responsible, but it is rarely stirs emotion. As Kissinger observed in his landmark first book, *A World Restored*, the dilemma of statecraft is that "it is not balance which inspires men but universality, not security but immortality."[25]

Obama caught a lot of flak for being uninspiring by explaining his foreign policy as "don't do stupid stuff." Hillary Clinton even dinged him for it, saying that this was not the doctrine of a great power. Yet in foreign affairs, like in medicine, avoiding mistakes is critical (recall the Hippocratic Oath, "First do no harm"), and leaders usually do not get enough credit for keeping us out of trouble. To avoid mistakes, Obama was usually careful to avoid rhetorical traps. He understood that while chest-thumping might be politically advantageous—and sometimes his advisors lamented that they wished he would do more of it—it establishes a logic that then one is expected to act on. This was certainly a lesson he took from the instances in which his rhetoric got out in front of him, such as with the red line in Syria.

Of course, restraint is not right in every circumstance. Just as doing "more" of everything is not a strategy, neither is doing "less" of everything. The test of leadership is choosing the right time to push more chips on the table. Obama is a calculating gambler willing to make big bets—consider the Iran nuclear deal, the Libya War, the bin Laden raid, and countless other special operations forces raids to kill terrorist leaders or free hostages. But he is not a bluffer.

To critics who say that Obama's restraint is simply "retreat"—an effort to reduce American obligations for its own sake—one must ask what a less restrained policy would look like, and how that would be balanced with other interests and made sustainable over time. Most critics elide such questions, preferring to emphasize the critique rather than grapple with the consequences of the alternatives they suggest.

Precision. Obama demands specific approaches for particular problems. To him, it is almost always better to wield a scalpel instead of a hammer. His approach is clinical, focused on the causal relationship between the action and desired effect. He needs to be convinced a recommended step will actually have a chance of working—and will intensively probe assumptions and thinking based on generalizations.

The emphasis on precision is also a reason Obama favors discrete instruments of power like special operations forces raids, "signature" drone strikes and targeted killings against terrorist plotters, and targeted economic sanctions—very precise tools that can be used against specific individuals. In a July 2015 speech before the Veterans of Foreign Wars, Obama made a special point of naming the terrorist leaders American forces had killed or captured in places like Pakistan, Yemen, Somalia, and Libya—names few Americans would be familiar with. By doing so, he was making clear he had no compunction about taking finely targeted lethal action.[26]

In this way, Obama has sought greater precision in how the US defined the enemy, replacing the amorphous "war on terror" framework with the more specific goals of defeating al-Qaeda and its adherents. And he has tried to replace the broad legal framework to authorize US military actions in the wake of the 9/11 terrorist attacks with a new congressional authorization tightly tailored to the fight against ISIS (so far unsuccessfully).

As a matter of strategy, precision helps the United States keep its freedom of action—or what Kissinger called "maneuver" and what military strategists describe as maintaining the initiative. Obama believed the US needed greater flexibility in its actions, and when approaching decisions he always sought to maintain flexibility for himself. It was always important to protect the president's "decision space," to pursue precise policies so as not to lock in a course that would turn out to be imbalanced and unsustainable—and therefore unwise.

Patience. A strategy needs time to unfold. In an era where everything is instant—opinions, access to information, answers—and the incentives call for greater and greater speed, maintaining strategic patience is especially hard. Obama's most significant successes—such as the Iran deal—required patience over years. On other issues—such as the rebalance to Asia, or the defeat of ISIS, or addressing climate change—even more patience is required. Again, this is reminiscent of Eisenhower, who said that the key to a successful foreign policy was the "element of time." In words Obama would echo over five decades later, Eisenhower warned in his farewell address against the "recurring temptation to feel that some spectacular and costly action could become the miraculous solution to all current difficulties."[27]

One part of patience is about giving policies time to work; another is staying persistent and sticking to the steady, often painstaking effort required to get results—especially when there are calls to quit and do something different. The work of diplomacy, former secretary of state George Shultz has said, is akin to the more mundane skills of gardening. It entails methodically working every day to keep alliances healthy, pulling the weeds before they rage out of control, and combating the dangerous pests that want to steal or destroy the fruit.

The gardening analogy captures much of what US foreign policy actually is—the steady pursuit of America's interests abroad through the constant nurturing of a complex array of actors, interests, and goals. And like gardening, successful foreign policy also requires one to be patient—not to get flustered by distractions, and to keep faith that with the right skills and circumstances (and a little luck), the desired result will be achieved with time. Perhaps it is no coincidence such successful strategists as John Quincy Adams, George F. Kennan, and Dean Acheson were also avid gardeners.[28]

Preferring sports to gardening, Obama describes his policy as a methodical one of "hitting singles and doubles," or where he compares himself to an NFL quarterback dropping back for a pass, in which "you can't be distracted by what's around you, you've got to be looking downfield."[29] Yet one must be sure there is time for the play to work before the defense closes in and you get sacked. Too much patience can lead a policy to be overtaken by events—what bureaucrats call "OBE"—missing the opportunity to act. The danger is that patience becomes a euphemism for inaction. What some consider as careful patience others perceive as spinning indecision—and yes, sometimes Obama has found himself playing catch-up.

To maintain support for a patient approach, the American people must understand it and have confidence it is working. It is not enough to do a good job executing a policy; one must also successfully sell it.

And in a world in which everything is expected to be done instantly, this is very hard to do.

Fallibility. Obama's willingness to acknowledge America's imperfections is one of the most controversial aspects of his leadership. However, he sees it as an essential part of generating American power and influence. America's greatness derives not from asserting perfection, but from conceding wrongs, learning from mistakes, and correcting course. Obama is willing to discuss openly the fact that America's record abroad is mixed, that while it has been a force for good, "at other times America's policies have been misguided, based on false assumptions…[that] undermine our own credibility, and make for a more dangerous world."[30] By admitting such things Obama has been ridiculed for being unpatriotic, "apologizing" for America. Yet Obama believes that self-criticism is a measure of American maturity and confidence.

The recognition of fallibility also cautions a leader to exercise power, especially military force, with great care. Obama believed in using force to achieve goals, and did so often. But he understands that, as he said in his 2009 Nobel Peace Prize speech, "war promises human tragedy." Therefore he always considered whether certain military actions would bring civilian casualties, potentially creating more terrorists. It was another reason he prized precision—in taking out the enemy, he wanted to limit the damage as much as possible.

The belief that no one is free of original sin, that no society is innocent, and that even the just exercise of power can bring tragedy draws on the arguments of Reinhold Niebuhr. Obama has studied Niebuhr, and has said he finds inspiration in the theologian's admonition that while the US should fight evil and hardship, it should do so with humility, remaining "modest in our belief we can eliminate those things." David Brooks, another Niebuhr admirer who talked with Obama in 2007 about the theologian's influence on him, explained Niebuhr's central lesson as reminding us of our imperfections because "we are never as virtuous as we think we are, and that our motives are never as pure as in our own accounting."[31]

For Obama, the fact that the United States is fallible is not an excuse for inaction or a license to withdraw. Nor does it mean he is uncomfortable with the exercise of American power, or that he believes that since the US has flaws, it is just an average country with no special responsibilities in the world. Instead, understanding fallibility is one of the things that makes the US remarkable—and by remaining honest about our flaws and seeking to overcome them, American foreign policy can be more effective. Such self-scrutiny is not to discard idealism. Instead, it helps guard against, as Niebuhr urged, an idealism that is "too oblivious of the ironic perils to which human nature, wisdom, and power are subject."[32]

Skepticism. When making difficult policy decisions, Obama is suspicious of those with quick answers and easy justifications. He believes in thoroughly interrogating issues, looking at them from every angle, and testing assumptions with rigor. Like fallibility, Obama's skepticism has deeper intellectual roots. As Harvard philosopher James Kloppenberg explains, this outlook is in the tradition of philosophical pragmatists like William James and John Dewey, embracing uncertainty, focusing on consequences, and remaining dubious of absolutes. Such skeptical thinking is "not for true believers convinced they know the right course of action in advance of inquiry and experimentation."[33]

Obama's skepticism is more than a philosophical disposition; it also shapes his view of Washington foreign policy expertise. He believes that on the issue that has mattered most since the end of the Cold War—whether to invade Iraq in 2003—most experts were wrong. At a more personal level, Obama and his core team always felt apart from—and never felt much respected by—the Washington crowd, many of whom popped off in the press and griped about not being consulted enough.

This fueled his confidence to defy the professional foreign policy elites. In his 2002 speech against the Iraq War, Obama criticized the "armchair, weekend warriors" who try to "shove their own ideological agendas down our throats." And as president, Obama derided the actions advocated by "somebody sitting in an office in Washington or New York [who] thinks it would look strong." When commenting on whatever the foreign policy grandees were advocating, some senior White House officials would quip "too much college, not enough knowledge."

This does not mean that Obama entirely discounts Washington experience—his administration has been well-stocked with Beltway veterans. But when listening to the Washington debate, he is troubled by the blending of policy and punditry, its obsession with symbolism and theater, and the lack of accountability. He concedes that the Long Game approach runs counter to the incentives that drive Washington. "It may not always be sexy," he says, and it "may not always attract a lot of attention, and it doesn't make for good argument on Sunday morning shows...but [it] steadily advances the interests of the American people." [34]

Again, it is Obama trying to be Warren Buffett in a foreign policy debate dominated by day traders.

Exceptionalism. The engine that propels Obama's strategy is American exceptionalism. One pursues the Long Game by forging a policy that is balanced, sustainable, restrained, precise, and patient. Recognizing fallibility and embracing skepticism are key to avoiding arrogance, being thrown off-course, or making unforced errors. This is *how* it is done. But *why* one does things this way is to pursue the United States' mission abroad, which is unique.

Obama has said that American exceptionalism is an "essential truth." His America is the strongest nation on earth (as he repeated for emphasis three straight times in his final State of the Union address, "It's not even close"). It is a force of ingenuity and innovation, respect and inspiration. And he recognizes that exceptionalism brings tremendous responsibilities—that because of its distinct power, American leadership remains "indispensable."

Exceptionalism is not the same as domination. What makes America different is that it can lead in multiple ways—it can be out front, or it can operate more behind the scenes. Obama believes that, in foreign policy as in life, just as there are times when you have to do most of the work, you sometimes get better outcomes when you let others take the credit. This is common sense. But it also is rooted in the idea of the paradox of American power—that while the US can do more than anyone else, it cannot do it all. That reality requires an exercise of power that is more nimble, clever, and persuasive.[35]

Nor is exceptionalism an assertion that the United States is flawless. Obama's America is not, in the words of Ronald Reagan's farewell address, a "shining city on a hill," a delicate perfection that must be carefully preserved. Instead America is a restless country, one that is chronically dissatisfied with itself, always striving to be better, reaching for more, seeking renewal. It is not an exceptionalism rooted in warm nostalgia of the past, or fear that the future will be taken away from us. What makes America exceptional is its ability to seek perfection relentlessly, not to claim it hubristically.

In this sense, one of the most important speeches Obama has delivered about America in the world actually doesn't say much explicitly about foreign policy.[36] It is his March 2015 address in Selma, Alabama, on the fiftieth anniversary of the "Bloody Sunday March," one of the pivotal events in the civil rights movement.

The speech was a sweeping paean to America's willingness to make itself better, and for how individuals can overcome powerful forces and do big things. Obama makes clear that America should be confident enough to be honest about its flaws and its abilities to overcome them, arguing that the country is not "some fragile thing." To Obama, the power of the Selma example is a key part of American strength—both at home and abroad.

So what presents the greatest threat to America's exceptionalism is not an outside force. It is from within. What's often missed about Obama's worldview is the fundamental optimism and deep confidence he has in the American people—the kinds of common citizens who, in the best traditions of Selma, have stood up to do the right thing time and again. But alongside this confidence is a substantial pessimism about American elites (which is ironic, given Obama is often accused of being elitist). His frustration about the state of the country's political debate—and how the US should respond to the changing world—runs just as deep. As he said in his final State of the Union address, one of the few regrets of his time in office is that the "rancor and suspicion" has only become worse. To remain exceptional, we must change our politics.[37]

Seen this way, Obama's effort to redefine America's role in the world remains incomplete. His Long Game approach has achieved some significant policy successes and avoided some grave mistakes. It has reoriented US foreign policy away from the "long war" and, in most of the world, restored the sense of admiration for America that was nearly squandered by 2008. And it has established a new center of gravity for Democrats on foreign policy—having avoided the disasters of LBJ and Jimmy Carter, or the frustrations of Bill Clinton. Future Democratic presidents will be measured by what Obama has done.

YET WITH SO many corners of the globe in flames, such a conclusion can seem hard to accept. The world of 2016 is indeed very complicated, and the next president will have her share of challenges to confront. But one must remember that, in fundamental ways, the world is always troubling, often uniquely so. Recall 1968, when over half a million US troops were bogged down in Vietnam, Soviet tanks rolled into Prague, and the American political system seemed to be ripping itself apart. Or 1979, with Americans held hostage in Iran, a worldwide energy crisis, and the Soviet invasion of Afghanistan. Or 2008, with the American economy on the cusp of the second Great Depression, the US military stretched to the breaking point through fighting two wars, and many parts of the world associating America with militarism, Guantanamo Bay, and torture.

History reminds us that the question is not whether the world presents challenges, but how best America can be positioned to deal with them. Considering the extent of today's global disorder, it is tempting to succumb to the narrative of grievance and fear—sharpening the divisions between "us" and "them," building walls longer and higher, and lashing out at enemies with force. Or to think it better that, to reduce exposure to such geopolitical risk, the US should divest from its alliances and pursue leadership that is "offshore." Despite all the talk of "strength," what all of these impulses reflect is a core lack of confidence.

We cannot submit to such pessimism. As Obama's presidency nears its end, the state of the world is indeed tumultuous and ever changing, but we have good reason to be confident. America's global position is sound. It has restored a sense of strategic solvency. Countries look to the US for guidance, ideas, support, and protection. The US is again admired and inspiring, not just for what it can do abroad, but for its economic vitality and strong society at home.

As the scholar Joseph Nye has correctly observed, it remains the American Century, an era of US "preeminence in military, economic, and soft power that have made the US central to the workings of the global balance of power, and to the provision of global public goods." Or as Warren Buffett declared in his more homespun way, "the babies being born in America today are the luckiest crop in history."[38] When it comes to being in a position to solve problems and give people an opportunity to improve their lives, the US is far better off than it was a decade ago. In 2016, America is great again.

This did not happen by accident; it is the result of policy choices. It is because of the Long Game. And as this story shows, it is not easy.

MAKING THE LONG GAME the new Washington consensus is still unfinished business. To be sure, some of the reasons why are attributable to Obama's perceived missteps—such as the Syria red line—in which the process tarnished the outcome and offered critics an easy target to caricature. Arguably, these are the moments when he diverted most from his instincts (in the case of Syria, setting a self-made rhetorical trap). However, the bigger problem for shaping America's role in the world still remains the way we—experts, think tankers, journalists, politicos—think about these issues and talk about them. We are all grappling with the "foreign policy breakdown," except today it is far bigger, much louder, and more corrosive than ever. Despite Obama's efforts, US foreign policy debate remains trapped in an endless loop of crisis. In fact, the debate is an inherent component of the crisis.

Stepping back from dissecting the separate issues that have dominated Obama's foreign policy—Syria and Iraq, Libya and Iran, Russia and China—it is hard to see a debate that is rising to the challenge. As Destler, Gelb, and Lake argued over thirty years ago, we continue to be our own worst enemy. Liberals and conservatives seek to outshout the other, with "each side seeking our salvation largely through the elimination of the other." Congress and the news media make debates more "noisy, partisan, and doctrinaire." And the professional foreign policy elite "deepens rather than bridges divisions."

Today's speed of communications, predominance of spin over fact, and splintering of the media environment make things exponentially worse—the answers have to be quicker, the stories more dramatic, the opinions sharper. Attention is fleeting. Memories are shorter. Everything gets packaged as "Breaking News" or subjected to a cable channel's countdown clock. While we chase around shiny objects, we tend to lose sight of the future. What all this creates, they wrote, is even truer today: "An American incapacity to conduct a steady and sensible foreign policy."[39]

So just as Eisenhower left office over a half century ago warning of the "unwarranted influence" of the military-industrial complex and its powers to distort policy, as the Obama era ends, we've seen the apogee of a different kind of ill, a "media-political-industrial complex" that exerts an influence over the making of national security policy that can be similarly damaging.

Because of this predicament, I conclude with a mix of regret and hope. Having been part of the foreign policy community both in and out of government for over two decades, I cannot claim to be above some of the ills that have caused this breakdown. But I am convinced that now, more than ever, America must continue to pursue a strategy that enables future presidents to operate sensibly and pragmatically in a difficult world. Barack Obama's Long Game points the way. Our challenge is to be confident enough to play it forward.

NOTES

INTRODUCTION

1. George F. Kennan, *Memoirs 1925–1950* (New York: Pantheon, 1967), p. 322.

2. Hal Brands, *What Good Is Grand Strategy? Power and Purpose in American State-craft from Harry S. Truman to George W. Bush* (Ithaca: Cornell University Press, 2014), p. 3.

3. Hal Brands, "Breaking Down Obama's Grand Strategy," *The National Interest* (June 23, 2014).

4. Brands, *What Good Is Grand Strategy?* p. 192.

5. The best example of this argument is Bret Stephens, *America in Retreat: The New Isolationism and the Coming Global Disorder* (New York: Sentinel, 2014); on retrenchment, see Stephen Sestanovich, *Maximalist: America in the World From Truman to Obama* (New York: Knopf, 2014).

6. Ryan Lizza, "The Consequentialist," *The New Yorker*, May 2, 2011.

7. See Atul Gawande, *The Checklist Manifesto* (New York: Metropolitan Books, 2009).

8. See David Milne, *Worldmaking: The Art and Science of American Diplomacy* (New York: Farrar, Straus, and Giroux, 2015), p 16.

9. See interview with Marc Maron, Podcast, Episode 613, available at http://www.wtfpod.com/podcast/episodes/episode_613_-_president_barack_obama

10. David Remnick, "Going the Distance," *The New Yorker* (January 27, 2014).

11. Robert Kaplan, *The Revenge of Geography* (New York: Random House, 2012), p. 20.

12. Quote from Robert Draper, "Between Iraq and a Hawk Base," *New York Times Magazine*, September 1, 2015.

13. Richard Holbrooke, *To End A War* (New York: Random House, 1998), p xvii.

14. Henry Kissinger, *White House Years* (New York: Little, Brown, 1979), p 54.

CHAPTER 1

1. See "Government Assessment of the Syrian Government's Use of Chemical Weapons on August 21, 2013," White House Press Release.

2. See Thom Shanker, C.J. Chivers, and Michael R. Gordon, "Obama Weighs 'Limited' Strikes Against Syrian Forces," *New York Times*, August 27, 2013; Karen DeYoung, "After Syria Chemical Allegations, Obama Considering Limited Military Strike," *Washington Post*, August 26, 2013.

3. See Jeffrey Goldberg, "The Obama Doctrine," *The Atlantic* (April 2016); "Remarks by the President in Address to the Nation on Syria," White House, September 10, 2013.

4. Quote from Goldberg, "The Obama Doctrine."

5. See, for example, Charlie Savage, "Barack Obama's Q&A," *Boston Globe* (December 20, 2007). Obama said: "As Commander-in-Chief, the President does have a duty to protect and defend the United States. In instances of self-defense, the President would be within his constitutional authority to act before advising Congress or seeking its consent. History has shown us time and again, however, that military action is most successful when it is authorized and supported by the Legislative branch. It is always preferable to have the informed consent of Congress prior to any military action."

6. For example, see Peter Baker, Mark Landler, David Sanger and Anne Barnard, "Off-the-Cuff Obama Line Put US in Bind on Syria," *New York Times*, May 4, 2013.

7. See Chuck Todd, *The Stranger* (New York: Little, Brown, 2014), p 431.

8. See Glenn Kessler, "President Obama and the 'Red Line' on Syria's chemical weapons," *Washington Post*, September 6, 2013.

9. Stuart Weiner and Lazar Berman, "Netanyahu to spend another $350 million so every Israeli has gas mask," *Times of Israel*, May 30, 2013.

10. Mark Landler and Eric Schmitt, "White House Says It Believes Syria Has Used Chemical Arms," *New York Times*, April 25, 2013.

11. "Senators McCain and Levin urge the President to Take 'More Active Steps' in Syria," March 21, 2013.

12. "Message from the ruins of Qusair," *Washington Post*, June 6, 2013.

13. "Obama should remember Rwanda as he weighs action in Syria," *Washington Post*, April 26, 2013.

14. Quoted in Dexter Filkins, "The Thin Red Line," *The New Yorker*, May 13, 2013.

15. "Public Opinion Runs Against Syrian Airstrikes," Pew Research Center, September 3, 2013.

16. See Michael Crowley, "Marco Rubio: The Hawk Turned Dovish on Syria in 2013," *Politico*, May 26, 2015.

17. Ted Cruz, "Why I'll vote no on Syria strike," *Washington Post*, September 9, 2013.

18. Rand Paul, "Why I'm Voting No on Syria," *Time*, September 4, 2013.

19. Peter Baker and Michael R. Gordon, "An Unlikely Evolution, From Casual Proposal to Possible Resolution," *New York Times*, September 10, 2013.

20. Adam Entous, Janet Hook and Carol E. Lee, "Inside the White House, a Head-Spinning Reversal on Chemical Weapons," *Wall Street Journal*, September 15, 2013; Anne Barnard, "In Shift, Syrian Official Admits Government Has Chemical Arms," *New York Times*, September 10, 2013.

21. Michael R. Gordon, "U.S. and Russia Reach Deal to Destroy Syria's Chemical Arms," *New York Times*, September 14, 2013.

22. Karen DeYoung, "Removal of Syrian chemical arsenal was result of unprecedented collaboration," *Washington Post*, June 29, 2014.

23. For the definitive academic treatment of this concept, see Alexander L. George and William E. Simons, *The Limits of Coercive Diplomacy* (Boulder: Westview Press, 1994).

24. Peter Baker, "A Rare Public View of Obama's Pivots on Policy in Syria Confrontation," *New York Times*, September 11, 2013.

25. Richard Betts, *American Force: Dangers, Delusions, and Dilemmas in National Security* (New York: Columbia University Press), p 271; quote from Goldberg, "The Obama Doctrine."

26. Quoted in Todd, p 447.

27. Goldberg, "The Obama Doctrine."

28. Quotes from Obama interview with ABC's George Stephanopoulos, September 15, 2013; and Goldberg, "The Obama Doctrine."

29. See Jeffrey Goldberg, "Netanyahu Says Obama Got Syria Right," *Bloomberg View*, May 22, 2014; Barbara Opall-Rome, "Israeli DM Cites Drop in Syrian Chem Threat," *Defense News*, June 1, 2015; and J.J. Goldberg, "Israel's Top General Praises Iran Deal as 'Strategic Turning Point' in Slap at Bibi," *The Forward*, January 26, 2016.

CHAPTER 2

1. Obama speech at DePaul University, October 2, 2007.

2. Quote from James Mann, *The Obamians: The Struggle Inside the White House to Redefine American Power* (New York: Viking, 2012), p 87.

3. Zbiginew Brzezisnki, *Second Chance: Three Presidents and the Crisis of American Superpower* (New York: Basic Books, 2007), p 154.

4. *The Audacity of Hope*, p 290.

5. *The Audacity of Hope*, p 290; also see Derek Chollet "A Real Alternative" *The National Interest* (September/October 2007).

6. Derek Chollet and James Goldgeier, *America Between the Wars: From 11/9 to 9/11* (New York: PublicAffairs), pp 288-289.

7. Ibid., pp 294-295.

8. Ibid., p 327.

9. Quote from Milne, *Worldmaking*, p 469.

10. *The Audacity of Hope*, p 293.

11. See Kevin Baron, "Revenge of the Liberal Foreign Policy Wonks," *National Journal*, June 5, 2014; and Mann, *The Obamians*, pp 45-65.

12. Derek Chollet, "A Consensus Shattered," *The National Interest* (Spring 2006).

13. See Matt Bai, *The Argument: Inside the Battle to Remake Democratic Politics* (New York: Penguin Books, 2008), pp 257-281; and Chollet and Goldgeier, *America Between the Wars*, p 322.

14. *The Audacity of Hope*, p 304.

15. See J. Peter Scoblic, *U.S. vs. Them: How Conservatism Has Undermined America's Security* (Viking, 2008); and Richard Betts, "U.S. National Security Strategy: Lenses and Landmarks," paper presented for the launch conference of the Princeton Project, November 2004.

16. See Chollet and Goldgeier, *America Between the Wars*, p 318.

17. Peter Beinart, *The Icarus Syndrome: A History of American Hubris* (New York: HarperCollins, 2010), p 385.

18. Quote from Goldberg, "The Obama Doctrine."

19. *The Audacity of Hope*, p 282.

20. Jonathan Schell, *The Time of Illusion* (New York: Random House, 1975), p 353.

21. George Packer, "Coming Apart," *The New Yorker*, September 12, 2011.

22. *The Audacity of Hope*, p126.

23. Quotes from I.M. Destler, Leslie H. Gelb and Anthony Lake, *Our Own Worst Enemy: The Unmaking of American Foreign Policy* (Simon and Schuster, 1984), pp 12, 25-26.

24. Quote from Goldberg, "The Obama Doctrine."

CHAPTER 3

1. Robert Gates, *Duty: Memoirs of a Secretary at War* (New York: Knopf, 2014) p 322.

2. Hillary Rodham Clinton, *Hard Choices* (Simon and Schuster, 2014) p 79.

3. See Geoff Dyer, *The Contest of the Century: The New Era of Competition with China—and how America Can Win* (New York: Knopf, 2014).

4. Milne, *Worldmaking*, p 508.

5. Clinton, "America's Pacific Century," *Foreign Policy*, October 11, 2011.

6. Ibid.

7. David Plouffe, *The Audacity to Win* (New York: Penguin, 2010), p 273.

8. Presidential debate transcript, September 26, 2008 http://elections.nytimes.com/2008/president/debates/transcripts/first-presidential-debate.html.

9. Clinton, *Hard Choices*, p 230.

10. James Traub, "When Did Obama Give Up?" *Foreign Policy*, February 26, 2015.

11. Ibid; and Goldberg, "The Obama Doctrine."

12. Clinton, *Hard Choices*, p148.

13. Gates, *Duty*, p 571.

14. Quote from "Who Lost Iraq?" *Politico Magazine*, July/August 2015.

15. Michael R. Gordon and Bernard E. Trainor, *The Endgame: The Inside Story of the Struggle for Iraq, From George W. Bush to Barack Obama* (New York: Random House, 2012), p 693.

16. Obama press conference, December 18, 2015.

17. Gates, *Duty*, pp 572-573.

18. This is the core argument of Robert Kagan, "Not Fade Away," *New Republic* (January 11, 2012), an article Obama read at the time and cited favorably.

19. Chollet and Goldgeier, *America Between the Wars*, pp 64-65.

20. Quote from Goldberg, "The Obama Doctrine."

21. Jeffrey Goldberg, "Hillary Clinton: 'Failure' to Help Syrian Rebels Led to the Rise of ISIS," *The Atlantic*, August 10, 2014.

22. See Mann, *The Obamians*, pp 241-254.

CHAPTER 4

1. Fred Kaplan, "Obama's Way," *Foreign Affairs* (January/February, 2016).

2. Marc Lynch, "Obama and the Middle East," *Foreign Affairs* (September/October 2015), p 23.

3. This section draws on Derek Chollet and Ben Fishman, "Who Lost Libya?" *Foreign Affairs* (May/June 2015).

4. An excellent depiction of these meetings is in David Sanger, *Confront and Conceal: Obama's Secret Wars and Surprising Use of American Power* (New York: Random House, 2012) pp 345-347.

5. See Michael Lewis, "Obama's Way," *Vanity Fair* (October 2012).

6. Gates, *Duty*, p 512.

7. Quote from Goldberg, "The Obama Doctrine."

8. Quote from Lewis, "Obama's Way."

9. Gideon Rose, "What Obama Gets Right," *Foreign Affairs* (September/October 2015).

10. Quote from Goldberg, "The Obama Doctrine."

11. See Alan Kuperman, "Obama's Libya Debacle," *Foreign Affairs*, (March/April 2015).

12. Obama, *The Audacity of Hope*, pp 309-311; quote from Goldberg, "The Obama Doctrine."

13. Quote from Jo Becker and Scott Shane, "Hillary Clinton, 'Smart Power,' and a Dictator's Fall," *New York Times* (February 27, 2016).

14. See Ivo Daalder and James Stavridis, "NATO's Victory in Libya," *Foreign Affairs* (March/April 2012).

15. See Charlie Savage, *Power Wars: Inside Obama's Post-9/11 Presidency* (New York: Little, Brown and Company, 2015) pp 638-649.

16. Quote from Becker and Shane, "Hillary Clinton, 'Smart Power," and a Dictator's Fall."

17. Quote from Jo Becker and Scott Shane, "In Their Own Words: The Libya Tragedy," *New York Times* (February 27, 2016).

18. Ben Fishman, "How We Can Still Fix Libya," *Politico*, February 28, 2016.

19. See Robert D. Kaplan, *Mediterranean Winter* (New York: Vintage, 2005), p 27.

20. Quote from Jon Lee Anderson, "The Unravelling," *The New Yorker* (February 23 & March 2, 2015).

21. See Goldberg, "The Obama Doctrine."

22. Quotes from John Lewis Gaddis, *Strategies of Containment* (New York: Oxford University Press, 2005), p 128; Fred Greenstein, *The Hidden-Hand Presidency: Eisenhower As Leader* (New York: Basic Books, 1982).

23. Clinton, *Hard Choices*, p 375.

24. Michael Crowley, "We Caved," *Politico Magazine* (January/February 2016).

CHAPTER 5

1. Hillary Clinton, *Hard Choices*, p 461.

2. Quote from Goldberg, "The Obama Doctrine."

3. Quotes from Franklin Foer and Chris Hughes, "Barack Obama Is Not Pleased," *The New Republic*, January 27, 2013; and Jeffrey Goldberg, "Obama to Israel—Time Is Running Out," *The Atlantic*, March 2, 2014.

4. *The Audacity of Hope*, p 308; Thom Shanker, "Warning Against Wars Like Iraq and Afghanistan," *New York Times*, February 25, 2011.

5. This draws on Derek Chollet, "The Shame of Srebrenica," *Foreign Policy*, July 9, 2015.

6. George Packer, "The Liberal Quandary Over Iraq," *New York Times Magazine*, December 8, 2002.

7. Philip Gordon, "The Middle East Is Falling Apart," *Politico*, June 4, 2015.

8. Quote from Goldberg, "The Obama Doctrine."

9. See https://www.whitehouse.gov/blog/2015/09/15/what-you-need-know-about-syrian-refugee-crisis-and-what-us-doing-help

10. Hendrick Simoes, "US to keep some F-16s, Patriot missiles in Jordan post exercise," *Stars and Stripes*, June 16, 2013.

11. Clinton, *Hard Choices*, p. 463.

12. Clinton, *Hard Choices*, pp 461-464; Panetta, *Worthy Fights*, pp 449-450.

13. See, for example, Mark Mazzetti, Michael R. Gordon, and Mark Landler, "U.S. Is Said to Plan to Send Weapons to Syrian Rebels," *New York Times*, June 14, 2013; and Michele Kelemen, "U.S. to Provide Military Support to Opposition in Syria," NPR, June 14, 2013.

14. See "On-the-Record Conference Call by Deputy National Security Advisor for Strategic Communications Ben Rhodes on Syria," June 13, 2013.

15. This section draws on Derek Chollet, "We Never Thought Training Syrians Would Be Easy," *Defense One*, September 22, 2015.

16. Remnick, "Going the Distance."

17. Quote from Greg Jaffe, "Hope fades on Obama's vow to bring troops home before presidency ends," *Washington Post*, October 12, 2015.

18. Goldberg, "Hillary Clinton: 'Failure' to Help Syrian Rebels Led to the Rise of ISIS."

19. Peter Bergen, *The United States of Jihad: Investigating America's Homegrown Terrorists* (New York: Crown, 2016).

20. For an accurate summation of Obama's view of the ISIS threat, see Peter Beinart, "How Obama Thinks About Terrorism," *The Atlantic*, December 7, 2015.

21. Quote from Goldberg, "The Obama Doctrine."

22. Roger Cohen, "Obama's Syria Nightmare," *New York Times*, September 10, 2015.

CHAPTER 6

1. See Kathryn Stoner and Michael McFaul, "Who Lost Russia (This Time)? Vladimir Putin," *The Washington Quarterly* (Summer 2015), pp 170–171.

2. See Angela Stent, *The Limits of Partnership: U.S.-Russian Relations in the Twenty-First Century* (Princeton: Princeton University Press, 2014).

3. Clinton, *Hard Choices*, pp 236–237.

4. Quote from Kaplan, "Obama's Way."

5. See White House Fact Sheet, "U.S. Assistance to Ukraine," December 7, 2015.

6. Stoner and McFaul, p 182.

7. See Michael McFaul, "The Myth of Putin's Strategic Genius," *New York Times*, October 23, 2015.

8. Obama Press Conference, February 16, 2016.

9. Quote from Goldberg, "The Obama Doctrine."

10. Obama Press Conference, October 2, 2015.

11. Quote from Goldberg, "The Obama Doctrine."

NOTES

CHAPTER 7

1. Gates, *Duty*, p 387.
2. On the Qom facility discovery and its exposure, see Clinton, *Hard Choices*, pp 424–425; and Sanger, *Confront and Conceal*, pp 179–183.
3. Clinton, *Hard Choices*, p 433.
4. Gates, *Duty*, p 391.
5. Gates, *Duty*, pp 391-392; Dennis Ross, *Doomed to Succeed: The U.S.-Israel Relationship From Truman to Obama*, (New York: Farrar, Straus and Giroux, 2015) p 367.
6. For Carter quotes, see Jeffrey Goldberg, "Can the U.S. Military Help the White House and Israel Move Beyond Iran?" *Defense One*, November 3, 2015; Michael Crowley, "Plan B for Iran," *Politico Magazine*, June 24, 2015; and Deena Zaru, "Carter: Bunker Busting Bomb Against Iran Ready To Go," *CNN* (April 30, 2015). Also see Julian Barnes and Adam Entous, "Pentagon Upgraded Biggest 'Bunker Buster' Bomb as Iran Talks Unfolded," *Wall Street Journal*, April 3, 2015.
7. Ross, *Doomed to Succeed*, p 362.
8. Gates, *Duty*, p 397; Ross, *Doomed to Succeed*, p 350.
9. Michael Oren, *Ally: My Journey Across the American-Israeli Divide* (New York: Random House, 2015), p 179.
10. Panetta, *Worthy Fights*, p 404.
11. Gates, *Duty*, pp 396-397; Oren, *Ally*, pp 179–182.

CONCLUSION

1. Reinhold Niebuhr, *The World Crisis and American Responsibility* (Association Press, 1958), p 81.
2. Franklin Foer and Chris Hughes, "Barack Obama Is Not Pleased," *New Republic*, January 27, 2013.
3. See Kagan's comment in *Has Obama Made the World a More Dangerous Place? The Munk Debate on U.S. Foreign Policy* (Anansi, 2015), p 68.
4. Obama's maternal grandparents, who raised him for several years, were from Kansas.
5. See Sestanovich, *Maximalist*, pp 66–90.
6. Evan Thomas, *Ike's Bluff: President Eisenhower's Secret Battle to Save the World* (New York: Little, Brown and Company, 2012), p 416; Peter Beinart, "He's Like Ike," *The Atlantic*, May 29, 2014; James Traub, "Obama's Not Carter—He's Eisenhower," *Foreign Policy*, March 7, 2014; Fareed Zakaria, "On Foreign Policy, Why Barack is Like Ike," *Time*, December 19, 2012.
7. Gaddis, *Strategies of Containment*, p 151.
8. David Brooks, "Obama Admires Bush," *New York Times*, May 16, 2008; Lizza, "The Consequentialist."

9. Jon Meacham, *Destiny and Power: The American Odyssey of George Herbert Walker Bush* (Random House, 2015), pp 585–588.

10. Quote from Goldberg, "The Obama Doctrine."

11. Meacham, p 599.

12. See Joe Scarborough, *The Right Path: From Ike to Reagan, How Republicans Once Mastered Politics—And Can Again* (Random House, 2013); and E.J. Dionne, *Why the Right Went Wrong: Conservatism From Goldwater to the Tea Party and Beyond* (Simon and Schuster, 2016), pp 464–465.

13. Quote from Meacham, p 217.

14. On the "transformational" aspects of Obama's ambitions compared to the "incremental" approaches of Eisenhower and Bush, see Joseph Nye, *Presidential Leadership and the Creation of the American Era* (Princeton University Press, 2013), pp 144–146.

15. Quotes from Sestanovich, *Maximalist*, pp 168–169.

16. Ibid, p 170.

17. John Lewis Gaddis, *Surprise, Security, and the American Experience* (Harvard University Press, 2004), p 15.

18. See Charles Edsel, *Nation Builder: John Quincy Adams and the Grand Strategy of the Republic* (Harvard University Press, 2014); James Traub, *John Quincy Adams: Militant Spirit* (Basic Books, 2016); and Robert Kagan, *Dangerous Nation* (Knopf, 2006), pp 198–199.

19. *The Audacity of Hope*, p 281.

20. Sestanovich, *Maximalist*.

21. See Sestanovich, "The Long History of Leading From Behind," *The Atlantic* (January/February 2016).

22. Eisenhower farewell address, January 17, 1961.

23. Quote from Goldberg, "The Obama Doctrine."

24. Quote from Goldberg, "The Obama Doctrine."

25. Henry Kissinger, *A World Restored* (Houghton Mifflin, 1957), p 317.

26. See Obama speech at VFW National Convention, Pittsburgh, Pennsylvania, July 21, 2015.

27. Eisenhower farewell address.

28. Derek Chollet, "Altered State," *Washington Post*, April 17, 2005; John Lewis Gaddis, "The Gardener," The New Republic, October 16, 2006; and Nye, *Presidential Leadership and the Creation of the American Era*, p 151.

29. Quote from "President Obama and Bill Simmons: The GQ Interview," GQ, November 17, 2015.

30. *The Audacity of Hope*, p 280.

31. David Brooks, "Obama, Gospel and Verse," *New York Times*, April 26, 2007; and David Brooks, *The Road To Character* (Random House, 2015), p149.

32. Reinhold Niebuhr, *The Irony of American History* (Charles Scribner's Sons, 1952), p133. See also Ross Douthat, "Obama the Theologian," *New York Times*, February 7, 2015.

33. James T. Kloppenberg, *Reading Obama: Dreams, Hope, and the American Political Tradition* (Princeton University Press, 2011), p xxxv.

34. See President Obama press conference with Benigno Aquino, April 28, 2014.

35. The is the core concept explained in Joe Nye's 2002 book, *The Paradox of American Power: Why the World's Only Superpower Can't Go It Alone* (Oxford University Press).

36. See Greg Jaffe, "Obama's New Patriotism," *Washington Post*, June 3, 2015.

37. "President Obama and Marilynne Robinson: A Conversation in Iowa," *New York Review of Books*, November 5, 2015.

38. Joseph Nye, *Is the American Century Over?* (Malden, MA: Polity Press) 2015; and Leslie Picker, "Warren Buffett, in Annual Letter, Rejects Candidates' Message of US Decline," *New York Times*, February 27, 2016.

39. *Our Own Worst Enemy*, pp 261–262.

BIBLIOGRAPHY

This book draws on my experiences during over six years in the Obama administration, starting with the 2008 presidential transition. Most of the issues covered are ones in which I had a direct, if sometimes modest, role. To refresh my memory and provide additional recollections, I have also consulted with many of my former government colleagues, as well as talked with numerous outside analysts, including journalists, who followed these events closely and provide a unique perspective.

To understand Obama's approach to the world, there is no better place to start than Barack Obama himself—his speeches, writings, and interviews over the years are an indispensable resource. Too often, analysts dismiss presidential rhetoric as ghostwritten spin, expecting the truth to be something that remains secret or unsaid. But Obama is a remarkably open and clear thinker; his foreign policy views are hidden in plain sight. His words, especially those from the many interviews he has given over the years (with everyone from political journalists and foreign policy thinkers to comedians and sportswriters), provide a unique window into how he has wrestled with issues, answered his critics, and explained the logic behind his decisions. The same is true for his most important national security advisors—especially Hillary Clinton, Robert Gates, and Leon Panetta—whose own memoirs are essential for insight into the Obama era.

Along with these direct sources, this book is informed by the many other thoughtful books and articles already written about the Obama presidency, the recent history of US politics and foreign policy, and the current debate about America's role in the world. In addition to the sources cited in the notes, these are the books I found most useful.

Axelrod, David. *Believer: My Forty Years in Politics.* New York: Penguin, 2015.
Beinart, Peter. *The Icarus Syndrome: A History of American Hubris.* New York: HarperCollins, 2010.

BIBLIOGRAPHY

Bergen, Peter. *The United States of Jihad.*New York: Crown, 2016.

Betts, Richard K.*American Force: Dangers, Delusions, and Dilemmas in National Security*. New York: Columbia University Press, 2012.

Brands, Hal. *What Good Is Grand Strategy?: Power and Purpose in American Statecraft from Harry S. Truman to George W. Bush*. Ithaca: Cornell University Press, 2014.

Bremmer, Ian.*Superpower: Three Choices for America's Role in the World*. New York: Penguin, 2015.

Brooks, David. *The Road to Character*. New York: Random House, 2015.

Brzezinski, Zbiginew. *Second Chance: Three Presidents and the Crisis of American Superpower*. New York: Basic Books, 2007.

Chivvis, Christopher S. *Toppling Qaddafi: Libya and the Limits of Liberal Intervention*. New York: Cambridge University Press, 2014.

Chollet, Derek and James Goldgeier. *America Between the Wars: From 11/9 to 9/11*. New York: Public Affairs, 2008.

Clinton, Hillary Rodham. *Hard Choices*. New York: Simon & Schuster, 2014.

Destler, I.M., Leslie H. Gelb, and Anthony Lake. *Our Own Worst Enemy: The Unmaking of American Foreign* Policy. New York: Simon & Schuster, 1984.

Dionne, E.J. *Why the Right Went Wrong: Conservatism From Goldwater to the Tea Party and Beyond*. New York: Simon & Schuster, 2016.

Dueck, Colin. *The Obama Doctrine: American Grand Strategy Today*. New York: Oxford University Press, 2015.

Edsel, Charles. *Nation Builder: John Quincy Adams and the Grand Strategy of the Republic*. Cambridge: Harvard University Press, 2014.

Gaddis, John Lewis. *Strategies of Containment: A Critical Appraisal of American National Security Policy during the Cold War*. New York: Oxford University Press, 1982.

_____. *Surprise, Security, and the American Experience*. Cambridge: Harvard University Press, 2004.

Gates, Robert M. *Duty: Memoirs of a Secretary at War*. New York: Knopf, 2014.

Gawande, Atul. *The Checklist Manifesto: How to Get Things Right*. New York: Metropolitan Books, 2009.

Geithner, Timothy F. *Stress Test: Reflections on Financial Crises*. New York: Crown, 2014.

George, Alexander L. and William E. Simons. *The Limits of Coercive Diplomacy*. Boulder: Westview Press, 1994.

Gelb, Leslie H. *Power Rules: How Common Sense Can Rescue American Foreign Policy*. New York: HarperCollins, 2009.

Ghattas, Kim. *The Secretary: A Journey with Hillary Clinton from Beirut to the Heart of American Power*. New York: Times Books, 2013.

Gordon, Michael R. and Bernard E. Trainor. *The Endgame: The Inside Story of the Struggle for Iraq, From George W. Bush to Barack Obama*. New York: Vintage Books, 2012.

Greenberg, David. *Republic of Spin: An Inside History of the American Presidency*. New York: W.W. Norton, 2016.

Greenstein, Fred I. *The Hidden-Hand Presidency: Eisenhower as Leader*. New York: Basic Books, 1982.

Haass, Richard N. *Foreign Policy Begins at Home: The Case for Putting America's House in Order*. New York: Basic Books, 2013.

Hill, Christopher R. *Outpost: Life on the Frontlines of American Diplomacy: A Memoir*. New York: Simon & Schuster, 2014.

Holbrooke, Richard. *To End a War*. New York: Random House, 1998.

Indyk, Martin S., Kenneth G. Lieberthal, and Michael E. O'Hanlon. *Bending History: Barack Obama's Foreign Policy*. Washington, DC: Brookings Institution Press, 2012.

Joffe, Josef. *The Myth of America's Decline: Politics, Economics, and a Half Century of False Prophecies*. New York: W.W. Norton, 2014.

Kagan, Robert. *Dangerous Nation: America's Foreign Policy from Its Earliest Days to the Dawn of the Twentieth Century*. New York: Knopf, 2006.

_____. *The World America Made*. New York: Knopf, 2012.

Kaplan, Robert. *Mediterranean Winter: The Pleasures of History and Landscape in Tunisia, Sicily, Dalmatia, and the Peloponnese*. New York: Vintage Books, 2004.

_____. *The Revenge of Geography: What the Map Tells Us About Coming Conflicts and the Battle Against Fate*. New York: Random House, 2012.

Kennan, George F. *Memoirs 1925-1950*. New York: Pantheon Books, 1967.

Kissinger, Henry. *A World Restored: Metternich, Castlereagh and the Problems of Peace*. Brattleboro: Echo Point Books & Media, 1957.

_____. *White House Years*. New York: Simon & Schuster, 1979.

_____. *Diplomacy*. New York: Simon & Schuster, 1994.

_____. *On China*. New York: Penguin, 2012.

_____. *World Order*. New York: Penguin, 2014.

Kloppenberg, James T. *Reading Obama: Dreams, Hope, and the American Political Tradition*. Princeton: Princeton University Press, 2010.

LaFeber, Walter. *The American Age: United States Foreign Policy at Home and Abroad since 1750*. New York: W.W. Norton, 1989.

Lewis, Michael. *The Big Short: Inside the Doomsday Machine*. New York: W.W. Norton, 2010.

Loomis, Carol. *Tap Dancing To Work: Warren Buffett on Practically Everything*. New York: Penguin, 2012.

Mann, James. *The Obamians: The Struggle Inside the White House to Redefine American Power*. New York: Penguin, 2012.

Meacham, Jon. *Destiny and Power: The American Odyssey of George Herbert Walker Bush*. New York: Random House, 2015.

Milne, David. *Worldmaking: The Art and Science of American Diplomacy*. New York: Farrar, Straus and Giroux, 2015.

Morell, Michael. *The Great War of Our Time: The CIA's Fight Against Terrorism From al Qa'ida to ISIS*. New York: Twelve, 2015.

Nasr, Vali. *The Dispensable Nation: American Foreign Policy in Retreat*. New York: Anchor Books, 2013.

Niebuhr, Reinhold. *The Irony of American History*. New York: Charles Scribner's Sons, 1952.

_____. *The World Crisis and American Responsibility*. New York: Association Press, 1958.

Nye, Joseph. *The Paradox of American Power: Why the World's Only Superpower Can't Go It Alone*. New York: Oxford University Press, 2002.

_____. *Presidential Leadership and the Creation of the American Era*. Princeton: Princeton University Press, 2013.

_____. *Is the American Century Over?* Malden: Policy Press, 2015.

Obama, Barack. *The Audacity of Hope: Thoughts on Reclaiming the American Dream*. New York: Random House, 2006.

Oren, Michael B. *Ally: My Journey Across the American-Israeli Divide*. New York: Random House, 2015.

Panetta, Leon. *Worthy Fights: A Memoir of Leadership in War and Peace*. New York: Penguin, 2015.

Plouffe, David. *The Audacity to Win: How Obama Won and How We Can Beat the Party of Limbaugh, Beck, and Palin*. New York: Penguin, 2010.

Rodman, Peter W. *Presidential Command: Power, Leadership, and the Making of Foreign Policy from Richard Nixon to George W. Bush*. New York: Vintage Books, 2009.

Ross, Dennis. *Doomed to Succeed: The U.S.-Israel Relationship from Truman to Obama*. New York: Farrar, Straus and Giroux, 2015.

Rothkopf, David J. *National Insecurity: American Leadership in an Age of Fear*. New York: PublicAffairs, 2014.

Sanger, David. *Confront and Conceal: Obama's Secret Wars and Surprising Use of American Power*. New York: Random House, 2012.

Savage, Charlie. *Power Wars: Inside Obama's Post-9/11 Presidency*. New York: Little, Brown & Company 2015.

Scarborough, Joe. *The Right Path: From Ike to Reagan, How Republicans Once Mastered Politics – And Can Again*. New York: Random House, 2013.

Schell, Jonathan. *The Time of Illusion*. New York: Random House, 1975.

Scoblic, J. Peter. *U.S. vs. Them: How Conservatism Has Undermined America's Security*. New York: Penguin, 2008.

Sestanovich, Stephen. *Maximalist: America in the World From Truman to Obama*. New York: Knopf, 2014.

BIBLIOGRAPHY

Sky, Emma. *The Unraveling: High Hopes and Missed Opportunities in Iraq*. New York: PublicAffairs, 2015.

Stent, Angela E. *The Limits of Partnership: U.S.-Russian Relations in the Twenty-First Century*. Princeton: Princeton University Press, 2014.

Stephens, Bret. *America in Retreat: The New Isolationism and the Coming Global Disorder*. New York: Penguin, 2014.

Stephens, Bret, Robert Kagan, Anne-Marie Slaughter, and Fareed Zakaria. *Has Obama Made the World a More Dangerous Place?: The Munk Debate on U.S. Foreign Policy*. Toronto: House of Anansi Press, 2015.

Thomas, Evan. *Ike's Bluff: President Eisenhower's Secret Battle to Save the World*. New York: Little, Brown & Company, 2012.

Todd, Chuck. *The Stranger: Barack Obama in the White House*. New York: Little, Brown & Company, 2014.

Traub, James. *John Quincy Adams: Militant Spirit*. New York: Basic Books, 2016.

Woodward, Bob. *Obama's Wars*. New York: Simon and Schuster, 2010.

ACKNOWLEDGMENTS

In writing this book I have accumulated many debts, and am deeply grateful to all of those who have helped along the way.

That starts with my bosses during the six years I spent in the Obama administration at the State Department, White House and Pentagon. Thanks to Secretary of State Hillary Rodham Clinton, Secretaries of Defense Leon Panetta and Chuck Hagel, and National Security Advisor Tom Donilon for giving me the opportunities of a lifetime.

My conversations with many former colleagues helped shape my thinking about foreign policy during the Obama years, and I'd especially like to thank Ben Rhodes, Michael McFaul, Jake Sullivan, Colin Kahl, Warren Bass, and Mark Lippert for their insights and friendship. I have also benefitted from many discussions about these events with some of the best informed and most astute (and often critical) observers of the Obama administration, including Les Gelb, Jeffrey Goldberg, Greg Jaffe, Robert D. Kaplan, Mark Landler, George Packer and David Rothkopf.

Since leaving the administration, I could not have asked for a better institutional home than The German Marshall Fund of the United States, and I owe a lot to my boss and friend, Karen Donfried, for her unstinting and encouraging support, including by providing so many thoughtful comments on a draft. I also could not have done this without the help of my closest GMF colleagues, Kelsey Guyette, Taylor Budak, and particularly Steven Keil, who also gave the manuscript a close read and offered many good suggestions.

ACKNOWLEDGMENTS

To assist with the research, I got indispensable help from Ali Wyne, an accomplished foreign policy thinker and writer now at Harvard, who has a very bright future ahead. At a critical stage in the drafting I also received an important assist from Jacob Freedman, an immensely talented former Pentagon colleague who helped ensure things read smoothly.

One of the great pleasures of being out of government is having the freedom to write and reflect, and I am grateful to those who gave me an initial opportunity to develop some of the ideas that appear in this book. That starts with Kevin Baron and the terrific team at *Defense One*, who in just a few years have created a must-read publication for anyone interested in US national security. I also wish to thank Gideon Rose at *Foreign Affairs*, David Rothkopf at *Foreign Policy*, Uri Friedman at *The Atlantic*, and Nicholas Gvosdev, formerly of *The National Interest*, for giving me a chance to think hard and first write about many of the issues addressed here.

I have benefitted greatly by being able to road test my thinking and arguments with some of the finest and most discerning scholars of recent American foreign policy. Peter Feaver at Duke University's Program in American Grand Strategy, and Will Inboden at The Clements Center for National Security at the University of Texas, invited me to participate in workshops that helped develop many of my ideas. And I especially thank Robert Jervis and the team at Columbia University's Saltzman Institute of War and Peace Studies for hosting several lively seminars to discuss this book.

Many friends and former colleagues read all or parts of the book, and I am deeply grateful to them for their willingness take time out of their busy schedules to share insights, help refresh my memory, offer editorial suggestions, and save me from embarrassing errors (of course, any remaining mistakes and the opinions expressed here are my own). I thank Ivo Daalder, Evelyn Farkas, Ben Fishman, Phil Gordon, Lisa Samp, and Matt Spence for their many comments and course-corrections. Kurt Campbell deserves a special shout-out not only for reading an early draft, but for welcoming me to his Iron Bell Run Farm, which is an ideal writers retreat. And in his own category is Bill Burns, the dean of modern American diplomacy who has been my mentor and friend for nearly a quarter century, who added to the book with his customary keen insight and wisdom.

I also received invaluable advice from several scholars: my longtime friend and collaborator Jim Goldgeier gave the entire book a careful read; RAND's Chris

ACKNOWLEDGMENTS

Chivvis offered numerous insights on Libya, and I learned a lot from his own fine work; Hal Brands, a rising star at Duke University and a leading scholar of US grand strategy, provided many thoughtful comments on the manuscript and offered numerous insights which are reflected here; and most of all Robert Jervis, my teacher for over two decades, has been an enthusiastic supporter of this project and made it better with so many smart suggestions.

The US government reviewed this manuscript to ensure it does not compromise any national security information, yet all statements of fact, opinion, and analysis are mine and do not necessarily reflect official US government views. I appreciate the assistance of John Powers at the National Security Council and Mark Langerman and his team at the Department of Defense for handling the review process so efficiently and with great professionalism.

Once again, a huge thanks to Clive Priddle. During the past eight years, this is the third book I have had the pleasure of working on with Clive and the PublicAffairs team, and I am very fortunate to have partners who are so talented, steadfast, and fun. Peter Osnos was an early champion and helped clarify my thinking, Melissa Raymond kept us on task, Marco Pavia helped copyedit and gave the book its elegant design, and Chris Juby made sure it got some attention. Thanks to all.

Finally, and most important, to my family: Lucas, Aerin and, most of all, Heather. For six years they had to deal with a distracted and stressed-out government official, and for the past year they have had to deal with just a slightly less distracted and stressed-out book author. Through it all, they helped me keep perspective and ensured our lives were full of joy. They are the reason this book was possible, which is why it is dedicated to them.

INDEX

GEORGE MARSHALL

DEREK CHOLLET served in senior positions during the Obama administration at the White House, State Department, and Pentagon, most recently as the US assistant secretary of defense for international security affairs. He is currently a counselor and senior adviser at the German Marshall Fund of the United States, an adjunct senior research scholar at Columbia University's Institute of War and Peace Studies, and a regular contributor to *Defense One* and many other publications. His previous books include *America Between the Wars: From 11/9 to 9/11*, coauthored with James Goldgeier, and *The Unquiet American: Richard Holbrooke in the World*, coedited with Samantha Power. He lives in Washington, DC, with his family.